THE GUARDIAN ANGEL

A VOICE FROM THE WILDERNESS

Colin Everard

MINERVA PRESS
MONTREUX LONDON WASHINGTON

THE GUARDIAN ANGEL
A VOICE FROM THE WILDERNESS
Copyright © Colin Everard 1996

All Rights Reserved

ISBN 1 85863 906 9

First published 1996 by
MINERVA PRESS
195 Knightsbridge
London SW7 1RE

Printed in Great Britain by
Antony Rowe Ltd., Chippenham, Wiltshire

THE GUARDIAN ANGEL

A VOICE FROM THE WILDERNESS

ACKNOWLEDGEMENTS

Dedicated to my love – the perfect wife and mother – Emy

I should like to acknowledge with deep gratitude the efficient and helpful assistance, and the humour, of my daughter Andrea.

I also wish to acknowledge the technical review, covering material from the first part of this book, performed by Mr Clifford Ashall, formerly Assistant Director and Head, Field Division, Centre for Overseas Pest Research, London.

For his encouragement and constructive support, I wish to acknowledge with gratitude the positive efforts of Mr Hutton G. Archer, Chief, Public Information Office, International Civil Aviation Organisation (ICAO), Montreal, Canada.

CONTENTS

ILLUSTRATIONS

THE AUTHOR

Colin Everard worked with countries of the Third World for forty years as an international civil servant and technical cooperation practitioner; as his story shows, he is no 'faceless bureaucrat'. In addition to visiting fifty countries for professional purposes, he lived in Ethiopia, Kenya, the Somali Republic and Uganda for many years; for his twenty years' work with the International Civil Aviation Organisation (ICAO), he was based in Montreal, Canada. The author is a Fellow of the Royal Aeronautical Society, a Fellow of the Chartered Institute of Purchasing and Supply, and a Fellow of the Institute of Management.

SPECIAL NOTE

Where reference is made to the work of the International Civil Aviation Organisation (ICAO) any views expressed are those of the author; these do not necessarily reflect the views of ICAO.

AUTHOR'S NOTE

The purpose of this book is not to present a 'success' story. I am not, for example, a political creature who somehow has to justify his past decisions and actions, always bearing in mind that the underlying intent is to illustrate the righteousness of his judgement.

Rather, what follows is a commentary of a somewhat unusual working life, which began shortly after the Second World War and extended until the early nineteen nineties. The experiences related often fly in the face of the image of a typical bureaucrat. This is a story of someone who, in a practical way, sought to be associated with an improvement in the human condition in developing countries; this purpose persisted over the years as the focus of his contribution, however humble.

Each of us holds a perception of the world in which we live. A good deal of the material which is presented in the following pages will seem exotic, especially for those who spend their lives in the developed world.

It is worth bearing in mind, however, that by far the largest part of the world's population lives in the Third World; what may seem to be extraordinary to an inhabitant of the developed world is the norm for someone who lives in the Third World. For most of my working life, the Third World was for me the real world.

My only regret with respect to the text which follows, is that the word 'I' appears on countless occasions. On the other hand, if one chooses to narrate anecdotes drawn from personal experience to illustrate some aspects of the developing world, then the usage of 'I' is often an inevitable consequence. If I had found some way to have avoided the use of 'I', it would have been more in keeping with my character.

For the first time in my memory my time is my own; to write this book is a luxury. I hope that the reader will accompany me through the pages which follow and along the way share my experiences with me. I also hope that what follows will contribute to a better understanding of some elements of the nature of the real developing world.

Vienna, January 1996   COLIN EVERARD

INTRODUCTION

In terms of time, this story begins shortly after the mid-point of our twentieth century. It was one of those dank November days in England, to be precise in south-east London. A misty drizzle permeated the air and made one's face feel slightly raw as it touched the skin. My brother and I, on our way to work, were walking quite quickly along a narrow lane which ran between little suburban gardens and the railway. As happened quite frequently, as we neared the station, we suddenly heard the approaching train, which meant a final sprint (our umbrellas tucked under our arms) past a man who noisily offered The Daily Worker, into the station and on to the eight minutes past eight train; occasionally we missed the 8:08 and caught the 8:11, which was a stopper.

The compartment we had entered was made to seat five people on each side, ten in all; on that particular morning I counted nineteen human beings in the compartment. Several of these people were suffering from colds and sounds of coughing punctuated the otherwise virtually silent atmosphere. As usual, one or two members of the sardine-like group insisted on holding newspapers slightly above their heads, trying to read the odd paragraph in the November gloom.

A number of thoughts ran through my mind that morning. Perhaps the most significant of these was a solemn question,

"Are you prepared to accept this type of situation as part of your everyday existence for the indefinite future?"

About halfway to London, I turned to my brother and quietly explained that I regarded the crush of the railway compartment to be, in basic terms, uncivilised. A few quizzical glances slowly veered in the direction of the voice which had broken the silence. With hindsight, I suppose that I left the train as a form of individual protest against conditions which prevailed at that time and which were certainly worse than most cattle have to endure in such countries as England today.

I also realised that there was something beyond the immediate protesting action which I had initiated. I was not happy with the way of life I was pursuing. My father had encouraged me to enter some sort of business activity and I had followed his advice. I was undergoing a systematic programme of exposure to various departments of a large clothing retailer and the intention was that, in due course, I would become a European representative for the company. Although I was still quite young (twenty one years of age) I had quickly developed an understanding of the merchandise and an effective way in which it could be marketed. Although periodically I was congratulated for my efforts by the management, unfortunately I found the activity to be, by nature, shallow. Although as time went by one could foresee a substantial income, for me at least something fundamental seemed to be lacking; however, what precisely was missing eluded my understanding.

Over the previous week or two, I had become increasingly conscious of a general feeling of dissatisfaction. At one point, I took a metaphorical step backward and tried to take an objectively hard look at myself. Perhaps if I could produce a reasonably accurate definition of my strengths and weaknesses, I would then be in a better position to choose an appropriate field of human endeavour.

I was a product of the Second World War and had attended Dulwich College during the war years. I had learned a lot at Dulwich and I had especially appreciated the all-round nature of my education; we were also strongly encouraged to participate in a number of extra-curricular activities. Separately, I gave some thought to intellectual capacity; at that time this was for me a question mark, simply because at that age the need had not really arisen for me to think through a situation.

As far as money and personal wealth were concerned, I had no ambition to amass wealth. On the other hand, I could not understand the merit of being poor; for example, I had never understood the Biblical reference to the effect that it is easier for a camel to pass through the eye of a needle than it is for a rich man to enter the Kingdom of God. Properly used, wealth is fundamental to the development of mankind. My personal attitude was that I would eventually have liked to be well off, but I would never be tempted by greed.

I also took into account the political situation which prevailed in England after the last war. I abhorred the basic tenets of socialism as it was preached, and practised, in England at that time. I could never accept the concept of 'public' ownership, which was patently false; the phoney policy of full employment had already led to over-employment and inefficiency in government-controlled services. I regarded the whole concept of a government-engineered Welfare State as demeaning. I could identify with compassion, but scorned the condescension which so frequently accompanied socialist dogma; and I detested the pseudo-intellectual political intolerance which was widely prevalent. In the political atmosphere of the time, I felt powerless; which was in fact the case.

I placed a high value on honesty and integrity and, contrary to the feelings of many at that time in England, I believed in the work ethic. In addition, my (albeit limited) work experience had revealed a significant talent in selling. "Selling" is used here in the widest sense of the term and involves not only selling merchandise but 'selling' ideas; in other words, convincing others to accept one's arguments.

Standing on that grey platform, I certainly recognised that I should go to my place of work that day; at the same time, I also knew that soon I would need to reach a conclusion about what I wanted to do with my working life. I caught the 8:11 and duly arrived at work, slightly late. A message had been received that the Deputy General Manager wished to see me as soon as possible. I had once met him briefly but had never been to his office. Within a few minutes, I was standing before him and, with an earnest look on his face, he recalled that I had recently undertaken a business trip and he had been reviewing my list of expenses; in a nutshell, he was unhappy with the list I had submitted and, apparently, was looking for some sort of explanation. I courteously informed him that the list constituted the actual expenses incurred and if he would explain the problem, I would naturally be pleased to give any necessary clarification.

The Deputy General Manager looked at me with a grave expression for some seconds. He then explained that the list of expenses was too limited and the costs shown were much too small. He asked me to consider that other members of the company also undertook business trips and, for the sake of consistency, he insisted that the costs should be appreciably raised. As a youngster of twenty one years of age I was at a loss for a response, simply muttering that I did not know how to cheat. I also took the opportunity to give notice of departure.

Continuing my reflections over the next few days, I eventually reached an overriding conclusion: during the period of my existence on earth I should endeavour to make a practical contribution to the well-being of others.

Amongst other things, I recalled my military National Service, two years previously, in what was then called the Somaliland Protectorate. The country had been afflicted by a plague of locusts and widespread damage had been suffered to grazing; and the crops grown in the few cultivated areas (mainly maize) had been devoured. For a period, I had been detached from normal military duties to support an anti-locust campaign.

I wrote to the Director of the Desert Locust Survey (Philip Stephenson) and received an early response to the effect that he had asked the Crown Agents in London to recruit me for a two year contract.

The interview with the Crown Agents was routine, except when I was asked a testing question towards the end of the interview; the main substance of the answer was beyond my knowledge. At that point, I had the temerity to inform the Interviewing Board that I was surprised to receive such a question; I had understood that the Crown Agents had been requested to employ me, rather than to involve me in a lengthy qualifying interview. I anxiously watched for a reaction from the good-natured (but serious) expressions of the several faces which seemed to be piercing my character. To my relief, first one and suddenly all dissolved in laughter, at which point the Chairman informed me that I seemed to be extremely well-informed on the subject and he felt that the members and himself should only wish me godspeed in the life which immediately lay ahead of me. He explained that I would be subjected to many privations and that I would need to make many sacrifices, but all of this would be in the interest of humanity. I responded that I was prepared for whatever would be required to make my work a worthwhile contribution.

The news of my appointment as a field officer of the Desert Locust Control Organisation was shared with my father. He expressed mixed feelings. He understood and accepted the motivation I had developed to work primarily in the interest of others. On the other hand, he did not accept that I needed to travel to another continent such as Africa to fulfil my desire. He pointed out, rightly, that there were several areas of London (and other major cities in England), where there would be much scope to improve the human condition. He wondered why I preferred to make a contribution in Africa, rather than in my own country. My response was that England was a developed country and its government should be in a position to bring the required resources to bear in order to tackle problem areas in the social situation; to me at that time, the key to the solution of social problems was a question of government priorities. In addition, as far as I knew, there were many people in England who could be trained for a field which had some bearing on an improvement of the human condition. But how many people were prepared to work in a developing country, with the associated challenge of harsh climatic conditions, quite different cultures and, as in this case, the existence of a huge locust problem?

In the first week of November 1952 I found myself again in the main town of the Somaliland Protectorate, which was Hargeisa. On this occasion, however, I had no connection with my former military colleagues, nor incidentally was I a member of the Colonial Administrative Service, which so effectively administered Somaliland at that time in the interests of the Somali people. I was a member of a far-flung part of a department which was based in Nairobi, Kenya, 1000 miles away. I was a civilian – and very much alone.

PART ONE

FLEDGLING DAYS

Chapter One

A Christmas Surprise

On arrival in Hargeisa I was driven to the Base of the Desert Locust Control, which had been established as an offshoot of the Desert Locust Survey; the Desert Locust Control Organisation was engaged in mounting anti-locust campaigns throughout East Africa, Ethiopia, the then Somaliland Protectorate, the then Italian Trusteeship of Somalia (these two countries were subsequently merged into the Somali Republic), Saudi Arabia, Yemen and Aden (the Wadi Hadramaut), with occasional reconnaissance visits to the Gulf States. The Desert Locust Control (DLC) Base was situated several miles from the town of Hargeisa and comprised a number of low rectangular buildings spread over about a quarter square mile; these buildings had been used to store ammunition, probably during the late thirties and early forties. The roofing material used for the buildings was corrugated iron which, although effective as a roof, was also a strong conductor of heat. Several of the buildings were surrounded by ten-foot high protective heaps of stones, of which there was an abundance. The Base was situated on the side of a stony hill, the general scene relieved only by a few stunted *acacia* trees; the trees came into their ephemeral own for brief periods once or twice a year, when a shower of rain would pelt the stones and permeate the dusty soil in which the *acacias* had somehow taken root.

I was told that I would be leaving for my first field assignment after four days of briefing and general preparation; the destination would be Jin-Ali in the Ogaden area of Ethiopia. I understood that the Ogaden was inhabited by Somalis and, under a treaty arrangement, part of the area (the Haud) was administered by the British government.

Having installed myself in a room reserved for transitory field officers such as myself, I lost no time in studying some briefing material. My concentration was, however, politely interrupted by a young Somali visitor who delivered a short note to the effect that someone who had met me about two years previously (during my military service in 1950), wished to invite me that evening for an informal dinner. I gladly accepted. On arrival at my host's house, I suddenly felt much less lonely.

The dinner party comprised about six friends, drawn from the limited expatriate community; they all seemed to have been associated at some stage with the Desert Locust Control Organization. For example, they spoke of Roger Courtney, who had been a hero of the British Special Air Service; sadly, Roger Courtney had died. I had known a friendly courting competitor of Roger's, Gerald Selby-Lowndes. Gerald had recently tried to traverse a river-crossing which was in flood and his vehicle had been dragged into the rushing torrent. He had left the vehicle, throwing himself in the direction of two of his staff, who were anxiously standing at the water's edge; due to the power of the water, his staff had not been able to pull him from the torrent and he had drowned in their hands.

During part of my detachment period two years previously, I had assisted Gerald Selby-Lowndes during the campaign mounted to deal with the huge invasion of desert locusts. Gerald was a man of charm and good humour. One image that I retained in my memory was of him sitting in a pair of shorts and sandals in an open Land Rover (I accompanied him in the front of the vehicle); behind him sat a retired Somali Sergeant Major with a large moustache. We used to start our work at about five thirty a.m. and when the time approached ten a.m. Gerald would suddenly say,

"Sergeant Major!"

There was an immediate response,

"Sah!" I would look round and there was the Sergeant Major sitting to attention. In front of him was a large basket-work box, which was full of bottles. Gerald would then turn to me and enquire what type of refreshment I would like; he invariably ordered a gin and tonic, which he maintained was a suitably long drink to replace some of the fluid lost by his body in the hot Somali sun.

Shortly after the guests had sat down to dinner, a middle-aged man enquired of the group whether they thought that Roger Courtney would like to share a drink; to my faint surprise, one or two guests smiled in a somewhat melancholic way and responded that it was a thoughtful idea. Without further ado, I followed the guests along a stony path through some bushes until we came across a plain tombstone, illuminated by our leader's torchlight. A stone ball was moved to one side at the head of the horizontal stone and a gin and tonic was duly poured into the hole, with positive mutterings all around.

In Hargeisa, the main diet revolved around mutton, chicken, or occasionally, wild buck (gazelle).   That evening's meal was no exception and we progressed with innocuous conversation until it was time for coffee. Our host then cleared his throat and, glancing in my direction, said that there were several members of the expatriate community in Hargeisa who remembered me from the period of my military service in 1950 and if in that small community my name should surface from time to time, I was sometimes referred to as "that lion man". Our host was sure that I understood what he was talking about and for the sake of himself and those present, could I tell them in my own words what actually happened to me during Christmas 1950?   Although I was slightly taken aback, I related the circumstances and facts of that fateful night.

Christmas is traditionally a time when families assemble and celebrate the birth of Jesus with good cheer. At Christmas in 1950 in the Somaliland Protectorate, there were young Subalterns who were far from home and who had no chance whatsoever of enjoying the good cheer of their families. John Whitmore, Chris Scott, and myself were three of those Subalterns. Jointly we decided to spend Christmas in the company of each other, far from what might have been to us a madding crowd. We felt that somewhere in the area of the top of a cool mountain pass would be a good place to spend Christmas; we duly departed for the Sheikh Pass which is roughly in the centre of Somaliland at the higher elevation of the escarpment which forms the edge of the main Somali plateau. We drove to the Sheikh Pass in what was termed a fifteen-hundred weight truck; we were accompanied by a driver and an askari (a soldier) of the Somaliland Scouts.   About forty miles south of the Pass, we called on an acquaintance to wish his family happiness at Christmas; before leaving him, he told us that he had recently heard that there were a number of lions in the area and he cautioned us to arrange for the askari to be on guard at night.

En route to the Sheikh Pass, one of our group shot a gazelle; on arrival, the animal was skinned, the skin spread over a bush and the meat placed in a large container.

That Christmas night had an unforgettably special quality. We had established a small camp area at about seven thousand feet above sea level. Although the rays of the late afternoon sun were pleasantly warm, once the sun had set it became cool; this was in pleasant contrast to the more usual Somali weather conditions of heat and blowing dust. Shortly after sunset, the fillet steak of the gazelle was cooked for dinner and a feeling of camaraderie and good cheer developed between us as we related to one another experiences of our young lives. Occasionally we raised our heads to the sky and we tried to identify one or two constellations from the glittering heavens, such as Orion's Sword or the Great Bear. In the thin air of that quite high elevation, we were very much alone; but not at all lonely.

It was Christmas Eve and I believe it was John Whitmore who, at about eleven o'clock, suggested that we should sing some Christmas carols. About midnight, we lazily went into our various sleeping bags which were lying on our 'Houndsfield' beds around our camp fire; before drifting into a contented sleep, I recall gazing at the gradually dying embers of the camp fire and the silhouette of our askari who had been designated to guard us.

Suddenly, I half woke up and realised that, although my movements were limited by the confines of my sleeping bag, I was no longer lying on the camp bed; from the feeling of unevenness under my back, I began to realise that I was lying on stony terrain. I opened my eyes and looking upwards could see a large dark form silhouetted against the night sky. My initial reaction was that I was probably dreaming and it seemed as though I was lying under the tailboard of a large truck. When the form seemed to slowly move, ever so slightly, accompanied by the sound of deep pants, I must have instantaneously sensed that I was in danger.

I have no recollection of how I managed to extricate myself from the sleeping bag, but I have a vivid memory of running blindly away from that large dark form. After running over the small sharp stones for thirty or forty yards, I could hear myself panting in the throat, almost as though one were desperately trying to escape the inevitable. I then saw the outline of a dense bush and I threw myself into its centre and, crouching, anxiously stared through the leafy branches, again panting, almost choking, audibly.

At this point, although I was horribly aware that some dreadful occurrence was in progress, I was still in a confused state. I was fully awake, but I really had no idea of what had happened, or for that matter what might happen in the next minute or two.

Looking anxiously out of that bush, my eyes strained into the darkness. Within a few seconds the situation became fearfully clear; a lion was padding its way, in unhurried style, towards me. As it approached, I simply froze. When the lion was about five yards from me, it halted and it seemed to raise its head in the night air; although it was dead ahead of me, I could not see whether it was looking directly at me. It stood there in an apparently unconcerned manner for a few seconds, turned slowly to its left – and padded away into the darkness. John Whitmore's voice cut through the night air,

"Colin, are you still in the land of the living?"

"Yes. Could someone please tell me what has been going on?"

"We had a lion, old chap!"

When I had returned to our Christmas group, limping due to cuts in my feet, through discussion amongst ourselves and questioning of our askari, it seemed that our nocturnal visitor had smelled the skin of the gazelle and had decided to investigate the smell, perhaps in the hope that he would be dealing with a wounded animal. According to the askari, the askari had started to doze but woke up sharply when he suddenly saw the lion standing near our group and the gazelle skin. The askari made a noise and the lion apparently decided to depart. He made a small jump over the embers of our dying fire and, on the other side of the embers, came into contact with a protruding part of the steel frame of my camp bed; the impact threw me from the bed on to the ground. The lion was probably a little surprised to find a sleeping human being enveloped in a sleeping bag, prostrated at the lion's feet under his head and mane. It was at about this time that John Whitmore woke up and clearly saw the lion standing near him. The remainder of what happened has already been described.

The completion of my narrative was followed by prolonged silence around our dinner table. At last, our host suggested that perhaps I should feel privileged to be still in the land of the living. At the same time, he opined that perhaps those present should also feel privileged to have heard the story recounted at first hand.

Do you believe in a Guardian Angel? Whether in fact each of us has a Guardian Angel may well be considered a moot point. I believe I have a Guardian Angel; my only regret is that he or she has been called upon to intervene on so many occasions!

Chapter Two

The Ogaden

The briefing which I received at the Desert Locust Control (DLC) Base covered not only the details of the duties I was expected to perform; the general locust situation at that time was also explained.

I learned that there were several types of locusts which, from time to time, could multiply into plague proportions. By far the most menacing of these was the locust which would remain our immediate enemy for a number of years to come: the desert locust *(schistocerca gregaria)*. About sixty countries were afflicted at various times by the desert locust, with much activity frequently reported in the Arabian Peninsula, Ethiopia and the area inhabited by the Somalis in the Horn of Africa. During desert locust plagues, heavy and widespread invasions occurred in the Ogaden area of Ethiopia. Once the locusts had bred, the whole area became heavily infested with the nymphs, commonly referred to as 'hoppers'.

The body of the young locust has a pinkish hue. Once temperature, humidity and other environmental conditions are right, the adults turn yellow and prepare for breeding. The female lays up to three pods of eggs over a short period, with each pod containing fifty to one hundred eggs. Depending on the degree of moisture in the ground, the eggs hatch some ten to fourteen days later and one would find areas of the bush country covered with blackish hoppers; the nymphs were at this stage described as being in the first instar. The hoppers would pass through five of the instars over a period of five or six weeks, each time shedding a skin before passing into the next instar. In the final instar, the wing buds could be seen and soon swarms would begin to form of immature (pinkish) locusts.

In order to survive, the locust needs to eat its own weight in food every day. The average weight of an individual adult is two grams; in avoirdupois terms, a half million locusts would equate to about one ton. The density of locust swarms is variable; however, often-observed parameters indicated densities between 100 and 200 million locusts per square mile. As an example, if one observed a swarm of, say, 400 square miles, even using the lower parameter figure, the swarm would contain of the order of 40,000 million locusts with an overall weight of 80,000 tons. As the 400 square miles of swarm swept over the land, it would therefore consume some 80,000 tons of crops and grazing each day, leaving behind desolation and the grim expectation for the subsistence farmers and their stock of at best, hunger and at worst, starvation. Its speed of flight in still air is about 12 m.p.h., which means that with a following wind of twenty or thirty m.p.h. locust swarms can cover long distances very quickly.

As its name implied, the objective of the Desert Locust Control Organisation was to control locust infestations. Although it was recognised that heavy and widespread damage could be caused to grazing in such areas as Saudi Arabia, Eastern Ethiopia and the northern part of the Horn of Africa, the possibility of incurring losses to crops in such countries as Kenya and Tanzania was regarded as a threat which justified significant public expenditure by the East African taxpayer to support anti-locust operations.

Shortly after the Second World War, the governments of East Africa had entered into discussions with governments of the countries to the north in the Horn of Africa, as well as with such countries as Saudi Arabia, Aden (the Wadi Hadramaut) and the Gulf States. Resulting from negotiations, it was agreed that the Desert Locust Survey should be formed. The DLS was primarily a multi-disciplinary scientific research organisation, whose staff included biologists (some of whom were entomologists), ecologists, geographers, chemists and meteorologists. These men and women pursued various avenues of research, many of which followed logically from the work of Boris (later Sir Boris) Uvarov, a Russian scientist who came to England in 1920 to work at the Imperial Bureau (now the Commonwealth Institute of Entomology). In 1921 he had published his 'phase theory' of locust behaviour and in 1928 a monumental book called *Locusts and Grasshoppers*. It had been through the research of Boris Uvarov that the reality of the so-called phase theory was clearly confirmed. His research established that locusts pass from a solitary to a gregarious state. The insect which was found in a solitary state could, under certain environmental conditions, become gregarious; once the previously solitary grasshoppers became gregarious, locust plagues would develop.

Because a severe locust plague did in fact occur from 1948-9, it was decided that in addition to carrying out field research, strong efforts should be made to develop methods to control the locust infestations. It was therefore decided to form an off-shoot of the Desert Locust Survey, which was called the Desert Locust Control Organisation.

If one's job was to participate in control measures, I wondered to what extent one should try to obtain some scientifically-based knowledge about locusts. The response was simple. At that time, apart from the research undertaken by Boris Uvarov, supplemented by research performed in laboratories in institutions such as the Anti-Locust Research Centre (ALRC) in London, relatively little research had been undertaken on this particular subject. It therefore followed that, apart from gaining an understanding of basic facts which were known about the behavioural pattern of desert locusts, there was little else to learn at that particular juncture; there were a number of theories relating to various aspects of research, but further time would be needed to test these theories.

Whereas the Desert Locust Survey needed to be staffed with good scientists, the Desert Locust Control Organisation needed personnel with a rather different emphasis, in terms of a person's qualities. Organisation and administration, linked with initiative and resourcefulness, were highly important. The ability not only to survive but to produce high quality work in isolated areas (within an unforgivingly tight work schedule) was also of fundamental importance; for example, during one assignment, I found myself working in an isolated area for seven months with only three Somali staff.

The working relationship between the Desert Locust Survey and the Desert Locust Control Organisation always remained healthy and productive; but the mission of each part of this collective effort had a distinct orientation. Whereas the personnel of DLS were recruited from the scientific community and therefore felt a common bond for that reason, members of the DLC tended to have a disparate background; however, the camaraderie and basic cohesion of the Organisation as a whole always remained strong positive factors.

It needs to be borne in mind that the problem of locust invasions was of ancient origin; for example, there are references in the Bible to the occurrence of locust plagues. The methods used in the first half of the twentieth century to control locusts tended to be limited to digging trenches into which the hoppers would fall, beating and burning, or simply creating a high level of noise in the often vain attempt to discourage locusts from settling on and devouring crops. These primitive methods were severely limited in effectiveness and could never be expected to protect widespread grazing, or crops grown on a relatively large scale.

As far as more modern methods of control were concerned, some success had been achieved in the forties using a minute percentage of arsenic mixed with bran. The problem with this method was to supervise properly its application; unless the bait was spread very thinly over the ground there would always be the risk that sheep or cattle might be attracted to the bran. Cases had certainly occurred of the bait mixture being dumped under trees and animals had subsequently died of arsenic poisoning.

In the late forties and fifties, such companies as Shell and Imperial Chemical Industries (ICI) devoted significant research effort to developing effective pesticides which could be applied in such a way that they would cause stomach poisoning to the locusts, but without adverse effect on sheep, goats or cattle. These insecticides were called dieldrin and benzene hexachloride (BHC).

In the early fifties the migratory routes of locusts were still not fully understood. It was known that locusts moved between breeding areas by, in general, travelling downwind towards convergence zones, sometimes covering more than one hundred miles in one day, depending on the wind speed. These winds often produced monsoon-like conditions, which were ideal for breeding purposes; it was essential that the sandy soil should be damp and soft enough for the female to extend her abdomen into the soil to lay her egg pod.

In order that the migratory details of the overall pattern of locust movements could be further examined, one of the duties of the field officer was to complete a reporting form whenever he found locusts. The columns indicated the date of the sighting of the locusts, the longitude and latitude, the distance traversed through the swarm, the colour of the locusts (or hoppers) and whether, in the case of yellow locusts, they were copulating; general remarks would refer to weather conditions.

As for the locust situation which prevailed in 1952, there had been a large invasion of the Somali Peninsula from Saudi Arabia, supplemented by a further invasion from Ethiopia; in terms of medium density swarms, the invasion would probably have covered an area of several thousand square miles. The locust swarms had gradually moved south-eastward, breeding along the way. This had resulted in heavy infestations of hoppers across the Somali Peninsula and extending southwards into the Ogaden.

Shortly before my departure, I was given final instructions concerning the payment of the staff who would be employed. It was explained that no bank existed near the location of the locust camp at Jin-Ali, which meant that I would need to travel about one hundred miles to Las Anod in the Somaliland Protectorate to obtain money. I was also informed that food was likely to be in short supply. It might be possible to obtain a few eggs from the local village and there was always the possibility that one could shoot a guinea fowl, partridge (yellowneck), or possibly a gazelle. However, I should understand that I would be too busy to spare much time shooting for the 'pot' and it was considered prudent to issue me with two boxes of tinned food; these were commonly referred to as 'rations'.

I had asked a carpenter to make me a wooden box in which I would keep my clothes and this was duly loaded into a Land Rover, together with tentage, rations and cooking utensils. In addition to the Land Rover, a truck (Dodge Power Wagon) would be filled with forty gallon drums containing water (two drums) and petrol (five drums).

Before my departure, I was given two final pieces of information. First, the main purpose in sending me to Jin-Ali was so that I could obtain first-hand experience of the nature of the work I was to undertake. An anti-locust campaign had been underway for almost two months; the field officer in charge of the operations in the area had reported that all was going reasonably to plan and he hoped that the control operations would be satisfactorily completed within the next few weeks or so. I was told that if the campaign continued to progress well, it was possible that the field officer *in situ* would be withdrawn and sent elsewhere, leaving me to oversee the completion of operations. Second, it was mentioned that various reports had been received from the Ogaden area relating to personal security; in the circumstances, the British Colonial Administrative Service had recently advised that unprotected civilians (such as DLC personnel) should call at the police station at Danot in the Haud area, which was adjacent to the Ogaden. Depending on the destination of the person concerned, the police officer in charge had authority to provide the civilian with an armed escort.

Fig. 1 — **The Horn of Africa** - The desert locust (schistocerca gregaria) affects some sixty countries. During plague periods the Horn of Africa proved to be the area most frequently invaded by large concentrations of locust swarms.

(Places referred to in the text are shown on the map.)

I duly left Hargeisa in a Land Rover, followed by the Dodge Power Wagon, complete with a team of drivers and a young man who would cook for me and generally assist with various domestic duties such as helping to put up the tent and organising the laundry. We headed south on the road to Awareh about one hundred miles away, the dust churning out behind us like smoke.

About seventy miles south of Hargeisa, we began to traverse a swarm of locusts which was moving eastwards. We stopped to view the spectacle. The swarm was of medium density and seemed to be of considerable depth; some of the yellow locusts were beginning to settle on the vegetation, as well as on the sandy soil which was visible between the bushes and *acacia* trees of that semi desert area. When we looked upwards and into the swarm, we could see locusts high above us, their silvery wings glittering against the sun. At that otherwise silent place, we could hear the constant hum of the swarm as it moved across the road. It seemed that the longer one watched the swarm, the more strongly one developed an empty feeling of powerlessness against the seemingly endless horde of insects. The menace was present in the millions.

My first reaction was that I should report the sighting of the swarm and immediately produced the form which would be used to record the details. We continued our journey and, from the mileometer, we noted that we had traversed the swarm from north to south for about eight miles; we had little idea of the east-west dimension. During the last mile or so, I had noted that more and more of the locusts seemed to be settling; they were yellow in colour and many were copulating.

En route to Awareh, we called at a small police post and I enquired of the sergeant whether he was in radio communication with Hargeisa. He responded that he would be able to transmit a message to Hargeisa and he would ask for the message to be urgently delivered to the DLC Base. I therefore summarised the report along the following lines,

"Urgent DLC Base via Police headquarters, Hargeisa. From Everard. Encountered mature yellow locust swarm about mile seventy south of Hargeisa, medium density, moving slowly eastwards, many settling. Copulating hard. For your info and any instructions. Reply immediately. Police post Awareh."

On arrival in Awareh, we drove to the police post and enquired whether a message had been received for Mr. Everard of the DLC; indeed it had and it read as follows,

"For Everard. Your message received. Stop copulating and kill them."

Where would the world be without wit?

Awareh was not unfamiliar to me, since two years previously I had spent the first months of my military service on detachment in the area. At that time, we had been involved with some minor internal policing duties, primarily to discourage tribal groups from clashing over the scarce waterholes. I called at the District Officer's complex and was delighted to find 'Bimbashi' (a Sudanese title) Aske in the office; he welcomed me and told me that a good deal of tribal warfare was in progress and that I should take whatever precautions I could against the intrusion of 'Shifta', the local name for bandits. He told me that recently he had asked the internal military force (the Somaliland Scouts) to support his efforts to maintain peace; a former senior military officer, Brigadier Given, had also made himself available to assist. During a skirmish a number of shots had been fired and one of these had removed a finger from Brigadier Given's hand.

The following day, we continued our journey through the bush until we reached Danot; as instructed, we called at the police post. The police officer in charge had been informed of our impending arrival; without delay two armed police constables were made available to look after us. Both were from the Issa tribe. The Issa are, along with the Danakil, generally recognised as being a fine people with brave fighting qualities. Since the Issa inhabited the north-western part of Somaliland, spilling over towards Djibouti, these men had no tribal affiliation to those who inhabited the Ogaden. Based on my experience amongst the Issa two years previously, once the constables joined us I felt confident that we would be well looked after.

The DLC camp at Jin-Ali was situated about seven miles north of the village. The camp area was protected by a *zariba*, which effectively was a fence (six feet high) of thorny *acacia* bush. Within the camp area was the 'office' which was a shelter constructed from the local bush. The rather primitive construction permitted one to work in relative comfort, mainly because the inhabitant was protected from the sun; at the same time, the bushy walls permitted any breeze to ventilate the interior. On one side was an open doorway, while opposite there was another opening which led into a tent, where one slept.

The locust campaign was in full swing and the field officer in charge of the area had employed about two hundred Somalis whose job it was to spread bait in front of the marching armies of hoppers; most of these were already in the fourth stage (instar).

In addition to the labourers who performed the work, there were others whose job it was to scout the area in search of new egg fields. A trained eye could spot where eggs had been laid and the presence of the eggs would then be confirmed through a brief digging operation. The 'scouts' were key reconnaissance personnel, since if one could receive information about egg fields a few days in advance, then one could plan the control operation more or less to the day, when the eggs would hatch into first instar hoppers.

In addition to the camp office, there was a living area for the Somali Supervisor and his staff. There was a fleet of about ten vehicles; these were mainly used to haul bait from the nearest depot some hundred miles away. The vehicles would also be used to deliver a few bags of bait to various designated points in the campaign area, where the bait would then be loaded on to burden camels for transportation to the scene of operations.

One major failing of the location of the camp was that there was no local water supply. It was understood that a limited amount of water might be available from time to time at the village of Jin-Ali; however, because of the number of personnel employed at the camp, the Jin-Ali Elders had decided that the village was not in a position to provide water on a continuing basis. Arrangements had therefore been made to obtain water from the next town (Galadi), which was just over the border in Ethiopia.

During periods of anti-locust operations, the routine of the field officer followed a pattern as demanded by the progress, or otherwise, of the campaign. One usually rose between five and six a.m.; over an early morning cup of tea, one would endeavour to assess the current situation and decide on adjustments to the execution of the campaign. For example, if the scouts had brought information the previous evening about a new egg field, then preparations would need to be made for a preliminary visit to the area to assess the extent of the egg field, after which logistic arrangements would have to be made in terms of personnel and materials. Stocks of water and petrol had to be checked every day in order that realistic requests could be made for replenishment. Much of the day was spent in either driving between the various work sites to supervise the work, or perhaps undertaking a walking trip with camels to visit the more inaccessible areas. The total area of operational responsibility of the field officer varied between two and ten thousand square miles, depending on the nature of the terrain and the density of the locust infestation.

After three or four days, the field officer whom I was assisting told me he thought I was making excellent progress and seemed to be quickly grasping the nature of the work; he also felt that I was developing a good understanding of what was important, as opposed to issues which were of lesser importance. He therefore suggested that I should take over part of his operations to gain first-hand experience; naturally, if I needed advice or guidance on any matter, he was available to assist.

I grasped the opportunity with much enthusiasm and used a great amount of energy in fulfilling my duties to the very best of my ability. Uppermost in our minds was that the time-frame at our disposal to achieve success was relatively limited. Once the hoppers had shed their skins for the last time and had become immature locusts, it would only be a matter of a day or two before, as though a secret trumpet had sounded (unheard by human ears), the locusts would rise up from the trees and bushes in a great cloud, only leaving us to consider the size of the swarm which had escaped.

After about two weeks, my colleague told me that he had received instructions that morning by radio to return to Hargeisa, as his services would be needed in another area. He was to hand the entire operation to me. He stated that he was confident that I could oversee the final part of the campaign, which in any case would draw to a close within the following three to four weeks, as the hoppers matured into locusts and flew off.

The handing over details were completed in a day or so and I then found myself in a position of responsibility for the successful completion of the campaign.

The vulnerability of our situation in terms of water became starkly clear when, about a week after the departure of my predecessor, the vehicle which had been dispatched to Galadi to collect water returned with empty drums. In discussion with the Supervisor and driver, it transpired that our staff had tried to smuggle a forty-gallon drum of ghee (liquid butter) over the border and this had been discovered. Initially, the Ethiopian Customs authorities had confiscated the vehicle and placed the accompanying staff under arrest. After a few hours of negotiation, the staff and vehicle had been released, but without water. The authorities then informed the staff that they should not expect to return to Galadi to collect water ever again.

Because of the potential seriousness of the situation, I immediately dispatched a short letter of apology to the Ethiopian Military Commanding Officer who was responsible for the public administration of the township of Galadi. I also took the opportunity to request him to receive me the following day for a short courtesy call.

Standing before a fort-like building the next day, I wondered what sort of reception might await me, if indeed I was to be received at all. After about ten minutes, I was asked to follow a soldier, who took me to the office of a young Amhara Captain; although somewhat reserved and formal, he nevertheless gave an impression that he had a pleasant disposition. He spoke no English but, like many professionals in Ethiopia at that time, spoke French quite well. After a few minutes of courteous exchanges, I referred to the problem of the water, explained the type of work in which we were engaged and informed the Captain that if it should not be possible for us to obtain water from Galadi, we would simply have to abandon the anti-locust campaign and leave the area. The Captain gave no immediate indication of his reaction. He glanced at me pensively for some seconds and then asked me whether I would like to join him for lunch; I happily agreed.

Lunch was eaten in a restaurant close by which served Ethiopian food and drink (anis). As the lunch progressed, the Captain became more relaxed and at one point I told him he gave me the impression that he was a happy man; was he really happy in a town such as Galadi? After all, he was a long way from Addis Ababa or Harar; the Somali population of the area could show hostile tendencies and I had understood that a number of incidents had taken place in which Ethiopian soldiers had been killed.

The Captain responded that, indeed, he was a happy man. He acknowledged that he worked in a hostile environment and that life was not always easy. He then turned to me and said he wanted to share a secret with me. I listened intently.

The Captain explained that until about a year previously, his professional career had been extremely successful in all respects. However, he had committed a grave error of judgement; he had fallen in love with the wife of a General. The beauty and personality of the woman made her irresistible to him; for her part, she had returned his deep and limitless affection. In plain language, he had had an affair with the General's wife.

The Captain was under the impression that his relationship with the General's wife had not been detected. However, when one day he learned that he was to be posted to Ual Ual (the scene of the outbreak of hostilities at the beginning of the Italian/Ethiopian war in the mid thirties), he realised that his affair was no longer secret.

The Captain further explained that he had languished in Ual Ual for several months, after which he received instructions that he should take over the military administration of the township of Galadi. He assumed that he would remain in Galadi for the indefinite future. He then turned to me and smiled in a charmingly sincere way.

After a few moments I thanked him for having taken me into his confidence and wondered whether I could ask just one question,

"When one takes into account the circumstances of your unhappy situation, why are you so happy?"

Without hesitation he explained that there were several 'punishment' military stations in Ethiopia; Galadi was regarded as by far the worst of these. The fact that he could not be sent to another location which was more unpleasant than Galadi was, for him, a good reason to be happy!

I immediately proposed a toast to the Captain's continued happiness in Galadi and wished him well in his future career; I was sure that with the resilient nature of his character, all would be eventually resolved in a reasonable manner.

I then quietly focused on the primary purpose of my visit and gently asked the Captain what his final decision would be in relation to our water supply. Without hesitating, his face broke into a flashing smile and he touched me jovially on the shoulder,

"As long as I am here, you can have as much water as you like, but please try and supervise your staff so that they will not again deviate from the law."

I thanked the Captain for his understanding and we left the restaurant. Fortunately, my Land Rover was waiting close at hand and the driver courteously opened the passenger door for me to sit at his side. Whereas I had felt well in the restaurant, in the hot sun outside I suddenly felt nauseated and somewhat drunk. The important thing was that I should give no inkling of my condition to the Captain; I shook his hand warmly and we waved one another good-bye.

Once out of sight of the township I lay on my side across two of the firm Land Rover passenger cushions. The return distance to our camp was thirty miles; the driving time was between three and three and half hours. Unlike the outward journey, when I had felt the Land Rover pitch and roll as it bounced over the stones, on the return journey I slept like a child and felt nothing of the road surface. Fortunately, for the remainder of our sojourn at the Jin-Ali camp we experienced no further water problems.

Although the locust control work was a new experience, I felt that it suited me well. I enjoyed the planning element, I was happy with the administrative aspects of my duties and I enjoyed being in a position where I could take day-to-day decisions based on operational needs. The labour force seemed to work quite well and did not resent my energetic supervision. Most of the workers showed a greater interest in receiving rations (mainly rice and dates) than in their wages; in other words, for them food was accorded a high priority.

Before his departure, my predecessor had explained that the workers should be paid twice a month. The procedure was that their names were entered on forms, which showed the number of days worked, the rate per day and the amount due; none of the workers could write, which meant that each had to place his thumbprint on the form as a signature.

One evening I assessed how much money would be needed for the next pay-day (a considerable sum) and the following morning I asked headquarters by radio that when a vehicle would next be sent, the driver should bring a cheque for the sum involved which I would cash (as previously instructed) at Las Anod in Somaliland.

A few days later, the cheque arrived and I told my Somali Supervisor that the following day I would be travelling to Las Anod, leaving him to supervise all matters during my absence. Meanwhile, the anti-locust campaign was continuing with all the force which I could bring to bear against the menace which could be seen marching in armies, by now in the fifth instar, across the local terrain, devouring all forms of vegetation as it progressed.

The journey to Las Anod was similar to most journeys in that part of the world; progress was slow over a bumpy, dusty road. When we eventually reached Las Anod, I drove around the small town and was surprised to find that most commercial establishments were closed; my immediate reaction was that perhaps these places had closed for a lunch hour. On enquiry, however, we learned that it was a Friday (the Muslim day of prayers and rest) and that all shops and banks would remain closed. I drove to the house of the District Commissioner; he expressed sympathy with the situation in which I found myself, but he explained there was nothing to be done to overcome the situation. He gently suggested that I might find it useful in future to keep some track of the days of the week. I explained that I would return to Las Anod in a day or two; without further ado, we drove back to our camp at Jin-Ali and arrived late at night.

The following morning I was woken in the usual way by a youngster who had brought me a cup of tea; the usual procedure was that he happily wished me a good morning and placed the tea on the wooden box which contained my clothes and a few personal belongings. But this morning, things were different. He wished me good morning; but at the same time he wanted to know where he should place the cup and saucer since there was no sign of my box. He was of course quite right; the box had disappeared.

I sprang out of bed, ran through the shelter and looked for our protective constables; they were sleeping peacefully on a blanket not far from the door opening. I felt this was no time for recrimination; after all, the constables could not be expected to stay awake for twenty-four hours at a time. They were excellent men and it was understandable that during the night hours they should fall asleep.

Having explained the situation to the Issa constables, both entered the shelter to take stock of the situation. My own assessment was perhaps more personal; at that particular point, the only property which was immediately available to me was a green silk dressing gown (given to me by my father) which had been draped over my bed, plus a cup and saucer which had remained on my camp table after coffee the previous evening.

While the reality of my personal situation was impressing itself on me, the constables were staring at the ground in the shelter. With fingers pointing to apparent imprints, they slowly moved towards the back of the shelter and into my tent. After staring for some seconds at the dusty area around my bed they drew my attention to various imprints in the dust; these were the imprints of butts of Italian rifles. They had no doubt that the thieves had stood over me with their rifles while the box was removed from the tent; fortunately I had not awoken.

The constables then announced that they would follow the large footprints of the shifta in an endeavour to identify who had stolen the box. They asked me whether the money which I had collected from Las Anod was in the box and I was relieved to respond that, although there was a small sum of money in one corner of the box, due inadvertently to having visited Las Anod when the banks were closed, I had returned the previous night without the large sum of money needed to pay the local wages. The constables asked me whether I wished to accompany them, or would I prefer to await the results of their search; I told them that I would prefer to assist. After a quick breakfast, the constables, the Supervisor and myself set off, following the footsteps up to the *zariba*, through a small opening and continuing over the terrain of loose, sandy soil.

By now the sun was rapidly climbing into the cloudless sky and the heat of the day gained strength. Since I no longer had clothes as such, I wore the green dressing grown; each of us was sweating profusely. The low *acacia* trees and bushes were green after recent rain and the topography was gently undulating. I marvelled at the speed at which we progressed, led by the constables whose practised eyes never seemed to leave the large footprints.

Suddenly we heard a shot; and then another. The constables crouched behind a bush and motioned us to move to one side. They soon detected the area from where the shots came and, without hesitation, both constables ran at full speed towards two figures who could be seen in their whitish Somali gowns about two hundred and fifty yards away. The Supervisor and myself watched our constables disappear in the bush and waited; several shots rang out.

After about ten minutes the constables reappeared and handed me some of my clothes, together with a small amount of money. Apparently, one of the shots of the police had passed through the clothes of one of the bandits and he had immediately dropped some of my belongings, which were being divided between the two men. The senior constable stated that the culprits were locust scouts, one of whom was called Warsameh Deria. A constable asked me whether I could recall the men, to which I responded that I remembered both well, since I had wondered why these men visited me with news of locust infestations more frequently than the other scouts. The simple fact was that both had wished to become as familiar as possible with the lay-out of my living and sleeping accommodation.

On our return to camp, the senior constable virtually took control of the investigation. He asked me to drive him to a certain village which, he explained, was the village where the two men lived. I looked on while he called for the Elders. Three Elders appeared and the constable stated that my belongings had been stolen by Warsameh Deria and his accomplice; the constable expected all items of property to be returned to me within forty-eight hours. The Elders remonstrated with the constable, stating that Warsameh Deria had not been seen for many weeks and they considered it unfair that they should be held responsible for his alleged actions. The constable was quite unmoved by these pleas; he repeated his ultimatum, after which he requested me to drive him back to camp.

After forty-eight hours had elapsed, the constable asked me to drive him again to the village of Warsameh Deria. He summoned the Elders, who immediately explained that the matter was outside their control. At that point the two constables rounded up 584 sheep and goats and dismantled three *gurghis*; a *gurghi* is a Somali mobile home which is constructed of mats placed over flexible branches. The constables also made enquiries about the relationship of various villagers with Warsameh Deria; resulting from this the brother-in-law of Warsameh Deria and a woman were escorted by the constables into our Dodge Power Wagon.

The man and woman, the 584 livestock and the dismantled *Gurghis* were all brought to the DLC camp, where an extension of the camp area was made by the erection of another *zariba*. The entire booty of the constables was then placed within the confines of the *zariba* and the Elders of the village were told that the relations and livestock would remain in the *zariba* until my belongings were returned.

That afternoon, a delegation of the village Elders, strengthened by a group of Elders from the town of Jin-Ali, visited the camp. Their first action was to present me with a goat. The Jin-Ali Elders then explained that it would be extremely difficult to recover my belongings since these had been shared between Warsameh Deria, his accomplice, plus two other men. The Elders stated that the four men had fled across the border to Ethiopia.

Before I could respond, the senior constable thanked the Elders for their explanation, as well as the goat. The constable stated that he sympathised with the Elders because it was already clear that some of the animals would die of thirst; he also had some doubts about the survival of the man and woman.

I then intervened to state that I hoped the Elders would do their utmost to recover at least some of my belongings. I requested the constable to let the woman return to the village; to my relief, the constable reluctantly agreed. I then asked about the man; the constable responded that he felt that, in the circumstances, the best course would be to inform the brother-in-law that he should find the thieves and explain to them that unless the stolen belongings were returned in the very near future, most of the animals would die.

The locust campaign continued. Learning from my recent experience, I travelled to Las Anod and stayed overnight with the District Commissioner. Early the following morning, I cashed the wages' cheque and immediately drove back to the DLC camp. I had made prior arrangements for the leader of each of the gangs of workers to be present and I arranged for most of the money to be disbursed immediately on arrival at the camp, thus reducing further risk of theft.

With only a short time remaining before the escaping locusts would depart in a swarm, renewed efforts were made to control the infestation to the greatest extent possible. In consultation with the Supervisor, I began to make plans to leave the area and suggested that the camp facilities should be quietly reduced and that any remaining supplies could be transported gradually by truck to Danot. I had in mind that the entire evacuation operation would be completed over a period of about a week, with myself and the Supervisor being the last to leave; the Supervisor suggested that it might be preferable to leave in the hours of darkness.

The field operations were beginning to be reduced as various areas of locust infestation had been reasonably controlled; efforts to finally bring the remaining heavily infested areas under control were intensified.

About three days before I anticipated leaving the area, a message was received from the Elders to the effect that practically all of my belongings had been recovered and I should be prepared to meet the Elders at midnight near their village in an open area. The area was known to one of the local employees, who undertook to show the Supervisor, the constables and myself the precise location.

What was not clear to us was whether we were being directed to some sort of trap. We took into account the animals which were still languishing in the *zariba* adjacent to our camp. If the shifta could liquidate our small group, then they could recover their livestock. None of us knew the answer to the proposition. It was up to me to make a decision, which I did.

With hindsight, if I had been about twenty years older, I have no doubt that I would have requested the release of the livestock and simply decided that the risk we were invited to take was not worth the reward. But a man in his early twenties often thinks quite differently from someone twice that age. After listening to the pros and cons of the implications of the proposal, I told my Supervisor and the constables that we should go to the designated place, accompanied by the man who knew the way.

We set off on foot at about nine p.m. I vividly recall a half-moon and the wonderfully starlit night. Our eyes soon became accustomed to that particular shade of darkness which is not of the dense, black type, but which has been lightened by the glittering heavens. We followed our man through the bush.

As far as sounds were concerned, there were few wild animals in the vicinity. In the Ogaden, most of the wild animals are found further south along the Webi Sciabelli river (in fact the name means "Leopard River"). Further south, our walk would have been accompanied by continuous cat-calling of jackals and the frequent cries of hyena. We did hear the occasional jackal; otherwise the night was silent except for the padding of our feet and the occasional monosyllabic exchange of comments between the group.

After we had walked about ten miles, our guide stopped and told us that the open area which I was supposed to enter at midnight was immediately ahead of us. I looked at my watch; we had about a half hour to wait. I suggested to the constables that it might be prudent for them to make a short reconnaissance of the area around the clearing, just in case there were armed men waiting in the bushes. The constables returned after about twenty minutes and stated that they had so far found no one; all was very quiet.

As midnight approached, I asked the constables to take up positions so that they could cover me with their firearms to the best of their ability; I also asked them to open fire if a shot should be fired from the perimeter of the clearing.

At midnight, I walked from the perimeter towards the centre of the clearing; after covering about fifteen yards, I stopped. I realised that if somebody wished to kill me, I was an easy target; although I felt vulnerable, at the same time I was somewhat strangely confident that all would be well. I glanced slowly around the edge of the clearing; there was no noise and no sign of movement.

A few minutes later, since there was no sign of movement, I began to think that I should withdraw from the clearing; as I was about to return to the perimeter, a slight movement ahead of me indicated that something was happening. A tall man approached, holding something against his chest; I could not discern his features. Within a few seconds, he was standing before me and he simply dropped his load on the ground; he then turned round and slowly walked away.

I knelt down and could feel some clothes and, to my surprise, a small heap of money. All of these belongings were wrapped in a blanket. I took hold of the blanket by the corners, ensured as far as possible that my belongings and money were enclosed and withdrew.

Immediately, the constables, my Supervisor and our guide gathered round and we set off on our return ten-mile walk. Once we had reached our camp, we examined the contents of the blanket; virtually all of my belongings and money had been returned.

The following morning the livestock were released and yet another consultation took place with the constables and my Supervisor regarding the next step. The constables and the Supervisor gave their opinion that my life was now in danger. They stated that it was likely that the shifta would organise an ambush; in their considered judgement, the correct course of action would be to return to Hargeisa via Danot without delay.

My reaction was that the campaign had been effectively completed to the maximum extent possible. I told the constables that I would take their advice; however, I stated that for one more day, I would inspect the various infestation areas in order to verify the degree of success achieved in controlling the locust infestations. I suggested that we should quietly leave the camp for Danot the following night.

Next day, I visited most of the infestation areas and found little residual locust activity. For security reasons I was accompanied by the senior of the constables, who seemed to be growing increasingly apprehensive about my safety. Bearing in mind that this excellent man was of the Issa tribe, I took his anxiety more seriously than would have been the case if he had come from another tribe.

On the return drive to the camp, we saw a Somali some distance ahead who was standing by the side of a large termite hill; sandy red termite hills (typically five to ten feet high) were commonplace and they were a feature of the area. The man seemed to be watching us in curiosity with his spear at his side. As we drove past him, he suddenly raised his spear and hurled it with lightning force at us; the spear passed just behind my head, flying straight over the back of the open Land Rover.

My instant reaction was to accelerate away from the danger. Calmly, the Issa constable turned to me and asked me to stop; I should turn around and try to chase the tribesman. I did this and we soon caught sight of him running through the bush. The constable jumped out of the Land Rover and shortly afterwards had caught the tribesman. He escorted him back to the Land Rover and instructed him to sit in the back. The man refused, whereupon the constable hit him with his fist with such force that the man collapsed over the back of the Land Rover; at this point, the constable raised the man's legs and pushed them into the back. He then came round to the front of the vehicle, sat down and asked me to drive back to camp. On our return, the constable stated that it was his business to deal with the attempted murder and he would settle the matter personally.

I requested a final meeting with the Supervisor and the constables; it was agreed that we would leave as quietly and unobtrusively as possible at about midnight by Land Rover. I then went for a short evening's walk; as seemed to happen on most evenings, the goat which the Elders had given me followed a few steps behind. The staff had christened the goat and it seemed to have become relatively domesticated.

On my return to the camp a youth came up to me and seemed to be trying to give me some information. I therefore invited him into the camp and, with the assistance of the Supervisor in interpretation, learned that the youth claimed to be an enemy of Warsameh Deria. He stated that Warsameh Deria had returned to his village the previous night; if the constables wished to capture the shifta, he would guide them to the man's *gurghi*.

After further consultations with the constables, we marginally decided to accept the offer and, again, we set off in the direction of the village of Warsameh Deria. We had left our camp rather late and it was already two thirty a.m. before we reached a point which was about three hundred yards from the small village. Our guide asked us to lie quietly in the low vegetation, because he expected Warsameh Deria and his accomplice to return to the village shortly. We lay quietly in the grass and low bushes.

Within five minutes, we heard voices close at hand and, almost immediately, I saw the silhouettes of two men, one of whom was tall and could well have been Warsameh Deria. The padding noise of their footsteps became louder and I suddenly developed an apprehensive feeling that they were so close to us that they might either step on us or fall over our prostrated bodies; as it was, they passed very closely in front of our heads.

After a few minutes the constables stated that they had seen the *gurghi* into which the men had disappeared and they intended to enter the *gurghi* and capture the men. If the men resisted arrest, they would be shot.

The constables stated that because it seemed to be darker than the previous evening, they preferred to wait for about two hours until the first moments of the dawn.

At the appointed time, one of the constables entered the small *gurghi*, while the other remained outside in case the culprits tried to flee. To the deep disappointment of the constables, the *gurghi* in question was found to be empty; an adjacent *gurghi* contained an old woman who was sleeping on the floor.

On our return to our camp, I felt that we had all suffered too much from climaxes and anti-climaxes. I identified myself strongly with the feelings of the constables and the Supervisor that we should leave as quickly and quietly as possible. That evening, we drove away from the camp area and in the direction of Danot without incident. The domesticated goat had now become a member of our close-knit team; with its new status, it travelled in the front of the Land Rover, sitting between the driver and myself. During the journey, it demonstrated from time to time that there are limitations in terms of domesticating a goat!

Once in Danot, I reported to the police officer in charge and thanked him sincerely for having provided me with security protection during a difficult period. We then continued our journey to Awareh where, to my surprise, I found the District Officer's complex deserted.

Since I felt that I knew Bimbashi Aske quite well, I drove up to his house. A number of people were enjoying food and drink and I made a sign from the door towards Bimbashi Aske. He immediately walked over and asked me what I was doing in Awareh on Christmas Day? I responded that I had come from another world and had no idea that it was Christmas Day.

After a great deal of feasting and drinking, I was shown a room with clean sheets and a soft pillow; I soon drifted into a wonderfully contented sleep. The following morning, I made contact with my staff and enquired if everything was in good order. They responded with smiles and said they had also been enjoying Christmas; even though they were not Christians, they felt they should be part of the festivities. Where was the goat? The answer could be seen on their faces. A goat had been sacrificed at Christmas time.

About five years later I briefly revisited Jin-Ali on an inspection trip. Understandably, as I approached the village my mind returned to the anti-locust campaign in which I had been involved in the area and, in particular, the theft of my belongings. The group of Somalis with me would certainly wish to halt in the village for a cup of tea; if I were to meet Warsameh Deria, what would be our reactions?

To my relief, there was no sign of the shifta. Towards the end of the tea drinking session, in a quiet, unconcerned way I asked those present if anyone remembered a man called Warsameh Deria. Immediately the tea-maker responded that everyone remembered Warsameh Deria because he was one of the most important and dangerous shifta of the region. He had been involved in many incidents involving bloodshed. Then another bystander commented that he had also known Warsameh Deria; the shifta had been killed about two years previously in a fight in the border area.

Glancing recently at an 1896 edition of the *Brockhaus Konversations-Lexikon*, referring to the inhabitants of the Ogaden the encyclopaedia includes the following statement:

The hostile mistrust (of the inhabitants), the enjoyment they derive from robbery and murder effectively closes the area to Europeans. The Englishman J.L. James succeeded in traversing the area in 1885 and was the first white man to do so. In London, he published *The Unknown Horn of Africa* in 1888.

Probably little has changed in the area during the last hundred years, although certainly the weapons which are now in the hands of the tribesmen are more sophisticated than those used in the last century.

On the day after Christmas (Boxing Day) our team returned to Hargeisa and, after debriefing and completion of various reports, we prepared for the next campaign.

Chapter Three

The Issa

In January 1953 I was briefed for the next assignment. Further locust swarms were expected to invade the Somali Peninsula and breeding would occur along the littoral during the first quarter of 1953. I should establish a camp at a small village called Sillil, which was about thirty miles from the town of Zeila. Zeila was an ancient town and had a number of Arab inhabitants. At one stage in its history, Zeila had been an important commercial centre; however, during the French colonial period Djibouti (thirty three miles to the west) had been well developed and was now a much busier seaport.

Preparations for the next assignment took about a week, after which our team departed from Hargeisa for our destination. We would travel about eighty miles to the town of Borama, the administrative centre of the Borama-Zeila District. We would then carry on for about a day's drive to Sillil.

Although I approached the impending assignment with enthusiasm, inevitably I was conscious of certain events which had taken place in the area about two years previously, during my military service. The Issa tribesmen who inhabited the area had suffered, in the mid-forties, from the loss of some of their livestock, caused by the animals eating the mixture of bran and arsenic locust bait; in other words, instead of the bait having been thinly spread in front of the infestation of marching hoppers, some bags had simply been dumped under some trees, with disastrous results. During my military service two years previously, when I had been asked to assist in anti-locust operations, the tragedy had been still uppermost in the minds of the tribesmen, who vowed to oppose any laying of locust bait.

As a young lieutenant I had been dispatched to support, as necessary, the government in imposing its policy of applying control measures to the invading locusts. The District Commissioner had arranged for a number of meetings to be held with the Elders of the tribe, to explain that arsenic would no longer be used in locust bait; he also went to great lengths to explain that the recently-developed insecticides would not harm the tribesmen's livestock, even if the locust bait was mindlessly dumped and eaten in significant quantities by the animals.

In spite of the efforts of the then colonial government to convince the Elders and tribesmen that they need have no more fears of loss of livestock, the Issa tribe defiantly refused to permit the laying of locust bait. Apart from simply refusing to co-operate, the Elders stated (rightly) that the tribe associated locusts with rain; they felt, with some logic, that if the locusts were killed then the rains would fail, with catastrophic effects to their livestock due to lack of ephemeral grazing.

The whole matter had come to a head near a coastal village called Luk Haiyah. The District Commissioner and his staff were camped on a small ridge about three miles from the coast; in addition to the staff of the District Commissioner, a small unit of the Desert Locust Control Organisation was present (with two truckloads of locust bait), plus my military section of a sergeant and eight askaris. Although on departure from Hargeisa I had been offered the use of a revolver, I had responded that I doubted if one would need such a weapon; I was therefore unarmed.

That night we heard a great deal of drumming, accompanied by high-pitched calls. The following morning, we were surprised to see hundreds of tribesmen in what the previous day had seemed to be a sparsely-populated area; the tribesmen were agitated and we seemed to be virtually surrounded.

Early in the morning, the District Commissioner called me and stated that he had been in radio contact with government headquarters in Hargeisa and that he had been instructed to implement the government's policy by laying locust bait in the area; to the extent that any of the tribesmen might decide to obstruct the government's policy, he might need to call upon the military, which would be our section, to restore order.

The District Commissioner then requested the locust unit, which was headed by a Somali Supervisor, to traverse an area close-by and spread locust bait from two trucks. He stated that he would follow the operation on foot and would stand in the area where the locust bait had been laid. He requested me to follow him, with my section of askaris, about fifty yards behind him.

The operation ensued and within a few minutes the symbolic laying of the bait was completed; the District Commissioner arrived shortly after in the area, with my section following as instructed.

There seemed to be a hushed lull for about five minutes; the wailing of the tribesmen had subsided, a breeze tempered the heat of the rising sun and, for that brief period, all seemed quiet.

Suddenly, we heard many shrieking voices and about two hundred tribesmen appeared from a nearby dry river-bed (a *toug*); all of them were running at high speed straight towards us. The District Commissioner walked slowly towards them and held up his hands, shouting "Stop!" When they were about eighty yards in front of us, they began to slow down and, eventually, most of the tribesmen stopped about fifty yards from the District Commissioner. He spoke Somali quite well and implored them to sit down with him; he would discuss the subject and answer all of their questions.

Our section had moved up to within ten yards of the District Commissioner and, looking beyond him, we could see the tribesmen clearly. All of them were carrying spears, some held shields in front of them, while others were swinging slings at their sides. Although they seemed to be listening to the District Commissioner, at the same time it was obvious that emotionally they were highly charged.

No sooner had the District Commissioner finished his brief statement when the leaders cried out loudly and the charge continued.

I had taken the precaution of ordering the section to kneel in the firing position; the askaris were prepared for action. The District Commissioner was standing immediately in front of the section, which meant that if some shots were to be fired, then we would have to wait until he retreated behind the firing line. As I approached him from behind, he turned round and, in an apparent state of deep distress and audibly sobbing, he asked me to restore order.

The Issa tribe has a reputation for producing some of the finest warriors and the constant warring between the Issa and Danakil tribes has been the subject of considerable storytelling. There was no doubt that the lives of the District Commissioner, the locust workers, my section of askaris and myself were in danger. It would be a matter of seconds before the tribesmen would be upon us; being heavily outnumbered, it was clear that we had little chance of survival. From a personal point of view, I felt especially vulnerable since I was unarmed. An image flashed through my thoughts: a dead man's penis protruded from his mouth, which also contained testicles. This had been what had stared me in the face when, after a recent tribal battle over water, I had briefly raised the canvas of a truck loaded with bodies.

Once I had rushed the District Commissioner behind our line, the order was given to open fire and, fortunately, this stopped the charge. I use the word 'fortunately,' because only one man was injured. As had happened on previous occasions (for example in the days of the Somali Camel Corps), it is too much to ask one Somali to fire on another; such was the case that day. The important point, however, was that the shooting had had the desired effect and with some encouragement from the askaris and myself, gradually the tribesmen crawled away through the grass.

Civil order had been restored, the injured tribesman was dispatched to the nearest hospital for attention and the government had made its point: the desert locust control operations would be implemented.

A few months after the incident, the District Commissioner was invited to Buckingham Palace, where he received recognition for his efforts in restoring order in a hostile and delicate situation.

In early 1953, as our Land Rover bumped along the road beyond Borama as it gradually descended to the coastal plain, it was understandable that I became conscious of feelings of apprehension. One could never underestimate the Issa. One general tribal characteristic that I found of some comfort was that the Issa tend not to involve themselves in treachery; in other words, the Issa would not give you a smiling welcome one day and deal with you as they might see fit in the days following. If they were to object to your presence, one would know straight away.

Eventually we reached the village of Sillil, where we were to establish our camp. I remembered Sillil well from my military days; this had been where my section and I had stopped for a few nights *en route* to Luk Haiyah. In the village of Sillil the sole permanent building, constructed of cement blocks, was a disused police station; Sergeant Abdi had suggested that we should temporarily use the small building as a base. There were two small rooms, each of which had a square window opening. The openings were windowless; however, they were barred, which gave the rooms the appearance of prison cells. Sergeant Abdi had arranged for my camp bed to be made up in one of the rooms; he hoped that the small window opening would permit sufficient ventilation for sleep. Each night, between two-thirty and three-thirty, he would wake me up and ask me to transfer to the other room. However, I should leave the camp bed in place; he had arranged for a mat and blanket to be available in the other room. He explained that this was a precaution. By chance, we had installed ourselves during the period of a full moon; he felt that this heightened the risk that the Issa might decide to kill me at night by aiming a spear at the head of my bed. If this were to happen, he hoped that I would already have transferred to the other room! And here I was, two years later, again in Sillil; I was keenly conscious of the fact that I was vulnerable and unprotected in all respects. I had no connection with the Colonial Administrative Service; nor had I police protection.

Shortly after my arrival, a delegation of six Elders came to the camp and presented me with a sheep. In the exchange of welcome and my thanks for the sheep, I stated that I had the feeling that I had met one or two of the Elders on a previous occasion. The senior Elder responded in a matter-of-fact way, stating that I was quite right; two of the Elders had been involved in the Luk Haiyah incident and had recently been released after two years in prison for having taken part in the disturbance. The spokesman added that he wanted me to know that the Elders fully understood that as a military man I had been following the orders of the government; in my new status as a civilian, I need have no worries about my personal safety and I was assured of their total co-operation. They understood the seriousness of the locust situation and they were satisfied that the bait which would be used would cause no harm to livestock. The Elders then stated that during the evening, they hoped that I and my team would be free to join them in a dancing party.

The type of dancing and singing performed by the Issa is markedly different to that of other Somali tribes. Whereas much of Somali dancing follows a somewhat routine pattern of rhythm and sound, Issa dancing is altogether more expressive, passionate and subject to sudden changes of rhythm.

That night, as honoured guests, we were treated to a wonderful spectacle of Issa dancing at its best. The singing and dancing was performed mainly by the men, although the women, standing back a little from the circle of warriors, contributed magnificently with their high-pitched, oscillating voices. The dancers, accompanied by a full-bodied chorus, started each dance fairly slowly and gradually quickened the pace until a crescendo was reached of intense body and leg movement. On occasion, the leading dancer would rush towards me with his spear at shoulder height, as though he was charging at full speed; just before he reached me, he would hurl himself to the ground and would briefly lie, prostrated, panting loudly. Each sequence of the dance seemed to lead to a more intense successor. The finale of the full chorus, with the women's voices at their shrillest, was accompanied by dancing which had now reached a new, and unforgettable, peak.

During the following two months, we energetically pursued the locust campaign. Shortly after our arrival, the area along the coast was invaded by locusts, which soon turned yellow and started breeding. As we had been positioned in good time, it was possible to locate most of the many extensive egg fields, which meant that the various gangs of labourers could be dispersed in readiness to spread the locust bait. Most of the littoral was accessible by Land Rover and truck, which greatly facilitated our work. Essentially, we were dealing with logistics and effective supervision of the control measures. In these relatively uncomplicated conditions, the campaign was conducted successfully and finalised in accordance with our plans.

Because further invasions and hopper infestations were expected from March onwards in the hilly area around Borama, I was requested to move the field base to Borama and establish a camp there in readiness for the anticipated campaign. Although I was a mere twenty two years of age, I had already gained a good deal of experience in anti-locust work and approached the next campaign with confidence.

One of the first tasks to be undertaken concerned the logistics of the general situation. Apart from the main north-south road, there were few roads in the area. In these circumstances, one needed to ascertain to what extent one could use camel tracks for motor transport; in addition, in the absence of tracks, it would be useful to have a reasonably clear idea of the network of dry river-beds, which were called *tougs*. Although the river-beds were usually dry, from time to time heavy rain in the mountains would cause flooding and one needed to be constantly alert to the possibility of a wave of water (sometimes three to four feet high) suddenly rushing down the *toug*. Occasionally, there was loss of life from a heavy flood of water and sometimes in the townships (for example in Hargeisa) vehicles might be washed down the *toug*.

Although our maps gave some indication of the *toug* network, these were often incomplete and occasionally misleading; in addition, as was the case in respect of the area north east of Borama, sometimes a white area on the map would simply show the words 'unsurveyed'.

After organising our camp near Borama, one of our first expeditions took us to an area called the Debrawein. This valley, which at one point became a gorge with high walls of rock, was regarded as virtually inaccessible. However, we had received reports that during periods of locust infestations, the wider parts of the valley were often severely affected. It therefore seemed prudent that, if possible, we should be prepared to undertake locust control operations in the area. In the absence of an access road, this would mean hiring about thirty burden camels to carry the sacks of locust bait and the rations for the gangs of labourers. If it might be possible to find a route into the area, however, then the logistics situation would become much easier.

Two Somalis and myself left by Land Rover with a guide and followed a camel track in the direction of the Debrawein. I had explained to the staff whom we left behind that I might return the same day, especially if we found the way to be impassable in terms of driving a Land Rover into the valley. If we did not return that day, this would probably mean that we had managed to reach the valley. We would take rations with us for three days and I hoped to return in two or three days.

To our happy surprise, we descended without much complication into the lower part of the Debrawein; and that afternoon we travelled for about two miles along the floor of the valley until it became quite narrow. At that point, we walked ahead for about a mile and found our way virtually blocked by some formidable black rocks; however, the stretch of rocks seemed quite limited, so we decided that the following day we would make strong efforts to navigate our way around the rocks. We hoped we were not trapped.

We endured the torment through the Debrawein for five days. Throughout the adventure, the sun beat down on us incessantly by day; the reflection from the rocks and the steep walls of what at one stage was a chasm, seemed to roast us. Human habitation was found only at the beginning of our journey. Nevertheless, we were not alone. There were packs of hyenas which visited us at night and, on one occasion, we met a lone tribesman who was furiously scaling some rocks and who disappeared over the top of a cliff-like formation; our driver explained that the man was in great haste because two or three lions had walked down the bottom of the Debrawein and he had just seen one of the lions carrying off a goat. As he disappeared from view, the man shouted to us and cautioned us to be very careful at night.

Once we had circumnavigated the main area of rocks, we agreed that we had reached a point of no return and that we should carry on in the hope that we would emerge soon at the other end of the Debrawein. As we forged ahead, we experienced countless obstructions and suffered many punctures from the branches of thorn trees which were strewn over the area.

Each night it was necessary for us to erect a *zariba* in order to protect ourselves from the wild animals. We took turns to act as sentinels during the night and the man on duty maintained a large fire. We felt that the *zariba* and fire would discourage the animals from coming near us, although the night air was punctuated by the cries of jackals, the 'laughing' donkey-like sounds of hyena, the low growls of lion and the coughs of leopard. One night, I was woken by a noise in the *zariba* and found myself looking from the inside through the *zariba* at a hyena on the outside.

The one redeeming feature of the area was that, for about three miles, there was running water. In the northern part of the Horn of Africa, surface water is extremely rare. In this case, it ensured that we were able to replenish our water container and therefore carry on with our journey.

I subsequently learned that during the thirties and early forties, a herd of elephants inhabited the Debrawein, taking full advantage of the availability of running water. Sadly, these animals were machine-gunned from the air and some were killed outright; others suffered bullet wounds. There are now no elephants in the Horn of Africa.

On the morning of the fifth day, I told my courageous Somali colleagues that we needed to recognise that we were probably near the end of our endurance. Our food supply was virtually exhausted and the running water which we had enjoyed earlier was now a few miles behind us. We should also recognise that, in order to continue our progression westwards, we would need much energy to mend the punctures, maintain our night camp and carry out all the tasks associated with our arduous journey. My personal view was that we would soon become relatively weak and, increasingly, we would find it difficult not only to continue our journey, but eventually to survive at all. I therefore suggested that unless we reached some sign of habitation that day, the following day we should leave the vehicle and walk in our group westwards until we reached the main north-south road.

In fact, at about four p.m. that day, we crossed a fairly smooth, gravelly area and, as far as I was concerned, I was prepared to continue progressing westwards. However, one of the Somalis turned to me and announced that we had just crossed the main road; my first reaction was that I found the assertion to be untrue. However, with some gentle persuasion, I was guided back to that smooth area and there indeed saw the main road; in that state of near exhaustion, for some reason it was difficult for the senses to accept that the road was in fact real and constituted the key to our delivery from the Debrawein.

We drove southwards in the direction of Borama and soon reached the village of Bawn. The degree of our hunger may be judged by the fact that when we entered a 'coffee shop', each of us walked across to a large cauldron in which lumps of mutton were being boiled; without hesitation, simultaneously, each of us reached into the water to grab a piece of meat, which was immediately subjected to desperate bites.

We returned to our camp that day. Over the ensuing recovery period of almost a week I took stock of the harsh lessons which the Debrawein had taught us. First, I had come face to face with a near-exhausted condition and I recalled the strange, sometimes irrational reactions associated with the condition. I had also learned that there are limits to an attitude which simply tells you to go forward; sometimes it may be more prudent to retreat and tackle a given problem by properly thought-through stages. And without doubt I had had a sharp lesson in endurance; especially under a hot sun and in generally hostile environmental conditions, there are certainly limitations to human endurance. The likelihood of this should be recognised sooner rather than later.

Soon afterwards, we began to receive reports of locust swarms moving eastwards from Ethiopia. Some of these would have crossed the Red Sea from Southern Arabia, whilst other swarms may well have emanated from the Takazze Valley in northern Ethiopia. It was estimated that the swarms would reach our area in seven to ten days. I therefore proposed that, having made a reconnaissance to the north-east, we should reconnoitre the area to the north-west of Borama, stretching from the north-south road to the border with Ethiopia. Specifically, we should visit Gocti and there obtain advice on the *toug* system, which could be accessed with motor transport, in the absence of roads.

We therefore left the following day for Gocti and a meeting was arranged with the village Elders. These men were informative, but did not appear to be friendly. I therefore invited them to share some dates and rice with us and suggested that we could sit as a group in the shade, against a wall of one of the few permanent buildings in the village. During the short meal, we obtained further information and the Elders sketched the *toug* system in the sand using small sticks. Shortly before the end of our 'working lunch', several shots rang out and we immediately realised that the shots were penetrating the wall above our heads; particles of mortar and dust enveloped us as the bullets hit the wall above.

I asked the Elders whether we should move or if they could kindly arrange for the shooting to stop. In a casual way one of the Elders simply replied,

"I am sorry if the shooting disturbs you. On the whole, our men shoot very well. We live close to the Ethiopian border; we have to make sure that we can shoot well because we are often attacked by shifta. After the attack, they take refuge over the border in Ethiopia. It is really nothing to worry about."

The discussion was brought to an end quite quickly and we continued our journey. We had copied the *toug* sketch and followed it with confidence.

Soon we reached one of the main *toug* arteries, at which point we were initially to move south east and, after a few miles, take a left fork past an island of vegetation; this was to lead us to a point which would be close to the main road. There had been no rain in the area and we found that we could travel up the wide, dry river-bed with ease.

When we reached the fork, I asked our driver to ensure that he took the left arm, leaving the relatively dense *acacia* and *sansevieria* vegetation on our right. Although he did this, unfortunately he was late in appreciating that we were traversing an area in which about ten wells had been dug. At that time, there was only one man in the area and he appeared to be working on one of the wells. As the driver tried to steer between several of the wells (which were quite close together), one of his rear wheels slid into one of the wells; the vehicle lurched to a standstill, with one of the rear wheels virtually out of sight.

After discussing the matter with our Somali Supervisor (Mohammed Abdi) and the driver, we decided to look for a piece of smooth wood; we would then try to jack up the sunken rear of the vehicle and move the vehicle forward using the engine, supplemented by our own pushing efforts. Without delay, we went to work and soon found a suitable piece of wood and began to position the jack under a rear leaf spring.

While we were working in the sand under the hot afternoon sun, we suddenly heard a voice and saw a very tall, muscular man watching us. After a few moments, he asked us what we were doing in the *toug*. We explained the situation, whereupon he firmly told us that we had no right to be in the *toug*. As far as he was concerned, *tougs* were for people and livestock; if one had a vehicle, then one's right was limited to using a road.

Initially, we did not take the man's comments seriously and ignored him. He then became agitated and stated that he would return with members of his clan and that they would be armed with spears. On his return, we would be dealt with. We treated our visitor with good humour and told him that we hoped that by the time he returned, we would have moved the Land Rover and would be well on our way.

About half an hour later, we felt that we had raised the rear part of the vehicle to such an extent that we should try to move it forward. Because of the soft sand, we decided to look for some bark which could be placed under the wheels. As we approached the vegetation at the side of the *toug*, our earlier visitor reappeared and was accompanied by about six other men; all were armed with spears.

Apparently looking to their leader for inspiration, the men began to dance and sing and soon transformed themselves into a highly agitated state. At this point, the Supervisor turned to me and told me that they were chanting,

"We must kill the white man, we must kill the white man."

In order to diffuse a situation in which the main participants seemed to be degenerating into a frenzy, I slowly walked towards the leader and smiled at him. Having learned a few words of Somali, I asked him to show me his beautiful spear; since he showed no inclination to do so, I approached him and stretched my arm out slowly to take hold of the spear, indicating that I wished to admire it.

As I stretched out my hand, the tall man took a quick step backwards, fixed me with an intense stare and raised the spear in a horizontal position to a level just above his shoulder. At this point I was seized with fear, accepting the hopelessness of my situation. My legs began to shake uncontrollably; momentarily, I anticipated that the steel of the spear would pierce my body. The quivering of the tip of the spear intensified as the man prepared to lunge at me and I was mesmerised by the glittering of the steel in the harsh sunlight.

The apparently inescapable situation in which I found myself must have given my Guardian Angel food for thought; and he must have realised that, if my life was to be spared, he would have to act very quickly. As on other occasions, he did not fail me!

Just at the moment when I expected the spear to be thrust into me, the tense silence was broken by a calm voice behind me. The words which were spoken were as follows,

"If you touch that man, I will shoot you between your eyes and I am a perfect shot."

During the minute or two when I had become drawn into a position of naked vulnerability, the Supervisor had slowly crept around the back and side of the Land Rover and had quietly removed my .22 rifle from the front of the vehicle. He then imperceptibly positioned himself, so that his elbows were supported by the vehicle; the bead of the rifle precisely covered the area between the eyes of the tribesman.

I did not turn round. Slowly, with a menacing look of extreme frustration, the tribesman lowered his spear and turned to look at the others in his group with questioning eyes. For my part I slowly retreated, walking backwards until I could see Mohammed Abdi to my left side, out of the corner of my eye. Mohammed Abdi looked cool and in total control of the situation. Whether he was imbued with the spirit of my Guardian Angel, or whether the Guardian Angel had personally intervened, I could not tell; the only point which was crystal clear to me, was that my life had been saved.

Within five minutes, we had moved the vehicle clear of the well and we continued our journey up the *toug*. The sketch map which we had made, based on the information given by the Elders, proved to be accurate and we returned to our camp that evening.

The following morning, I reported the incident to the District Commissioner; I was referred to a District Officer who had specific responsibility for the Gocti area. I was asked whether, if I were to meet the man again, I would recognise him; certainly I would. I was then provided with two armed policemen and requested to help in identifying the man, who would then be arrested and brought to trial.

We immediately departed for the area of the wells; as on the previous day, the first man to appear through the trees at the side of the *toug* was the tall tribesman. I immediately told the constables that this was their man; they instructed him to sit in the back of the Land Rover, as he was under arrest. The tribesman ignored the constables until one of the constables, who was considerably shorter than the tall tribesman, took the tribesman by the arm, in order to lead him to the Land Rover. At this point, the tribesman looked down scornfully at the constable and told him that unless he immediately let go of his arm, the constable would lose his head. The constable appeared visibly shaken and relinquished his hold. After further threats and counter threats, eventually the tribesman was coaxed into the Land Rover and was duly brought before the District Officer.

The District Officer received me in his office and explained that, because of a shortage of staff, he was performing two roles: the first was as a police officer-in-charge and, second, as a magistrate. He then placed a policeman's cap on his head and asked that the tall tribesman should be brought into his office, whereupon the tribesman was charged with attempted murder. He was told that a hearing would be held before the magistrate in three hours' time; until the hearing began, he would be held in custody by the police. The tribesman appeared unconcerned and stated he would be happy with whatever outcome was decided upon.

At the appointed time the tribesman was brought before the magistrate; the police officer's cap had now been jettisoned and the District Officer was attired in clothes appropriate to a magistrate. I was called as a witness and orally repeated the written report which I had submitted that morning. The tribesman was asked whether he had anything to say, at which point he asserted that he was acting in the conviction that the Land Rover should not have been driven in a *toug*, and especially in the area of the wells. He agreed that he had intended to kill me; however, after thinking over the matter, he was pleased that in fact my life had been spared and he regretted any discomfort that might have been caused to me. He stated that he felt that he should be allowed to return to his village, although he could not guarantee that he would never again threaten intruders who were traversing the *toug* area.

Eventually, the magistrate gave his opinion that the man was guilty of attempted murder. Normally, he would have deserved a sentence of at least two years' imprisonment; however, since the man appeared to be repentant, he would be sentenced to two months' detention. Because of the short duration of the sentence, the tribesman would not be sent to prison as such, but would remain in a detention area which was adjacent to the District Commissioner's Office in Borama.

The way in which the rough justice had been exercised surprised me and it was evident that, measured against the accepted norms of the application of the law, there were many loopholes and drawbacks. Perhaps during a period of inadequate staffing there was little or no alternative. Possibly, the philosophy applied was that rough justice was better than none at all. Whatever the philosophy, the Issa tribesmen appeared to accept the way in which justice was exercised and on the whole the tribesmen seemed to maintain a respect, sometimes affection, for the British colonial system.

During the following weeks, yet another locust campaign was planned and conducted. The hilly conditions created considerable difficulty, especially since much of the terrain was stony. Nevertheless, with our knowledge of the *toug* system, the primary problem of logistics was to a substantial extent overcome and the campaign was relatively successful.

A month after the trial of the tribesman, I happened to be in the area of the District Office at Borama, when my eyes fell upon the tall tribesman; he was exercising in a compound, which was under police guard. I asked whether I could visit him and this was agreed. On seeing me, the bored expression of the tribesman immediately changed and his face seemed to light up with interest; he smiled in a good-natured way and approached me.

When I asked him how life was treating him, I immediately realised that this was a rather silly question. The man did not respond, but stated that within a few weeks he would be released and he would like to pay a visit to our camp before returning to his village. I responded that we would be pleased to see him.

When the man eventually appeared, he seemed to be making a conscious effort to behave in a pleasant way. The scorn with which he tended to treat others and his threatening disposition had been replaced by a polite, quiet, good-humoured nature. We showed him around our camp and explained the purpose of the vehicles, the petrol, various types of equipment and the locust bait. The tribesman then turned to me and asked whether he could make a request. During his period in detention, he had developed an admiration for my Somali colleagues and myself; his question was whether it might be possible for him to be employed by the DLC as a watchman. He would not ask for wages, but if it might be possible for us to give him some food, this would be appreciated. The main point he wished to make was that he felt he owed us a debt and if he could work as a watchman then, to some extent, he would feel that at least part of the debt would have been repaid. I responded that he would be employed from that day and that he would receive wages and rations at precisely the same level as other watchmen. He assured us that as long as he was on duty, whether by day or by night, we could be assured that no one would enter the camp for the purpose of theft. The man proved to be true to his word and, until leaving Borama in early June, no outsiders dared to linger in the vicinity of our camp.

On the day that we returned to Hargeisa, I shook hands with the tribesman. He explained that he had considered volunteering to accompany us, even though he understood that it was likely that we might well be sent to an area some hundreds of miles away, far away from the Issa tribe. He had considered the matter fully and had concluded that he had certain responsibilities within his clan and it was high time that he returned to his village. He told us that if we should ever return to the area, he hoped that we would lose no time in contacting him. He liked us and he would look after us. He paused and, for a moment, looked a little discomforted. He then firmly looked me in the eye and said,

"I am sorry that I wanted to kill you. At the beginning, I made some empty threats and thought that you and your group would be frightened and would run away. But instead you ignored me and when I returned with my spear, you tried to take it from me. I could not control my anger and I became very upset. Although I wanted to kill you, I am pleased that I did not, because this was not my intention. Now I feel so sorry about it all. Goodbye – Nabadgylyo."

Fig. 2   *The author - Somaliland, 1953.*

Fig. 3　Part of a locust swarm in South Eastern Ethiopia which covered an area of 1000 square kilometres-equivalent to the area of Greater London (photograph courtesy of Clifford Ashall).

Fig. 4   *Sir Boris Uvarov K.C.M.G., F.R.S. A Russian
scientist who came to Britain in 1920. By his Phase Theory
of locusts published in 1921 he first explained the mystery of
locust plagues.*

Fig. 5   *A termite hill in the Ogaden. It is more than twice the height
of Senior Research Officer, Cliff Ashall.*

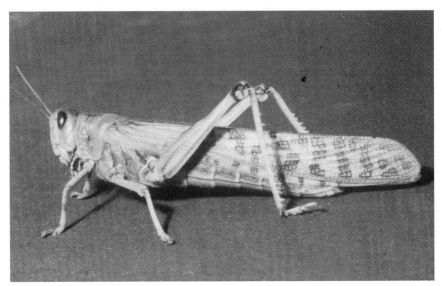

Fig. 6   *The Enemy - The desert locust (schistocerca gregaria) weighs two grams and its length is about 7.5 cms. (3 ins.) It can consume its own weight in food each day. (Photograph courtesy of Clifford Ashall).*

Fig. 7   *A 'toug' (Wadi). In the absence of roads, 'tougs' often served as a passage for transportation.*

Fig. 8 *Issa tribesmen near Sillil. In addition to his spear, one of the tribesmen carries a shield, which is made of thick hide.*

Fig. 9   *Burden camels loaded with locust bait (author standing on far left).*

Fig. 10   *'Mountain' burden camels - between El Gal and Durbo.*

Fig. 11   *En route to Cape Guardafui.*

Fig. 12   *The Tip of the Horn of Africa - Cape Guardafui.*

Fig. 13 *Mother dromedary with one day-old offspring.*

Fig. 14   *Tribesmen in the Ogaden are frequently armed; their firearms often date from the Abyssinian war in the thirties.*

Chapter Four

Las Anod

The journey from Hargeisa to Las Anod is monotonous; one's view is of semi-desert, the low scrub occasionally turning to a patch of green around the *tougs*. For the last hundred miles of the three hundred mile journey, the alternating dirt and sandy road becomes more bumpy as an extensive plain of clay and gypsum rock is traversed.

We established our camp about a mile or so from the township of Las Anod. The seasonal summer *kharriff* was beginning to blow from the south-west, producing vast clouds of blowing dust during the daylight hours. We were to experience the dusty conditions during the whole of the summer. As far as the DLC personnel were concerned, I was happy that our team of Somalis remained almost intact. Through the various experiences we had shared, and with a knowledge of each other's personalities, we worked well together. As time went by, I felt increasingly confident of the competence of the members of our team and I hoped that they also were conscious of the fact that I was a firm believer in supporting one's staff and, to the maximum extent possible, delegating duties. Each treated the others with courtesy and respect and during the total period of about fifteen months when we worked together, I cannot recall a voice raised in anger; what I do recall is a great deal of hard work (as may have been demanded at any time of the day or night), thoughtfulness and good humour.

Awaiting us at the Las Anod base was the local Somali Supervisor who would be directly assisting me during the next seven months; his name was Haji Nur. I had requested that the Supervisor who had assisted us in Borama and who had saved my life, should continue to work with me; to my disappointment, I had learned that he had been involved in 'gun-running' and had been sentenced to a prison term.

Haji Nur was an elderly man by Somali standards, probably in his fifties. He seemed to be well-experienced and had a good sense of humour; in addition, he had been involved in the British military campaigns against the 'Mad Mullah'. On one or two occasions, we visited the large fort at Taleh and we would sit under the massive walls at night while he narrated various stories about the efforts of the British to overcome what was, in fact, a fairly widespread rebellion against a thinly dispersed colonial administration.

Apart from the severe climatic conditions which became part of our everyday life, a basic problem which existed for Europeans who stayed in the Las Anod area was that the local water was undrinkable due to the widespread gypsum deposits; effectively, this caused havoc with one's digestive system. In consequence, it was necessary to fetch water from an area called Hudin, which was fifty miles north of Las Anod.

Once a week, we would travel with a Land Rover and Dodge Power Wagon to a rocky outcrop at Hudin; the Dodge Power Wagon carried six empty forty-gallon water drums. On arrival, we would scramble over stones and rocks for a hundred yards. In front of a hole at the bottom of a rocky cliff was a boulder, around which perhaps twenty or thirty baboons would be sitting. The ambition of the baboons was to remove the boulder and gain access to the water supply. As we came into sight, the baboons would climb up the rocks which framed the outer part of a cave and they would sit on a ledge about thirty feet above the entrance.

Three of us would then push the boulder to one side and we would enter the cave carrying empty jerrycans; each had a capacity of four and a half gallons. As we approached the water, the rock roof of the cave slanted steeply downwards, which meant that we were soon lying on our stomachs. I would then inch my way towards the water; the jerrycan would be placed laterally in the water and, when as much water as possible had been collected in the jerrycan, it was pulled towards my body and then pushed to the next man, who repeated the exercise until someone at the mouth of the cave could carry the water over the stones and rocks. The water would then be poured into one of the drums.

The weekly procedure took hours to complete, but we accepted that there was no alternative. Eventually, the boulder would be replaced in the mouth of the cave and we would drive back to our base with our supply of water.

The area over which I was to maintain surveillance against locust invasion extended over about ten thousand square miles. Initially, much of the time was spent in travelling over parts of the region to maintain systematic surveillance. Often, the reconnaissance journey would last two or three days and those parts of the area which were inaccessible to motor transport were traversed on foot, sometimes using burden camels to carry necessary supplies.

Most of the area was inhabited by the Habr Awal tribe; all were Sunni Moslems. Outside the townships, wealth (or lack of it) could be assessed by the number of camels owned by a particular individual. A man who owned ten or fifteen camels would normally have one wife; once a man had acquired about twenty camels he would be ready to marry a second wife. A man with eighty to one hundred camels would be regarded as well-off and would usually have four wives. In addition to camels, the Habr Awal maintained substantial flocks of sheep and goats and, in the few areas where permanent water could be found, a few head of cattle. In general the people were friendly and peaceful.

On one occasion we were traversing a bush area to the south of Las Anod on foot. In the heat of the afternoon I saw a figure lying motionless in the sand; as I drew closer I could see that we were looking at a small, middle-aged woman who was clad in clothes which gave her the appearance of being poor. She was apparently asleep (perhaps sick or dying) and in front of her hands we could see the only material property which she had with her; this was a blackened kettle. I knelt down quietly by her side in an endeavour to form some judgement concerning her condition. If, for example, she had been suffering from malaria we could have offered to have carried her back to the road, after which we could have transported her to a hospital in Las Anod.

As I was peering at her and trying to assess her condition, the woman briefly opened her eyes. She must have been astonished to see a white man's face so close to hers. In any case, she jumped up and slapped me on the side of my head, heartily shouting what was probably some form of abuse. I turned to one of the Somalis in our group and enquired the reason for the woman's hostile reaction. The Somalis laughed gently and then told me that the woman appeared to be in perfect health and she was apparently taking a rest. When she had woken up she had jumped to the conclusion that someone wished to steal her kettle, in which she was carrying valuable water. I asked the Somalis to reassure her that we had no intention of depriving her of her only visible property.

In August the *kharriff* began to lose its velocity; by the end of the month, the force of the wind had greatly subsided. Soon the north-easterly wind began to make itself felt, which we knew would lead to rainfall within the next week of two. The same wind would also carry locusts from the hilly areas some three to four hundred miles to the north.

By the end of September, we began to sight locusts; initially, the swarms were quite thin, but during the next two or three weeks a number of medium density swarms invaded the area. Some of these swarms were up to one hundred square miles in extent and, after recent rain, the locusts soon matured and bred. The resulting egg fields extended over hundreds of square miles.

Because of the size of the area for which I was responsible and the widespread laying of locust eggs, I requested additional supplies of locust bait, as well as several more heavy vehicles. I also asked that, if possible, another field officer should be dispatched to take over part of the locust control operations in the area.

The ensuing campaign proved to be highly exhausting, although it was eventually successful. The escaping swarms were small in extent and many of the locusts would die from natural causes; some would also fall prey to attacks by birds, thus reducing the escaping swarms even more.

During the period of the campaign, I received a message that the senior field officer, based in Hargeisa, would be visiting us for about two days to inspect the work. I welcomed the visit and looked forward to discussing our strategy and the tactics which I had developed to give effect to the strategy. The senior field officer asked me to meet him at a point near Bohotleh, south of Las Anod. The inspection visit went well. As rain was threatening on the second evening, I suggested that we should pull our respective camp beds into a tent, instead of sleeping under mosquito nets in the open.

The following morning, my visitor told me over breakfast that I had been talking in my sleep. I responded that I could well believe this; I had been alone with a few Somalis for about four months and possibly through lack of the opportunity for conversation, I may well have resorted to talking in my sleep. The point was acknowledged; however, my visitor explained that what he found interesting was that I was not speaking English. He spoke no Somali, but gave his opinion that he thought I had been speaking Somali.

The Somali language is generally acknowledged to be complex and often impossible for Europeans to pronounce properly. Because of this, most of my colleagues had discouraged me from trying to learn the language. At that time, Somali was not a written language, although Kirk had tried to produce a grammar of the Somali language in the early part of the twentieth century. An associated difficulty in communicating in the language was that, in general, Somalis were not used to foreigners trying to speak their language; in consequence, unless the language was pronounced perfectly, including tonal nuances, the Somali listener tended to look at one uncomprehendingly, as though as to show that he had no knowledge of the language which was being spoken to him. The sounds of the foreigner simply sounded foreign. I had made no conscious effort to learn the language as such; from time to time I had asked my Somali colleagues to pronounce the equivalent of such words as 'good morning', 'goodbye', 'water', 'locust'.

After the departure of my inspecting visitor, we continued to pursue the anti-locust campaign with great energy; the aim was to control the hopper infestations to the maximum degree achievable.

Three weeks later, I was undertaking a reconnaissance journey by Land Rover with our driver, an assistant and a cook. During those journeys, in order to alleviate the interminable nature of the journey, the Somalis would tell one another long stories. Each phrase was acknowledged by the listeners with a 'hai-yeh, hai-yeh'. During one of these story-telling sessions, I quietly mentioned that I had just missed the previous sentence and could it please be repeated. The driver slowed down, stopped the vehicle and switched off the ignition. He stared at me and said simply,

"Mr. Everard, you are speaking our language". I looked at the puzzled faces of my three helpers, nodded my head and said in Somali,

"Yes, I have understood the whole story, except for the last sentence. Would you kindly repeat it?"

Apparently, I had learned to speak the Somali language fluently and with excellent pronunciation through a process of immersion; just as a child learns a language, initially I had learned to understand and this was followed by speaking. As the weeks passed, I spoke easily with increasing confidence. A few years later I found myself at a government tea party in Mogadishu and spoke Somali with my hosts and their Somali guests. One or two of the guests asked me where I had learned to speak so well and with such a pure accent; the simple answer was that the Somali I had learned was the language which was spoken in the interior of the country, untainted by Arabic, Swahili or Italian vocabulary, which often creeps into the language in the country's coastal areas.

The ability to speak Somali was of considerable benefit in terms of the work we had to undertake. It also meant that one could really understand what was being stated, without the 'twist' sometimes injected by interpreters. Occasionally, we would meet a tribesman in a desolate area and I would ask him where he had come from and whether he had seen any locusts; or perhaps he had experienced rainfall. Sometimes the man would answer in a natural way; or one might see a look of confusion on the man's face and he would indicate that he did not seem to understand. At that point, I would quietly tell him that I was speaking to him in his own language and, if he listened carefully, he would understand what I was saying. From that point, there were no further problems.

The locust control campaign proved to be different to the earlier campaigns in which I had been involved. First, the general area was flat and was therefore easily accessible; the drawback was the vastness of the campaign area. Second, our team was not subject to personal danger. The Habr Awal were tolerant by nature and our presence seemed to make little impact on their everyday lives; to the extent that we needed information or assistance, this was readily offered.

Because the large area had been the subject of invasion by waves of locust swarms over a period of a week or two, the campaign lasted longer than usual, as the eggs progressively hatched into first instar hoppers. Instead of adopting the usual approach of employing gangs of labourers to spread the locust bait in the various infested areas, we were able to spread most of the bait directly from vehicles. This was done manually. Mechanical spreaders were brought into use only later.

During the last two weeks or so of the campaign, the infested area was systematically traversed by vehicle and to the extent that hoppers or young locusts were present, these were dealt with.

I travelled with one of the teams performing the work and we set off for what we anticipated would be a solid week's work. There were few villages in the general area. When at dusk the Land Rover and Dodge Power Wagon would stop, we would cut branches for a *zariba,* a fence. Unfortunately, we had seen no gazelle that day and we therefore ate rice and dates, accompanied by soup. While we were eating I noticed that the Supervisor seemed to be not only quiet but somewhat withdrawn. I therefore asked him if all was well, whereupon he told me that he was feeling ill and had probably contracted malaria. I was the only member of the team who slept on a camp bed; the other members slept directly on the ground, usually on mats. I therefore suggested to Haji that he should use my bed; I would sleep on his mat. We helped him into bed and shortly afterwards he developed a high fever and began to shake uncontrollably.

Because the cries of several hyena were clearly audible in the chorus of nocturnal sounds (mainly caused by jackals), I took the precautionary measure of organising three-hour guard duties by a driver, a helper and myself. The guard on duty would ensure that the fire was maintained at a good level and in the event that wild animals would come very close to the *zariba,* then the guard would wake us up. At about ten p.m. I quickly fell asleep on the Supervisor's mat.

At about two a.m. I woke up; a fairly heavy object was moving steadily over the blanket which covered my legs. My initial reaction was to raise one of my legs and push the object away from my body. Since this seemed to have little effect and the weight persisted, I stood up; I then heard the guard say that a large snake was moving over my blanket. I jumped away from the general area, took hold of my rifle and appealed for someone to bring some light. The fire was flickering at a low level and the paraffin lamp gave only a weak light. I carried the paraffin lamp towards my blanket and could clearly see the snake resting on the blanket. Perhaps because of the illumination, the snake suddenly became active and as it raised its flat head some inches above the ground I realised we were dealing with a cobra; its length would probably have been six feet. Raising its head higher, the cobra moved in my direction and its head began to sweep laterally through the air; evidently, it was seeking an object which it could strike. Although we had been given a tin which contained a 'Snake-Bite Outfit', I felt less than confident that we could follow the snake-bite procedure in a timely way before the lethal venom would take effect.

I then noted a hole next to the sleeping mat and realised that the area we had chosen for rest was shared with the home of the cobra.

Enclosed as we were within the small *zariba*, our options to organise a quick escape were distinctly limited; it was equally clear that the cobra could strike at any moment. I therefore handed the paraffin lamp to the guard and asked him to hold it as closely as possible to the scything head of the cobra; he should approach the snake as closely as he could dare.

By the dim light of the lamp I then did my utmost to aim at the head of the snake and, after a few seconds, squeezed the trigger. There was no noise; the cartridge did not fire. With a mixture of frustration, hopelessness and fear, I wondered what we should do next. The cobra responded. The snake moved quickly to its hole and had soon disappeared from sight.

We agreed that it would not be safe to remain within the *zariba* and each of us found a place to sleep in one of the vehicles. I slept in the back of the Dodge Power Wagon and snatched a few hours rest before it was time to commence the day's work. My sleep was interrupted on one occasion by a nightmare; I awoke in the sitting position feverishly pressing the blanket around my legs. Fortunately, this time I was dealing only with an unpleasant dream and I hoped that the cobra would stay in its hole.

Some two weeks later, I declared the campaign at an end. Inevitably, there would be an escape of locusts, but the swarm would be thin and scattered to such a degree that many of the locusts would not survive predators for long.

After seven months of operations in arduous conditions, I felt drained to the point of near-exhaustion. The team members were also extremely tired, although we were pleased that Haji Nur had recovered from his bout of malaria. We drove steadily back to the DLC Base in Hargeisa and wondered what was in store for us in terms of our next assignment. I was ready to tackle the next spell of duty whatever might be involved; but I also secretly hoped that I would find a way to recover from the strain of the previous seven months.

Chapter Five

A Change of Direction

On returning to Hargeisa in November 1953, I met the senior field officer and asked him what he had in mind for me in terms of the next field posting. With a faint smile he handed me a letter and suggested I should open it forthwith. The letter was signed by Philip Stephenson, who was the Director of the Desert Locust Survey and Desert Locust Control Organisation. He simply stated that my efforts over the past year had been watched with interest. In view of the success achieved, the Director had decided that I should be promoted to administrative officer; my first posting would be to Asmara, from where locust control operations in the then Eritrea and Northern Ethiopia were organised.

Although satisfying in certain respects, promotion in the DLC did not carry a great deal of weight as such. By nature, the DLC was not a strongly structured type of organisation; in order to be successful, it had to maintain a high degree of flexibility and its personnel came from different backgrounds. In addition, the age range of field officers was wide. For example, while I had just reached the age of twenty three, one of my colleagues Colonel ('Call me Charles') Copeman was a man of fifty-eight; most field officers were in their thirties or forties. We all recognised that there needed to be a management hierarchy (however loose) and that this would include such work as administration, accounting, logistics control, as well as one man who occupied the position of senior field officer. However, our dedication to our work, the total respect in which we held one another, the faith which we unquestionably accorded the judgement of our colleagues (at whatever level) transcended conscious feelings of relative rank. The respect in which we held one another was of far greater importance than a rank which any of us might hold.

After a year's administrative work in Asmara, I was appointed as the head of operations for Eritrea and Northern Ethiopia. I had just celebrated my twenty-fourth birthday.

After taking stock of the situation I wrote a fairly long memorandum to the Director in Nairobi and set out my thoughts and proposed plans.

Our knowledge of migratory routes of the desert locust had increased greatly during the first half of the fifties. A substantial amount of scientific work had been initiated to gain an understanding of the yearly pattern of locust invasions; this pattern inevitably depended to a significant extent on the winds which were prevalent at any given time, including those of the upper air. Important advances had already been made in the effective use of aircraft for reconnaissance purposes; also aerial spraying techniques, which were the subject of prolonged experiments, were beginning to show promise. All of the information which these initiatives provided were supplemented by the constant routine of reporting, which was part of the daily work of the field officers on the ground.

Although considerable progress had been made, there were still many questions relating to the whereabouts of locust swarms at any given time. If some of these questions could be answered, our knowledge of migratory routes would be enhanced; in turn, this would enable us to plan our anti-locust control measures more effectively. Several of us had our 'pet' ideas; it would be an exaggeration to call these ideas theories.

There was a good deal of support for the notion that at certain times of the year locusts would harbour in the Takazze Valley of central Ethiopia. Due to high mountains and hostile tribesmen, no locust information-gathering had been undertaken in the area. I proposed to traverse the Takazze Valley in order to cover the gap in our picture of locust movements in Ethiopia.

The foot trek, using mules, was due to start in March or April 1955. About a week before I was due to leave, a message was received that certain problems in Hargeisa between the senior field officer and the government had led to the departure of the senior field officer. I should transfer to Hargeisa to take up my duties immediately, due to the impending locust invasion. With hindsight, perhaps my Guardian Angel had assessed the challenge of seeing me safely through the dangerous Takazze Valley as difficult, possibly insurmountable. In any case, this was one expedition which, although I felt it was important from the locust information gathering aspect, could no longer be pursued.

In early May 1955, I therefore found myself again in Hargeisa, although this time as the senior field officer. I would be responsible for the success of anti-locust operations throughout the northern part of what is now the Somali Republic.

Shortly after my arrival, I carried out an extensive journey to visit all of the field officers who were working in the area. At the age of twenty-four, I would have shown understanding if any of the field officers had mentioned that they found me to be a little young to hold a position of supervisory responsibility; in fact, each in his turn and in his own way, made a point of letting me know that they were delighted to be part of a far-flung team with myself as head of operations.

Over the next eighteen months, many campaigns throughout the area were mounted to combat the heavy invasions of locusts; each invasion was followed by breeding and heavy resultant infestations of hoppers.

In November and December 1956, the expected rains along the northern escarpment and on the plateau of the interior were only patchy; from the reports we received, in the north-eastern part of the country the rains had completely failed.

We immediately appreciated the importance of this development. In order to breed, locusts need humidity and rainfall; for example, if the ground should be dry and hard, even if the adults mature into yellow locusts, the female will not be able to pierce the surface and extend her abdomen into the ground to deposit her egg pod. If the rains were to fail over a widespread area, this would mean that few of the eggs would hatch and, effectively, part of the new generation of locusts would be wiped out.

There was also another important factor, albeit problematical. If locust swarms were to become decimated by natural causes, it might occur that the survivors would develop a solitary rather than gregarious existence, as explained by Boris Uvarov in the phase theory which he had developed in 1921. If this occurred on a large scale, then effectively the plague would come to an end.

During the winter period of 1955-56 I exhorted the field officers to do everything possible to achieve the maximum degree of success in their locust control operations. Although we did not pretend to know whether, in fact, we could influence the behavioural pattern of the locusts, at least if the various campaigns could be successful with a small resultant escape, then we would have provided encouragement to the locusts to revert to a solitary state.

We subsequently received a report of swarms moving eastwards along the line of the escarpment through Erigavo; as was usual, the locusts would descend on to the coastal plain for breeding. What was unusual, as far as the locusts were concerned, was that the rains had failed in that area.

Because the disposition of field officers was somewhat sparse in relation to the tremendous amount of work in hand to prevent the next locust generation from developing, I decided to handle the infestation in the north-eastern part of the country myself.

A week later I arrived in Erigavo, where I called on the District Commissioner. The District Commissioner welcomed me and then proceeded to give me various pieces of information that he had received regarding locust movements. He confirmed that the rains seemed to have failed. He then wished me 'bon voyage', but added that since he had received one or two reports that the tribesmen of the area seemed to be adopting a hostile attitude, he intended to give me an escort of armed policemen. However, he would need to call the policemen from another area and therefore they would follow forty-eight hours after me.

As we traversed the coastal plain by Land Rover, we came across a few scattered locust swarms of low density. Moving eastward, we noted the effect of lack of rain; much of the vegetation seemed quite dry. We then began to find areas which had apparently been invaded by dense swarms of locusts; the locusts had found it impossible to penetrate the dry, hard surface of the ground and had settled on the trees at night. During the night, the females had dropped their egg pods on to the ground. We found many *acacia* trees with a yellow 'carpet' beneath them; the 'carpet' was constituted of locust eggs. The eggs would dry within the next few days.

Eventually, we decided to establish a camp in broken country near the foothills of the escarpment. The reason for this was that, although few locusts would survive on the coastal plain due to the dry conditions, we had been told by a local tribesman that there had been rain in the mountains and a number of areas were infested with hoppers. Over the following two days we carried out a reconnaissance on foot and decided to commence control operations in the mountains.

During mid-afternoon on the second day, I was walking with a Somali locust scout in the broken country at the foot of the mountains during mid-afternoon; we were about eight miles from our camp and were traversing the area to see whether there might be some hopper infestations.

As we walked through the bush, I could see that we were approaching a *toug*; I also noticed some movements of tribesmen. Remembering the cautionary words of the District Commissioner, I stopped and asked my Somali scout if we were approaching a village, or perhaps some wells. Before he could reply, fifteen tribesmen ran towards us from the *toug* shouting,

"Kill him! Kill him!"

As the men rapidly approached, they began to hurl large stones at me. I turned away from them and ran as quickly as I could. After two hundred yards or so, I wondered whether I was still ahead of them or if, perhaps, they were gaining on me; I therefore stopped briefly and looked behind me. Some of the men had dropped out, but about six were running steadily towards me. I turned away again and continued running and suddenly felt a large stone brush against my right ear; my immediate reaction was that if the stone had been two or three inches to the left, then it would have struck my head. After having run another two hundred and fifty yards, I came to the edge of a deep *toug*. I stopped briefly and looked at the height of the walls; I concluded that they were about thirty feet high. I wondered whether I should try to slide down the wall and escape across the *toug*. When I looked round and saw the menacing tribesmen, the decision was obvious. I began to slide and then fell down the wall into the *toug*; I ran across the bottom of the *toug* and somehow managed to scramble up the other side. I looked back and the tribesmen were shouting insults in my direction and one or two tried to hurl stones, which fell far short. Without further delay, I returned to our camp. It was only then that I realised I had sprained my ankle; the ankle took a few days to recover. Separately, our drivers and helpers had been told by two of the local Elders that the Elders objected to our presence; unless we left without delay, our lives would be in danger.

Our Somali staff advised me to leave the area, but I explained that the armed escort should soon arrive and I hoped that this would discourage the local people from any further interference. We were working in accordance with the policy of the government and the Elders had no right to contravene the policy; if they wished to make special representations on the subject then this could be done by them peacefully.

Shortly afterwards, the escort arrived and was, in fact, accompanied by a District Officer. He told me that he had wanted to visit the area in any case and had persuaded the District Commissioner that this would be a good opportunity. I explained the situation to him and the incident which had occurred.

Within a matter of minutes, my staff announced the entrance of two Elders, who were accompanied by three or four men of the group which had pursued me. When we explained the situation to the District Officer, he gave instructions to the policemen that they should arrest the visiting group.

The following morning, the District Officer had the men brought before him and all admitted that they had participated, whether directly or indirectly, in the incidents of the previous day. I was asked whether I recognised any of the men as having been from the group who had pursued me and I immediately pointed to three of the men. The accused were then asked whether they had anything to say; they all admitted that they had contravened the policy of the government and had taken part in the incidents of the previous day. They had been under the impression that I was unprotected and they were astounded that the District Officer and the policemen had arrived on the scene immediately. They said they now regretted their actions and had not intended to kill me. The District Officer, in his capacity as magistrate, then sentenced the men to terms of imprisonment. He also warned them that if there were any further attacks on our group, those responsible would be severely dealt with by the government. From that day, we started our operations and continued with our work, unmolested, for the next three weeks.

Each day's work followed a similar pattern. I would rise at 3.30 a.m. and eat a quick breakfast. Burden camels which carried sacks of locust bait would have already left our camp at about 2.30 a.m.; since these animals walked at about two and a half miles per hour, they were sent ahead. I would leave at 4 a.m. and walk eighteen miles to a point at the bottom of the foothills of the escarpment. I was accompanied by a Somali helper; he not only guided me, but also carried a goatskin of water which was to refresh us from time to time as the day wore on.

After reaching the scene of operations, the sacks of bait which had been carried by the burden camels would be transferred to waiting mules. We would then spend the day walking in the foothills, systematically covering the area and controlling the hoppers as we found the bands marching through the bush. During the period of the ensuing three weeks, the area was controlled.

Overall, the impact of the countrywide operations was significant and the volume of escaping locusts was, relatively speaking, low; the locust swarms were of thin density and many of the locusts would fall by the wayside, as they moved southwards on the monsoon wind.

The degree of control achieved would also be enhanced through the effectiveness of the airspray unit. Led by Ludwig Martel (a Polish Battle of Britain pilot), experimental aerial control measures were being developed, mainly using Micronair equipment. The insecticides which were used were formulations of benzene hexachloride, Acrodel (ICI) and Dieldrin (Shell).

Initially, the approach adopted in aerial spraying was to create a 'curtain' of spray through which a locust swarm would fly; logically, as the locusts flew through the curtain, a droplet of insecticide would touch their bodies, sufficient to kill them. In fact, at the beginning of the experiments this did not happen, primarily because the extremely rapid movement of the wings of the locusts dispersed the droplets of insecticide and, at the same time, protected the body of the insect from contact.

Another part of the problem concerned the volatility of the insecticide; depending on the density of the air, the wind and the size of the droplets, there was a tendency for the insecticide to move upwards instead of downwards.

Eventually, it was found that the optimal time to spray locusts was as the temperature dropped a little in the late afternoon or very early evening, when the locusts would begin to look for vegetation on which they could roost. As the swarms settled on the trees, the locust density tended to be high and much of the insecticide found its mark. In addition, since the minute droplets made contact with the vegetation, the locusts would die of stomach poisoning as the ravenous insects devoured the leaves.

The aerial locust spraying techniques which were developed bore little resemblance to crop spraying. In contrast to maintaining a constant height above the ground, locust spraying often took place in mountainous or broken country; this required frequent and sudden changes of altitude. During spraying sorties, a careful watch needed to be kept on the contours of the terrain so that one could climb out safely. The spray was applied at thirty to fifty feet above ground level. At all times, the highest standards of airmanship had to be maintained.

Within the next three years, the methods of controlling locusts would become altogether more mechanical. Apart from developments in aerial spraying, which progressively became more effective, attention was also paid to spraying techniques on the ground. One of the research projects of the Desert Locust Survey developed a system under which the exhaust gases of the Land Rover would be used to activate a spraying mechanism attached to the exhaust pipe. A Land Rover would carry a drum of insecticide (Acrodel or Dieldrin) and could spray large semi-desert areas by traversing the countryside ahead of the marching bands of hoppers. With hindsight, as we moved from manual to mechanical control measures, one could say that from 1956-1957, the perfecting of anti-locust control measures was well underway, which would lead to total technical effectiveness within a few years.

On my return to Hargeisa in 1956 shortly before Christmas, I received a dinner invitation from the Governor of Somaliland. Since I had no direct relationship with the government and worked for the East Africa High Commission (based in Kenya), the invitation was unexpected. I happily accepted and enjoyed the dinner hosted by His Excellency. After dinner, the Governor invited me to walk into an adjacent room for a short chat. The Governor told me that he was extremely pleased with the way in which the various locust campaigns were being conducted and he added that he felt our team of field officers had contributed to giving our Organisation a high reputation in the country. He had asked the Chief Secretary to the government to write to the Administrator of the East Africa High Commission to place on record the government's appreciation of our efforts. He then went on to say that he had kept in close touch with the actions initiated by myself in various respects; in a nutshell, he had great respect for the way things were going.

The Governor then went on to explain that the Colonial Administrative Service was looking for good people and it was his opinion that I fitted the required criteria in terms of my work attitude, energy, enthusiasm and other personal qualities. He then told me that he had prepared a letter to the Office of the Colonial Secretary in London in which he was recommending that I should be recruited to the Colonial Administrative Service. Before dispatching the letter, which he intended to do the following day, he felt he should keep me informed and no doubt I would be hearing from the Colonial Office in London shortly.

I thanked His Excellency for his kind words, as well as the excellent dinner. I then explained in a quiet way that I felt happy in the work which I was doing and, although naturally I appreciated his consideration, I wished to state clearly that I would remain in the work which I had been recruited to do. I would not wish to transfer to the Colonial Administrative Service.

The Governor looked at me with incredulity. Did I not understand the benefits of becoming a member of an élite service with the guaranteed security of a permanent appointment, not to mention the resources which would be available to support me which were inherent in the Colonial Administrative Service? There could be no comparison in the status of a member of the Colonial Administrative Service and a far-flung member of the East Africa High Commission.

I appealed to his Excellency for understanding and apologised for not, apparently, being sufficiently conscious of the status element. Nevertheless, I believed in what I was doing and would continue along the same course. I shook hands with the Governor and we returned to the dinner group.

Whether His Excellency was conscious of the impending 'wind of change', which resulted in a substantial reduction of the Colonial Administrative Service, I do not know. What we do know is that, within a few years, many fine British colonial administrators had been compensated for loss of career and had left the service. It would only be a matter of a few years before the Colonial Office was replaced by the Commonwealth Office and the Overseas Development Administration (ODA).

In early 1957, I received a letter from the Director; he was pleased with the way anti-locust control measures had progressed over the previous twenty months or so. He wished to continue a policy under which I would be exposed to as many facets of anti-locust work as possible; with this in mind, since the DLC liaison officer to Somalia would be away from his post for about four months, I should take over the duties during the period of the liaison officer's absence. On completion of the short assignment, I should take some leave, after which the Director had in mind that I would be appointed as the Organisation's senior field officer for Kenya, Tanzania and Uganda. I acknowledged the Director's letter with pleasure. At the age of twenty-six, I had confidently settled into a management role; as a liaison officer to Somalia, I would now have some opportunity to be exposed to an element of diplomatic challenge as well.

Chapter Six

The Tip of the Horn

The main thrust of the DLC liaison officer's work in the then UN Trusteeship of Somalia was to use his good offices to encourage the government to undertake effective anti-locust control measures. Locusts had no respect for national boundaries and the Trusteeship of Somalia was a geographical extension of Somaliland to the north, as well as the Ogaden area of Eastern Ethiopia: in a nutshell, it was part of the main focal point within which there was a high level of locust activity.

As far as the cost of mounting anti-locust campaigns was concerned, the Somalia government allocated a certain sum of money from its annual national budget to cover the costs of staffing a locust control department; in addition, the government met certain capital costs of equipping the department with vehicles and machinery.

During periods of intensive locust activity, the government budget to conduct effective control measures was inadequate. An arrangement had therefore been entered into between the government and the East Africa High Commission (acting on behalf of the governments of Kenya, Tanzania and Uganda) under which, once the Somalia government's locust control budget had been exhausted, an application could be made for additional funds to ensure continuity of the anti-locust effort. Typically, the government's locust control budget ceiling was reached after eight or nine months of the financial year, at which point a request for additional funds would be made in writing to the DLC liaison officer who was based in Mogadishu.

Under the original terms of the UN Trusteeship arrangements, it had been foreseen that about twenty years or so would be needed for the creation of an effective Somali government infrastructure. The Italian government had developed comprehensive plans covering the training of staff across a broad spectrum of services. Correctly, the government had recognised the difference between the undertaking of training courses by Somali government personnel and the work experience needed by the trained staff to perform the duties of a particular job.

By the time I arrived in Mogadishu in 1957, Somalis were participating strongly in political activities within the main townships, including Mogadishu. Although a few thousand Italians were still present in the country, none of these participated in the affairs of the country at the political level. As far as the bureaucracy was concerned, most senior positions were held by Somalis, although quite frequently Italians were present in an advisory capacity in the various ministries.

Shortly after my arrival, an announcement was made to the effect that the Trusteeship Council of the United Nations had directed that the country should be brought to independence far sooner than had been originally planned. The new time-frame envisaged a period of five years, instead of the twenty-five years foreseen earlier.

Although I was not directly involved with the affairs of the government, at the same time I recognised that developments within the Somali government would have a direct impact on the effectiveness of our work. For those on the spot, such as myself, the drastically shortened period to prepare for independence could lead to only one result: administrative chaos and possibly, at the political level, bloodshed.

For those with a direct knowledge of conditions in former colonial countries, the decision to rush to independence was misguided and irresponsible. A cynical view was that this was a 'cut and run' decision. Bearing in mind the fragile (sometimes total lack of) infrastructure, there could be no rational defence of simply walking out of those countries which had been created by a handful of developed countries during the last main era of colonisation, about a hundred years previously.

The 'wind of change' was an inevitable development. The fact that, under certain political pressures, it blew away a cadre of experienced colonial administrators before their successors could gain experience was, without question, a shameful political act; the (sometimes bloody) price will continue to be paid for many years to come.

In 1957, although the political outlook for Somalis was ominous, those on the spot had to make the best of what they knew would become a bad situation. I therefore spent much time emphasising the importance of the part which Somalia would play in the control of the locust scourge and took every available opportunity to ensure that

Ministers of the government and representatives of the international community were kept fully aware of the important locust control measures which were in hand.

One of the many problems which affected the overall effort was the need for DLC field officers to obtain visas when they crossed the border from Ethiopia into Somalia and vice-versa. The visa situation in Ethiopia was onerous and time-consuming. I felt that if some loosening of the visa requirements could be agreed to by the Somali government, it might then be possible to approach the Ethiopian government and propose that similar reciprocal arrangements might be considered.

I therefore requested an appointment with the Minister of the Interior and, a few days later, found myself sitting in front of him in his office. The Minister was a well-educated man, with a quick sense of humour and suave in appearance; as tended to be the case with other Ministers, he wore a well-cut suit, rather than Somali dress. His large office was well-appointed and he sat with confidence behind an imposing desk; occasionally, he glanced pensively through one of the large office windows towards the sea.

The Minister listened attentively as I explained the visa problem; I touched on the advisability of field officers being issued with multi-entry visas, possibly with a validity duration of a year. While I was talking, I gradually became conscious of a noise outside the Minister's office, which seemed to be increasing; from time to time, one heard high-pitched voices apparently clamouring to be heard. At one point, the Minister gently smiled and apologised for the vociferous noise which could be heard on the landing outside his door; he explained that the Somali government wished to afford its citizens their full democratic rights and every day a number of citizens assembled in the various ministries to appeal for assistance in one form or another. As an aside, the Minister stated that the poor people had no idea that they would receive no help whatsoever from the government. As he finished his explanation, one could hear intermittent thuds on his door. Apologising for his interruption, he asked me to continue on the subject.

Having explained the background to the problem, I began to touch on possibilities which might be considered in terms of alleviating the visa situation. Just as I was reaching the last part of what I wished to say, there was a sudden crack of the door bursting open and some fifteen Somalis ran into the office, shouting with high-pitched voices. These men were followed by a group of policemen. Initially, the Minister looked alarmed, but when he saw the policemen he nodded to a sergeant and, without further ado, the intruders were beaten about the head and body. Most of the men ran from the office; three had been hit with such force that they lay prostrated on the floor. The policemen dragged them out and closed the door.

The Minister, who had been glancing out of the office window, turned to me in a relaxed way, smiled handsomely and simply said,

"You were saying, Mr. Everard?" The meeting ended shortly afterwards; without result.

The Somalia locust control department was well organised and, except for an Italian accountant, it was staffed entirely by Somalis. I spent the first few weeks familiarising myself with the way in which the department worked; during these visits I made a point of conveying a message that the resources of the Desert Locust Control and the Desert Locust Survey were available to support the national effort, as required. I also made reference to the periodic requests for supplementary funding and explained that, since the money had been contributed by the East African taxpayers, I was sure that the local personnel would understand that the East African governments expected the money to be spent properly.

Shortly afterwards, looking out of my office on an upper floor, I noticed a Land Rover of the locust department which had been parked at a building site some two hundred yards from my window. I walked up to the driver and questioned him regarding the purpose of his journey; he responded that the Permanent Secretary (the top bureaucrat) in the Ministry of Agriculture was overseeing the construction of a new house. The man in question appeared shortly afterwards; he explained that my predecessor had given his agreement that one of the Land Rovers could be used by the Permanent Secretary. I responded that I assumed that this would be for official duty and certainly not for the purpose of supervising the construction of domestic housing.

A month later, on driving through the city, I was struck by the number of vehicles which I saw which had a yellow locust painted on the door. I therefore diverted to the locust department and asked the senior officer if he could explain why so many official vehicles were to be seen in the city. I was told that elections would shortly be held countrywide and that the government had decided to requisition all of the locust department vehicles for election purposes. Primarily, the vehicles would be used to transport government supporters to voting booths on election day. There were altogether eighty-four vehicles of various types which were available for anti-locust operations. I asked the senior officer whether he knew that the purchase of the vehicles had, partially, been financed by the East African governments. He responded that he was aware of the fact; however, I should understand that he was powerless to contravene the instructions of the government and, specifically, his Minister.

When I returned to my office, I found a letter awaiting me; this was a request to transfer a substantial sum of money to supplement the government's budget for locust control measures. The request was signed by the Permanent Secretary whom I had met earlier and who had been supervising the construction of a new house.

I took no action on the request. After receiving one or two telephone calls from the Permanent Secretary's office and that of the Minister, I received a visit from the Permanent Secretary. He told me that he was surprised that I had delayed authorising his request; the main purpose of his visit was to carry to the Minister my authorisation for the release of funds. I told him that I was concerned regarding his use of the vehicle. In addition, I had been told that the government had requisitioned the entire locust control fleet of vehicles for political purposes; if that were true, then I would certainly not authorise the release of funds until all of the vehicles had been returned to the locust department and the cost of their operation refunded.

The following day I was summoned to the office of the Minister. After a formal welcome, it was clear that His Excellency was irritated and he lost no time in coming to the point. He had received a report from his Permanent Secretary saying that I was officially conducting myself in a difficult and uncooperative manner; he had no time for explanations in such circumstances and I should understand that my presence would only be tolerated provided that I gave unhesitating assistance to the government. Specifically, the government urgently needed money to support the operation of the locust department; he demanded that I should authorise the release of funds within twenty-four hours, otherwise I would face deportation. I would be required to pack up my belongings and leave the country immediately.

The Minister's eyes flashed for a few seconds, before they fixed on me with a furious stare. I smiled at him. Eventually, the prolonged, pregnant silence was broken when he said, "You don't look very worried".

I explained that my reports indicated that the vehicle fleet was being used for purposes other than for control measures against locusts. Until I was satisfied that any additional funds requested would be used for official purposes, I would never sign the authorisation for the release of funds. As for the deportation threat, the Minister should understand that I was in a position to leave the country immediately. At the same time, the Minister should understand that I would give a full report on the whole matter to the governments of East Africa; I would also recommend to my Director that my successor should be altogether more rigid and less flexible than myself. Without further ado, I thanked the Minister for having afforded me time and left his office.

Two days later I was again summoned to the Minister's office. The man I met on this occasion was quite different from the stern and irrational individual who had threatened me two days previously. As I was shown into his sumptuous office he sprang out of his chair and, smiling, gave me a brief embrace. When I had sat down, he explained that he had personally looked into the whole matter and he confirmed that the reports I had received were correct; the vehicles were being used for purposes other than controlling locusts. On behalf of the government he apologised and stated that all of the vehicles would be returned to the locust department compound within the next few days. He then added that, unfortunately, the government did not have sufficient money to buy petrol for the return journey of the vehicles and he wondered whether I would kindly authorise the release of funds from the bank for this purpose.

I thanked His Excellency for the information and noted the government's apology. Regarding the issue of providing funds to enable the vehicles to be returned by the government, I deeply regretted that I could not help. Further, until all of the vehicles had been returned, I would not be in a position to consider any authorisation to release funds. Second, since it seemed that the Minister had initially received incorrect information concerning my own conduct from his Permanent Secretary, I wondered whether the Minister considered that the Permanent Secretary should apologise?

The Minister smiled and said that he had been giving the question some thought; he had reached the conclusion that his Permanent Secretary was not the right person to hold the post. He had consulted with other ministries and had tried to have the Permanent Secretary transferred elsewhere. I should understand that political relationships were extremely sensitive and, unfortunately, the Minister had not been successful in having the man transferred.

At that moment, a messenger appeared and placed an envelope on the Minister's desk. On opening the letter, the Minister's face lit up and he looked at me with some self-satisfaction. He said,

"I have solved the problem. I spoke last evening with my friends who are the Ambassadors of the rich countries and I told them that we have a senior bureaucrat, of the highest integrity, who needs further training for his work to prepare him for promotion. This letter tells me that immediate arrangements are being made for the Permanent Secretary to receive a fellowship (bursary) to attend a course overseas. I hope that this will mean the absence of the man for at least a year!"

The Minister then touched a bell switch and a messenger was asked to request the Permanent Secretary to attend a meeting in the Minister's office immediately. When the Permanent Secretary appeared shortly afterwards, His Excellency told him that he recognised the wonderful work which the Permanent Secretary had been undertaking. In the view of the Minister, the hard work should be recognised. In addition, it was the Minister's view that the Permanent Secretary needed a change; some sort of promotion was being considered. In the circumstances, arrangements had been made for the Permanent Secretary to attend a long course of instruction overseas.

The Permanent Secretary looked stunned and his lips quivered nervously. He then gathered himself and announced that this step had been taken without consultation with him and he would refuse to go. The Minister responded that he well understood why the Permanent Secretary would prefer to stay in Mogadishu; nevertheless, the Permanent Secretary would attend a course overseas and, if necessary, the Minister would arrange for the Permanent Secretary to be escorted to the aircraft under armed guard. I never saw the Permanent Secretary again.

Over the next week or so the vehicles were gradually returned; some of those from outlying districts had run out of petrol and were under tow. Eventually it was reported that all of the vehicles were present; in future, there would be strict control to ensure that they were used only for the purpose of locust control measures. I visited the compound and arranged for all of the vehicles to be mechanically checked by the maintenance personnel, after which the government was requested to bring each of the vehicles to a mechanically sound state.

With the touchy incident behind us, we should go to work. During discussions with senior members of the national locust organisation I enquired whether they had carried out a reconnaissance for locusts in the extreme north-east of the country, in other words in the area of the tip of the Horn of Africa. The response was that this had not been done, partly because few reports of locusts had been received from the area; in any case, they regarded the area as inaccessible.

Just as some of us had ideas about the possibility of locusts harbouring at certain times in the Takazze Valley in Ethiopia, I was intrigued concerning the locust situation in the north-eastern part of Somalia. As far as migratory routes were concerned, we expected locust invasions of the Somali Peninsula from October or November onwards, as the north-east monsoon wind established itself over the Horn of Africa. During the first quarter of the year, locust swarms generally moved eastwards along the line of the Somali escarpment; as far as we knew, in a general sense the swarms would 'hold up' in the mountains during the summer months, that is while the south-westerly *kharriff* was blowing across the Somali Plateau. Although we did not know in precise terms where the swarms were harbouring, we used to refer generally to the area of the Erigavo hills.

In fact, we did not know where the locusts settled, since aerial reconnaissance had failed to find them. On the other hand, we recognised that the effectiveness of aerial reconnaissance during the spring and summer months was limited due to the relatively high density of dust and sand particles which were present in the air during the *kharriff*.

Over the previous few years, we had received few reports of locusts in the area of the Erigavo hills and mountains; around Erigavo, the escarpment rises to some seven thousand feet. I had therefore become intrigued by the disappearance of the swarms during the summer months.

The importance of the subject was obvious. If the swarms were found to be concentrated in a certain area, the next step would be to assess the possibility of destroying the locusts, which in turn would reduce the breeding potential. This could be considered either as a ground operation or, more likely, by aerial spraying.

My presence in Somalia gave me the opportunity to pursue the subject further and, possibly, satisfy our curiosity. I therefore planned a journey to the tip of the Horn of Africa, namely Cape Guardafui.

We travelled from Mogadishu in a northerly direction towards Belet Uen, but forked right at Bulo Burti. The initial part of the journey followed the river called the Webi Sciabelli (Leopard River) and the green vegetation which thrived along the river was a feast for the eyes. Once we had left the river *en route* to Galcaio, we soon found ourselves in semi-desert conditions with low scrub and the occasional *acacia* tree. As we approached Galcaio, our vehicles were filled with dust as we bumped over a plain of gypsum rock. We continued in a northerly direction as far as Gardo and then turned eastward to Scusciuban, an alliteration of the sound of rushing water.

Travelling in a northerly direction from Scusciuban, I found myself passing a fairly extensive mobile camp; on enquiry I was told that an Italian company was prospecting for oil. I spoke little Italian; however, I was invited to stay the night and was asked to join the team at seven p.m. for a communal dinner. The dining hall was filled with the excited voices of the Italian prospecting personnel; eventually my host shouted above the din and asked me whether I could imagine what his men were talking about. I responded that perhaps they were discussing the Suez Crisis or the German question, at which point he smiled and simply replied, "Women!"

After a three day journey, we halted near the top of the mountainous escarpment at a small village called El Gal. The villagers told us that although the Italian authorities were beginning to survey the area with the intention of constructing a road, there was no road linking El Gal with the coast. It would be necessary for us to hire burden camels. It was explained that although camels were not usually used on mountainous tracks, the local people had bred a smaller type of burden camel; these animals would be quite capable of walking through the mountains to a coastal fishing village called Durbo.

We set off in the late afternoon, with two camels carrying our belongings and water. The camels were controlled by a man who shouted various commands. For example, one of these warned the camels to be careful; as soon as the animals heard the caution, they would stop and test the ground ahead with their feet until the animals were satisfied that the ground was firm enough to take their weight.

After descending into a valley in the late evening we made a small camp; we carried on at five a.m. the following morning. Once in Durbo I made contact with a Somali District Officer, who kindly made his small cross-country vehicle available to me, stating that I could drive the vehicle with my helpers to Alula and decide at Alula how I should reach Cape Guardafui.

At some points on the littoral, we found ourselves driving close to low cliffs, which narrowed our passage between the sea and the higher ground. The surface of parts of the cliffs had been cracked and sometimes broken by myrrh trees, whose bulbous roots had somehow taken firm hold. My mind went back to a visit to the Valley of the Kings in Upper Egypt and a wonderful wall painting (in the palace of Queen Hatchepsut), which depicted myrrh being collected in about 1500 B.C. from the Land of Punt, which was later to be called Somaliland. The aromatic tree was an important ingredient for scent.

Alula is a small town which is the administrative centre for the tip of the Horn of Africa. I was told that it would be difficult to reach Cape Guardafui, because after a few hours the track would come to an end at the foot of some cliffs which extended into the sea.

We drove eastwards towards Cape Guardafui and reached the end of the track at Bereda just before nightfall. There we asked the villagers how we should reach Cape Guardafui. They advised us that the best way would be to travel by canoe during the night to Olloch, from where one could walk to Cape Guardafui.

The villagers offered to put two canoes at our disposal, stating that departure time would be at about ten p.m. I asked the villagers about locust movements; although they had seen a number of swarms over the years, they were preoccupied with, and distracted by, the menace of hyenas. They stated that the destruction of hyenas was of much greater importance to them than controlling locust swarms.

At ten p.m. I was invited to sit in a canoe and I enquired whether I should paddle or assist in any other way. The answer was immediate,

"You are a tall man and skill is necessary to paddle the canoe in the sea, so that it will not capsize. The sea is shark-infested. The best thing for us would be if you could lie on the bottom of the canoe and remain as still as possible!"

The next eight hours proved to be the most comfortable part of the journey. The canoe made its slow progress in a smooth and stable way, following the shoreline about two hundred yards out to sea. The moon was clear and the air was pleasantly warm; with the gentle lapping of the sea against the sides of the canoe, the experience was positively refreshing.

At six a.m. the following morning, we reached Olloch and the canoe was beached some way from the shore as the water was shallow. I left the canoe with the helpers and waded through the surf towards the village which had been established on a sandy slope just above the sea. As we walked out of the sea, the villagers streamed towards us. Clearly, the villagers were surprised to see us and some of them touched my skin; most of these individuals had never before seen white skin and were clearly intrigued by the difference between the colour of their skin pigmentation and my own.

I asked them about locusts and received some information. However, their main preoccupation was on the subject of hyenas. If I came from an Organisation which could kill locusts, then why could I not kill the hyenas which constantly threatened their livestock and, sometimes, their children?

At eight a.m. we began the walk towards Cape Guardafui. The first part of the walk remains unforgettably imprinted in my mind. It was extremely hot and the soft sand burnt our feet as we tried to force our way upwards. The first part of the journey was strenuous and it seemed to last an eternity; as we took each step forward, the soft sand dragged us back.

Eventually, the trying first stage of our walk was left behind and we continued for a few hours over a gently rising plain until, at last, the lighthouse at Cape Guardafui came into view.

The lighthouse was maintained and operated by Alfredo Polidari. Although he spoke no English and my knowledge of Italian was superficial, somehow over the next day and a half we managed to communicate effectively. Alfredo had looked after the lighthouse for two years and was proud of his ability to maintain and operate it; he gave me a detailed guided tour of the lighthouse complex. All was immaculate and clean; the metal parts of the equipment were highly polished, which added lustre to the general appearance.

Evidently, Alfredo was a self-sufficient individual. He had lived on Cape Guardafui with three or four Somalis for two years. Although he was totally preoccupied with the maintenance and operation of the lighthouse, he seemed well-versed in current affairs and referred to the Suez Crisis, the German question and other events of the day with knowledge.

If someone has been virtually alone for a protracted period, when the person receives a visitor it is quite normal that the person begins to talk, sometimes uncontrollably. During my visits to various field officers, the tendency for them to talk continuously for long periods was much in evidence. As far as Alfredo was concerned, he showed no inclination to talk at great length; on the contrary, he was interested in the purpose of my visit, asking questions and listening to the answers with interest.

Alfredo explained that he had recently accepted an offer of a short holiday in Mogadishu, but had cut it short; he had not enjoyed the noise on the streets and the general hubbub of the city! He also explained that he rarely received visitors. He had been visited a year previously; there had been two men, one of whom was a Catholic priest. Unfortunately, the priest had suffered a heart attack and had died. Alfredo then pointed towards the grave which he himself had dug about a hundred yards from the lighthouse.

After having spent two nights at the lighthouse and having obtained as much information as was possible about movements of locusts, I told my helpers that we should leave, returning the way we had come. Apart from the information I had received, we had walked over the general area and collected samples of many species of the vegetation and these were placed in a press; subsequently, they would be sent to the herbarium in Nairobi for further examination. It later transpired that at least one of the plants we had collected had become an addition to the recorded African plant species.

On the second evening, I let Alfredo know that we would be leaving the following morning; apart from telling me he had enjoyed our visit, he announced that he wanted me to have an English breakfast before my departure. He hoped the meal would strengthen me for the return journey. Next morning, Alfredo asked me to make a final tour of the lighthouse and he would send someone to call me when the breakfast was ready.

About an hour later I found myself sitting at a rustic table in a small room, with Alfredo opposite me. In front of me was a perfect place-setting for breakfast; suddenly Alfredo looked rather worried, jumped up and found a linen napkin which he handed me, apologetically stating that it should have been in place before. The culture and civilisation of that small room seemed foreign in the desolate surroundings and heat of Cape Guardafui.

Alfredo then asked me if I was ready for breakfast, at which point a large plate was brought which was more than covered with an enormous omelette; a part of the monster hung over the edge of the large plate. I looked at the omelette and my immediate reaction was that I could not possibly eat it. At that stage of my life I was fit and healthy, which meant that in any case I ate relatively little food.

I managed a flicker of a smile and told Alfredo that I was overcome by the magnificent English breakfast. If he would bring a plate, I would cut the omelette in half so that we could share it. He looked at me in a good-natured way and simply said,

"I never eat breakfast."

He then went on to explain that he had heard and read a good deal about the English breakfast and he was taking the opportunity to watch an Englishman eat his breakfast. He had thrown twelve eggs into the omelette!

I immediately realised that I had no alternative; slowly, I managed to eat the whole omelette. I can still remember the look of satisfaction on the face of Alfredo.

We returned to Durbo over the next two days, using the same route; the overnight canoe journey proved to be as pleasant as the earlier one. We reached the fishing village of Durbo, west of Alula, by about midday and the helpers suggested that we should return to our Land Rovers at El Gal that evening. I responded that it would be unpleasant to walk in the heat of the afternoon and felt that perhaps we could leave at about 3 p.m.; from this time, the temperature should progressively cool. We should be able to reach an altitude of about three thousand feet above sea level by nightfall; we could then walk the remaining part of the journey to El Gal the following morning.

At about 2.30 p.m., we were making final preparations for the walk and the helpers were loading the camels. A man then began to talk to us and it transpired that he too would be walking to El Gal: we invited him to walk with us. He then explained that the camel track which we had used was a rather long route; he knew a much shorter route and offered to show us the way if we would like to use it. We were fatigued and the prospect of a shorter walk proved attractive. We therefore asked the camel driver to meet us with the camels near the top of the escarpment; by the time he arrived we would be waiting for him by the track.

At 3 p.m., the group of four of us (including our new-found guide) set off and, initially, we made good progress. After about an hour, the terrain became steep and rocky. Our guide explained that once we had reached the top of the ridge, it would be a steady walk to the track where we were to meet the camels. We laboured long and hard up the mountain and, after scrambling for two hours, we became extremely tired. Our guide had stopped his easy conversation and looked a little anxious. Shortly after we had carried on, one of my helpers collapsed with exhaustion; when I asked for the goatskin of water to help revive him, I found that the rest of the group had already drunk about two thirds of the available water. After a few minutes, the man slowly began to regain consciousness and we told him that we would try and half-carry him onwards with his arms on our shoulders.

After another hour's hard scrambling (by this time no one spoke), we had reached what seemed to be the crown of the mountain; we then stopped to rest.

I noticed that the lips of the guide were quivering and I looked at him with concern. He then announced that he had missed his way and we had climbed a mountain which was too far to the west; in order to gain the ridge where we were supposed to meet the camels, we would have to descend into a valley and climb the side of the next mountain.

At this juncture, the helper stared at me with piercingly deadly eyes; with a look of hate on his countenance he blurted out, "Shall we kill him?"

For one ghastly fleeting second, I felt I could identify with his exasperation. Then I simply responded, "No!" But I could understand his frightening emotion.

Not only had the guide misled us, but one of our group had collapsed with exhaustion and the remaining helper and myself were in a pitiful state of fatigue. I for one felt terribly alone on the mountain. The barren mountains were uninhabited. Although the sun would soon set, it was still hot. If we were soon to find that we were all in a state of collapse from exhaustion, would we be able to summon the strength to forge ahead the next day after an overnight rest on the mountain? Would we be prey to wild animals? How long could one maintain one's strength without water? We could not evade such questions; and we did not know the answers. All we did know was that we had made a dreadful misjudgement; we had separated ourselves from our water!

I gathered myself and announced that we had no option; we must try and reach the ridge before the camels, otherwise the camels would pass and we would be without water.

We scrambled down the mountain and into the valley; as we began to climb up the other side, I realised that dusk would descend within the next forty-five minutes. We were beyond the point of goading one another to greater efforts; the only question was whether we could keep going at all.

The final part of the climb up the mountain entailed scrambling over some huge rocks; fortunately, the man we had been dragging had now partially recovered and I tried to explain to him that if he could keep moving for another half hour, we would be on the ridge. When we were almost through the final wall of rocks, my foot slipped and I fell a few feet; although I was only shaken, at the same time I realised that the inside of my ankle had been gashed. We tied a rag around my ankle in a vain endeavour to stop the bleeding.

When we reached the camel track on the ridge it was dark; we sank to the ground amongst the bushes in a semi exhausted state. By now, the silent night air felt cool and I hoped that a breeze would bring more relief to our weary limbs. As a faint wafting of air filtered through my shorts, which were saturated with sweat, I began to feel more lively. I wondered about the whereabouts of the camels; were they in the area, or had they already passed?

Perhaps the Guardian Angel had felt the need to keep a watch on us; after all, in terms of co-ordination, the planned separate movements of the camels and our group had turned out to have been a terrible mistake. In any case, within two minutes of our arrival on the track, we heard the unmistakable noise of wooden camel bells; although we were exhausted, we managed to generate mild feelings of relief.

The next morning, fed and rested, we walked the remainder of the journey to El Gal. At lunchtime, we began the long drive back to Mogadishu.

The first town to be visited was Scusciuban. By the time we had arrived at about 6 p.m., my foot had swollen to such an extent that I could not see the contour of the ankle. I enquired whether there were any medical facilities in the town and was directed to a small house. To my great relief, the house was inhabited by an Italian doctor; Dr. Parisi worked for the World Health Organisation (WHO), mainly in the field of malaria.

I was happily surprised to meet Dr. Parisi, since there were few qualified medical doctors in Somalia at that time. He examined my ankle and explained that I would need to stay in Scusciuban for at least two days; specifically, I would remain in his bed and he would sleep on a sofa in his living room.

Without further ado and announcing that he would unavoidably hurt me, he cleaned my infected ankle, after which my whole foot was swathed in bandages.

On our return to Mogadishu, a comprehensive report was prepared covering our expedition and a number of possibilities were highlighted which merited further exploration. In fact four years later, in 1961, I was to make another expedition to the area and was able to focus on the main areas where locusts would harbour during the summer months, before beginning their flight to the south for breeding from September to October. Although locusts were found over a wide area, the expansive, saucer-like Hemistio Valley seemed to be the main harbouring area for the large swarms. If their presence would be confirmed in future years, they could be sprayed from the air and to the extent that this would be successful, the next generation of locusts would be correspondingly snubbed out.

Alfredo, the lighthouse keeper, was still enjoying his lonely work; in that remote region, in his friendly way, he asked me whether I happened to be 'passing again?' I asked him how many visitors he had received during the previous four years. He became thoughtful for a few moments, then he made his response,

"One."

On completion of my four-month assignment in Mogadishu, it was time to take some leave. Because of the difficult nature of our work, the amount of leave granted was generous. I looked forward to a holiday of three and a half months in Europe. Initially, I would visit my parents and a few relations; after that I was not sure how I would spend my time. In discussion with a colleague, he suggested that the best approach to adopt when taking a holiday that was really needed (and he expressed the view that I deserved a good rest), would be to pursue an activity which would totally preoccupy me. Why not learn to ski?

Chapter Seven

Emy

In February 1957 I found myself in Victoria Station in London, doggedly maintaining my course towards the train which would transport its passengers to Folkestone. I was not used to the hundreds of people who were equally intent on heading in various directions; I felt hemmed in. Having been in London for a few weeks, I missed the quietude, space and seemingly limitless horizons of the desert conditions to which I had grown accustomed. Based at my parents' house in London, I had undertaken several long walks to explore various districts; I had come to realise that, however differently I wished them to be, these walks (each of several hours' duration) would never be a substitute for the physical exertion which had become part of one's everyday life in Africa.

As I approached the train, I looked forward to a skiing holiday in the mountains of Austria. The travel agent (Erna Low) had organised a holiday 'package', which meant that I need not be concerned with the travel arrangements. I should return to the enjoyment of life in England and Western Europe and try to overcome the hankering I still retained for the life I had left behind. The purpose of the long holiday was, after all, to readjust to Western 'normality'.

As I sat in my reserved seat at a table for two, I looked around and noticed that the railway carriage, which was planned with open seating throughout its length, was steadily filling up; the seat opposite mine was empty. My eyes fell on a magazine on the small window table in front of me; I assumed it had been left by a passenger who had disembarked from the train on its arrival in London. Looking through the window, there were the usual scenes of small groups of people; among others, I saw a middle-aged couple who, apparently, were seeing off their daughter.

The train would leave at any moment and, more or less unthinkingly, I took hold of the magazine and began to glance through its pages. I was soon immersed in an interesting article and was hardly conscious of the train's departure.

Suddenly, I was startled by the voice of a young woman; I soon realised she was sitting opposite me. She said in firm tones,

"Do you usually steal other people's property?"

Although I was taken aback by what I felt was a somewhat exaggerated assertion, I humbly apologised, closed the magazine and pushed it politely in the direction of the confrontational voice.

"Since you have started reading my magazine, you may as well finish it; but don't forget to give it back to me before we leave the train, please."

I continued reading; at the same time, I could not escape certain thoughts. I had briefly noticed the young woman on the platform; she was good-looking and well-dressed. But sitting in the train opposite her, for some reason I did not wish to look at her directly; I tried to continue reading the article, but I was intrigued by the approach that she had adopted when she talked to me. I was also perplexed by her accent, or lack of it. The young woman seemed to speak English perfectly, but without any sort of accent which would give a clue regarding the area in which she may have been brought up. I wondered to myself why there was no discernible accent. After some minutes, I had finished the article and returned the magazine courteously with a smile.

Now I could see the young woman. She was of medium height, good-looking and her hair was brown; she wore a loose red sweater beneath a woolly, llama coat. In spite of the earlier brief verbal attack, the girl had an open expression and smiled easily. And she had temperament!

"Where are you heading for?" I asked.

"Kitzbühel. I am Austrian and I am going to do some skiing. And you?"

"Fieberbrunn."

"That is about twenty kilometres from Kitzbühel. How long are you going for?"

"At the moment, I am booked for two weeks. If I enjoy the skiing and like it there, I may stay for a few more weeks."

"You must be quite rich; and you are still young."

"No, it is just that I have a job in Africa and sometimes I have to work in difficult conditions. So instead of being given a short holiday each year, depending on the country in which we work, we are sent home after eighteen or twenty-four months for three or four months' rest."

"What do you do?"

"I work for the Desert Locust Control Organisation in East Africa and so far I have spent most of my time working with Somalis."

"Do you know Peter Haskell, the Director of the Anti-Locust Research Centre in London?"

"Well, I have met him. Do you know him?"

"Yes, I trained as a biologist at King's College, London University. As part of the entrance examination, I chose to write an essay on locusts."

"I find this a remarkable coincidence. I wonder what the statistical chance would be that I should sit in my reserved seat and meet someone who not only knows what a locust is, but has also studied in the field. My name is Colin Everard; may I ask you yours?"

"I was baptised Emilie, but everyone calls me Emy. The rest of my name is von Bertele-Grenadenberg. Since the war, the Austrians no longer use 'von' so I call myself Emy Bertele."

The journey to the Austrian Tyrol took about twenty-four hours. I talked to Emy on the way, helped her with her suitcase when we transferred to the Channel ferry and in the evening asked her whether she would like to have some dinner in the restaurant car. The response was somewhat hesitating; Emy would have dinner with me, but only with a clear understanding that she would pay for her own meal.

The following morning, as we passed through the Austrian landscape, I was impressed by the beauty and the sheer majesty of the mountains. Eventually, we reached St. Johann, where I would leave the train and take another; this would travel to Fieberbrunn. I told Emy I had enjoyed our conversations enormously and I thought she was a very nice girl. I hoped we would meet again and perhaps I would ring her in Kitzbühel. In case we should not meet again, I would take a snap of her in the train from the platform, which I did.

I called Emy two days later and the following evening took the bus to Kitzbühel. We were to meet for a glass of wine; on arrival, Emy introduced me to an English friend called Peter. I recall a feeling of irritation. This was to be an evening which I would spend with Emy; I certainly had no wish to be in the company of another man and I suggested he should leave, which he did. Emy then explained that she had asked Peter not to meet her that evening, but he had insisted on making an appearance.

What Emy did not explain (simply because it did not concern me), was that one of the reasons she had taken a holiday in Austria was that she felt that it was time to think of marriage. There were three front-runners; she hoped that during her skiing holiday, she might be able to decide which of these men she should marry.

I enjoyed Emy's company, although at that time I did not develop strong feelings of affection towards her. Certainly, I was not infatuated with her; and there was no question of love. Our relationship was friendly, but somewhat formally correct. I enjoyed her intelligent wit and I liked her good looks and appearance. And I also admired her wide general knowledge; Emy seemed to be equally at home talking about music (including opera), or sports activities (including cricket!), or literature, or current affairs, or architecture – the list seemed inexhaustible.

In those early days of our acquaintance, the quality I most appreciated in Emy was her sense of humour. My own is somewhat over-developed and I had often previously encountered problems with girls who took strong exception to my tendency to tease them. Emy not only withstood the teasing, but frequently turned the tables on me; from the beginning, Emy never allowed herself to take me too seriously.

I saw Emy on several occasions during my stay. One evening, I was introduced to her uncle Bili and aunt Melitta in Kitzbühel; Emy explained that several members of her family were taking a skiing holiday in Kitzbühel. While we were drinking a glass of wine, I was asked what my plans were. I responded that they were quite vague for the next few weeks. I had thoroughly enjoyed my introduction to skiing and I was thinking of extending my stay in Fieberbrunn. After a short discussion between Emy's uncle, her aunt and herself, I was asked whether I would like to visit Vienna. Emy's uncle would be travelling to Vienna within a day or two and he would give Emy a lift so that she could visit members of her family. Without doubt I also would enjoy a visit to the capital city of Austria.

Uncle Bili drove us to Vienna. During the six hour journey, Emy and I talked continuously. We discussed education and I was told quite firmly that unless one had a command of English, French and German, then one could hardly claim to have reached an elementary standard of education. Another point which Emy made, with some force, was that she had already seen in her young life violence and civil strife. Emy had no wish to go into details, but her memories were associated with the period spent by the family in Slovenia; the family's experiences during the time of the Partisans had not been pleasant. Arising from this, as far as Emy was concerned she would always enjoy happy events; there was so much to enjoy in the world which was positive, so why should one indulge in the negative aspects of our existence? In particular, why do some people delight in introducing negative distortions to what should be straightforward situations? Why concentrate on sadism, decadence, degradation of the human spirit and depressingly sordid subjects, for example, instead of enjoying positive creativity and happiness. We should laud those who spread positive, cleverly-engineered creativity, joy and happiness; we should encourage them to greater efforts.

At last we arrived in Vienna and I shall never forget the courteous way in which Bili saw me established in an hotel near the Palace of Schönbrunn.

Vienna was a delight and, with hindsight, those days enabled us to get a 'feel' for our respective personalities. We enjoyed one another's company and, perhaps unconsciously, we were happy to do things together.

Although Emy spent much of her time with her grandmother and other relations, we made one or two walks through the old city. One afternoon, a poster caught our eye which announced that the Opera Ball would take place two or three days later. If we could get tickets, would we like to go to the Opera Ball; why not? It seemed a nice idea, but one problem which immediately emerged was the question of evening clothes. Both of us had come to Austria to ski and we certainly had no clothes which would be suitable to wear for the Opera Ball. Emy mentioned that a friend was in Vienna and it might be possible for her to borrow an evening dress from Almuth, which fortunately was to be the case. Almuth was a good friend of Emy; later, Almuth was to marry Emy's uncle Peter.

In my case, I told Emy that I would hire some tails (a 'Frack') for the evening. Unfortunately, I had to announce a day or so later that although I had explored every conceivable avenue, it seemed that every "Frack" which was available for hire in Vienna had already been reserved; I was at a dead end. Did this mean we would have to abandon our idea of attending the Opera Ball? What a pity. It would have been such a great event in our young lives!

Emy thought for a few minutes and then called her uncle Peter; she explained to her uncle that he and I were about the same size and she wondered whether it might be possible for me to borrow his 'Frack'.

On the evening of the Opera Ball, Emy and I met at uncle Peter's house, where we changed into the evening clothes. I had never before worn a 'Frack' and, in trying to dress myself, I encountered problems with the white waistcoat and white tie. At one stage, while I was unsuccessfully trying to make an adjustment to the waistcoat, uncle Peter appeared and smiled good-naturedly.

"You are an Englishman. Do you like Scotch whisky?" he asked; he spoke with a quite strong German accent.

"Well, yes," I responded. A strong scotch and soda was then brought; uncle Peter smiled and said,

"Chin-chin. Let me help you." He then approached me and dressed me from head to toe; problem solved!

Uncle Peter had generously arranged for a car to take us to the Opera Ball; as the car was brought to a halt in front of Vienna's magnificent Opera House, we felt that we had arrived in style. The grandeur of the Opera Ball was something completely outside my experience. We enjoyed the occasion tremendously. For the whole of the night, wherever we strolled in the Opera House, our ears were filled with enchanting music. At about five a.m. we enjoyed the traditional gulyas, before I returned to the hotel and Emy rejoined her family.

After several days of sightseeing and great enjoyment in Vienna, it was time for me to start thinking of a return to my work. I felt that I had been very fortunate in meeting Emy. I mentioned to her on one occasion, however, that I had reached a conclusion that I seemed to be the sort of person who was unsuitable for marriage; in any case, I was 'wedded' to the locust life.

As for Emy, she held a position in foreign relations with the American company Dupont in London. In this position, with her solid scientific background, good looks, charming personality and ability in languages, she was an excellent representative of the company, whether in England or in Europe.

In the spring of 1957 I returned to Africa and assumed duty as the senior field officer for East Africa, based in Nairobi. I told one or two of my friends about my enjoyable holiday, including the fact that I had met a lovely, charming girl. One of my colleagues (Charles Rennie) suggested that I should invite Emy to spend a holiday in East Africa; Charles Rennie was about ten years older than myself and gave me an impression that he was much more experienced in these matters. I respected his advice, but responded that things had not really reached a point where I could reasonably make such a suggestion. Charles told me to bear his advice in mind. If eventually Emy were to visit East Africa, he would assist by arranging for her to stay with married friends.

During the next eighteen months I corresponded with Emy, sometimes enclosing photographs of scenes of our work. From time to time I received delightful responses; from our correspondence, it was clear that Emy had a good idea of the type of life I was leading and the conditions under which we worked.

In mid 1958 I told Charles Rennie that I would accept his advice. The fact was that I had met a delightfully unusual person and if Emy should be able to visit East Africa, I was sure that she would enjoy herself. I therefore asked Charles Rennie if he could make some arrangements for Emy to stay with friends and I wrote to Emy, explaining that if she could fly to East Africa, from that point on my friends and I would make sure that she would have an enjoyable holiday.

In July 1958, I waited at Embakasi Airport in Nairobi hoping to catch a glimpse of a pretty, somewhat courageous young woman who, although ostensibly on holiday, was in fact coming to spend some time in a highly unusual environment. After the arrival of her aircraft, I waited patiently and watched the various passengers arrive; there was no sign of Emy. Just as I was concluding that all of the passengers must have disembarked, Emy appeared. I was relieved and held out my arms to embrace her; in response, Emy held out her hand and shook mine,

"How do you do, Colin?"

While driving Emy to the friends' house where she would stay, I asked her why there had been a long delay before she appeared in the arrival area. Emy explained that when the aircraft had been parked, she had seen a man standing on the apron. The man had lost most of his hair and was considerably overweight; Emy had peered at him for a number of minutes, wondering if the man was in fact Colin Everard. She eventually concluded that the man was probably not myself; Emy then admitted that she had been greatly relieved when, upon seeing me, the correctness of her assessment had been confirmed.

Within four days of the arrival of Emy in Nairobi, we had fallen in love. Both of us knew that this was no fleeting infatuation. We had known one another for about eighteen months and, although a substantial part of the period had been spent in exchanging letters, each of us knew sufficient of the other's nature and personality to feel totally confident that we should spend the rest of our lives together. From that point, we would be together; and wherever my work might take me, Emy would be there.

What were our natures and what qualities did we value? First, in basic terms, we felt we were decent people, that is to say a couple who recognised the importance of loyalty and all that is implied in loyalty. We both enjoyed arguments (not quarrels!) and we found our arguments, laced with much humour, to be stimulating and enjoyable. I loved Emy's simplicity and naïveté, including her seemingly innocent questions, which were invariably dead on target.

As we travelled through life together, Emy demonstrated a will to achieve uncompromising standards; on the rare occasions when her standards cannot be adhered to, she exhibits admirable qualities of rationalisation. A natural constant which shows through all these qualities is an infectious 'joie de vivre'. Emy enjoys her life, our four daughters, her relations, her friends. And in their turn they enjoy Emy.

No one has seen Emy badly dressed, simply because this is something outside her experience. As a young married couple living in Nairobi or Mogadishu, we could never have afforded an appropriate wardrobe so that Emy could maintain her standards of appearance. Undeterred, Emy immediately set about making her own clothes. As a young girl, Emy had received some lessons in dress-making and had made clothes for her sisters; now she developed her skills to dress herself. For years, her clothes were constantly admired; they always reflected the height of fashion. Some years later, when we had the opportunity to have, for example, leather clothes made in Thailand, Emy chose her clothes with such skill that she epitomised fashionable elegance.

Although at all times lacking in ostentation, Emy is a deeply religious person. Not only was Emy instructed in the Catholic religion from a young age, but she has practised the religion with a constancy that few could match. I can recall only one Sunday in the last thirty-seven years when Emy was not able to attend a Sunday mass; at the time we were travelling by train across the Gobi Desert between Beijing and Ulan Bator in Mongolia. Religion has given Emy tremendous strength over the years. At various times, courage has been demanded of Emy. Whether escaping with her family after Tito had incorporated part of southern Austria into Yugoslavia at the end of the last war, whether on the point of a gun in Uganda, sitting in a jet transport aircraft where the door was opening with consequent loss of pressurisation, enduring a difficult birth of one of her children, or being left alone while her husband had to travel, Emy's faith has invariably supported her and carried her through the most trying situations.

All her life, Emy has enjoyed reading; the surroundings or circumstances are never allowed to impinge on her concentration. For example, during a rail journey between Beijing and Ulan Bator, only tea was available on the train; the restaurant car served no food. When the train stopped at a station before traversing the Gobi Desert near the Mongolian border, I suggested that I should try to obtain some food. After a good deal of difficulty with communication, I bought a jar of pears and some biscuits. When I returned to the platform, I found that another train had entered the station, which meant that I would need to walk around one end of the newly-arrived train to regain access to the train and compartment which I had left. After what seemed to be quite a long walk, I rounded the end of the newly-arrived train only to find that the train from which I had disembarked was no longer there.

Carrying the pears and biscuits, I ran back to the main station and asked what had happened to the train; my pleas were met with blank faces, simply because my Chinese listeners did not understand English. With consternation, I tried to explain that my wife was on the train; I needed to know its whereabouts. After a few minutes, a German-speaking woman explained that she was leading a tourist group from the train which had just arrived. She would ask her Chinese colleague to assist with interpretation. The officials in the station appeared totally unconcerned and gave no clear information regarding the whereabouts of the train I had left. Eventually, the Chinese interpreter (who spoke German) told me that sometimes trains were taken to a nearby maintenance depot for repairs; perhaps my train was in the depot.

From the platform, I could see a large, high shed about a kilometre from the main station. It was a cool morning with brilliant sunshine, but from where I stood I could not see into the shed; straining my eyes in an endeavour to see what was in the interior of the large building, I could see only a dark enclosed area. It seemed that there were no windows in the building.

I walked in soft sand towards the shed and reached the open entrance about ten minutes later. Looking around, I could see several Chinese workers staring at me; should I enter the darkened interior of the building? Would the Chinese workers report that I had entered the building and, if my entry was unauthorised, would I be arrested?

The decision was simple. The fact was that I had lost my wife! I entered the blackness and waited for a minute or so, hoping that my eyes would become accustomed to the darkness. I could see the form of a train and I walked along its side; I remembered the number of the carriage, as well as of our compartment. The train was empty and no human voice broke the silence of the darkened shed. After some minutes I began to discern the train more clearly; looking up, I could see that there was quite an extensive hole in the roof of the building and the sun's rays were shining through. Then I recognised the number of the carriage and entered the train; I walked along the corridor until I reached the number of our compartment. I slid the door open and, with a feeling of enormous relief, saw my wife sitting in the rays of the sun, book in hand.

"My dear Emy, what are you doing here? The train has been shunted into this huge shed, apparently for repairs. All the passengers have left. But you are still reading."

Emy looked at me with a smilingly questioning expression.

"Well, I am reading Durant's, 'The Age of Louis XIV', and I have excellent light. I really have no idea where we are, but I would like to finish the chapter."

After a little gentle persuasion, Emy accompanied me with her book to the main station, so that we could wait for our train to reappear and board it for Ulan Bator. Before reboarding, Emy finished her chapter!

To revert to our beginnings together in Nairobi in 1958, since we had fallen in love, we thought that we should be married without delay. We considered the option of returning to England so that our marriage could be celebrated with our families. However, we concluded that the sooner we were married the better; this would mean that we would be married in Nairobi. A day or two before we were to be married, we were strolling through some gardens which were bursting with gorgeous colours of bougainvillaea. Emy looked somewhat pensive and turned to me with a look of innocent simplicity,

"You know, we have fallen in love, but before marrying you I should have checked whether you have a job and that sort of thing; how much do you get paid?"

I explained that I was employed on a two-year contract basis and, up to then, I had served through three of the contracts; I hoped my contract would be renewed, but one could never foresee the future. Emy replied simply,

"It's good to know that you have a proper job."

Like many young people, we discussed whether we should consider living together before our marriage. We rejected the idea. This would have been an affront to Emy's faith. From my point of view, I felt strongly (and still do) that a couple who believe that they can learn to make physical and spiritual love properly within a short time, are indulging in fantasy and delusion. There is a gulf of difference between a bit of fun and consummation of the marital state. In any case, why spoil a natural process of sexual enjoyment by pretending to make 'instant love'? Unqualified commitment to each other in a lifelong relationship, confirmed by marriage, was of overriding importance. We would also become passionate, but it would not be the passion of a quick-fire 'fling'.

Emy and I were married in St. Austin's church in Nairobi on 27th September 1958. Philip Stephenson gave Emy away and my old friend Charles Rennie was best man. In the absence of relations and close friends, the priest had arranged for a young woman to act as bridesmaid. On reflection, since Emy had never met the designated bridesmaid, she felt that this well-meaning gesture was not entirely appropriate; instead, she invited a good friend of mine, Diarmaid Harvey-Kelly, to be her 'bridesmaid'. As a good friend, we felt comfortably close to him; he performed the role perfectly!

The small reception after the marriage was held in Charles Rennie's house. Although we knew few people in Kenya at that time, the reception was nevertheless memorable. A number of colleagues and friends were present. One of the bachelors, Hector McMichael, came over to me at one stage and, in his characteristically pensive way, announced that he felt that I was indeed lucky to have found Emy. I certainly agreed. He then told me he had met a number of women in his life, but so far had met no girl of Emy's type; this was a pity, because Emy appealed to him very much! Did I have any advice for him? I was faintly amused by his directness and, on the spur of the moment, told him that Emy had sisters; the next 'in line' would be a beautiful, artistically talented, fun-loving, bubbly girl named Marceline.

During his next visit to England, Hector McMichael visited Emy's family house in Purley. Shortly afterwards, Marceline and Hector McMichael were married!

Our honeymoon was short, mainly because a great deal of work was brewing. We spent our honeymoon in the highlands of Kenya, at the Brown Trout Hotel. On arrival, we found a small group of people in front of the main entrance to the reception area. Out of curiosity, we joined them and found that they were admiring a brown trout which had just been caught. One of the group turned to us and gave a graphic description of how the fish had been hooked; he then announced that the weight of the fish was seven pounds, which was a record. Emy looked at me and, with an expression of slightly mystified irritation on her face, said,

"We didn't come here to fish, did we?"

Another member of the group then announced that he was in charge of the reception; we must be Mr. and Mrs. Everard who had ordered the wedding suite.

We settled down as a young married couple in rented accommodation. Since Emy was a qualified scientist, she was immediately employed as a research assistant at the experimental laboratory of the Desert Locust Survey in Nairobi. While Emy was nurturing various generations of desert locusts, I prepared for the control measures which would be needed when an impending invasion of desert locusts materialised in Kenya.

The first year or two of marriage, in particular, are a delight. The married couple are certainly deeply in love; at the same time, inevitably there are traits of character and qualities which each will need to learn, and adjust to, with respect to the other. Emy and I were no exception.

As far as cooking was concerned, as a young girl Emy had routinely cooked breakfast for nine every morning: her parents and the seven brothers and sisters. Although Emy was an accomplished cook, she decided to develop her skills further and became extremely successful. Not only did she look after her husband, but the children were brought up on a balanced diet of natural foods. Invariably, bones and leftovers of vegetables were kept and subsequently used as a basis for soup. Canned or 'instant' food has only been accepted as a rare exception.

After we had left Africa to live in Canada for twenty years, Emy continued to develop her cooking skills. Her dinner parties became almost legendary, not only for the hors-d'oeuvres and main courses but, especially, for the delicious Austrian 'Torten'.

Before I had met Emy, my approach to food was typically English: one needed to eat to live. After a few years of married life, and having been continuously spoiled by Emy's superb cooking, although I did not wish to admit it, from time to time I felt that I should live to eat.

A few years after our marriage, when I was transferred to work in Uganda, I continued the enjoyment of playing golf. Since I had not had the opportunity to play golf during my years in the Horn of Africa, I relished the prospect of playing regularly at a small club in Uganda. For her part, Emy had played tennis for her college at university, but had not played golf. Without hesitation, Emy told me that she would not wish to become a 'golf widow' and immediately enrolled for some lessons. A year or so later, we were playing happily together and have continued to do so ever since. As she was steadily improving, I offered to buy her a new set of golf clubs if she were ever to achieve a handicap of 18. About a year later I asked Emy how her golf was getting on; she responded that she had just been given a new handicap by the Ladies Golf Union – 18.

Before leaving Uganda in 1966, we were invited to Kitale for Christmas by some farmer friends. Emy was her usual bubbling self, exuding happiness – and full of wit. After a magnificent Christmas dinner, our host and hostess invited us to sit with them in front of a cosy fire; they felt personally close to us. After some light-hearted conversation, our hostess became more serious,

"May I ask you a personal question? Do you two ever argue?"

I thought quickly for the right answer; but before I had a chance, Emy responded,

"I never argue with Colin; he is always wrong!"

Between 1959 and 1970, Emy gave birth to four children. All were girls and we often commented that one was more beautiful than the next. In their different ways, each strikingly beautiful daughter has grown and developed into a distinctive individual with interesting, and stimulating, characteristics. In their various professional pursuits, they have already achieved much and contribute positively within the society in which they live and work; they must take credit for their achievements. And their mother must also be recognised for having brought them up with love and constant attention to standards over the years. Now it is their turn to do the same within their own families; and they seem to be managing admirably.

In 1984 I was returning from an exhausting mission to Asia. The flight time between Tokyo and Montreal would have been about fifteen hours. Normally, I used to spend most of the time on the aircraft in reviewing papers or completing reports. On this occasion, I recognised that I was extremely tired; if I had attempted to work, inevitably I would have found myself in a situation of diminishing productivity.

I had difficulty in sleeping and began to meditate on the lives which Emy and I were sharing. As I had left our house in Montreal, on that particular occasion our young daughters had been playing near our front porch and each had a small pipe in her mouth; each was blowing soap bubbles through the pipe. As the bubbles appeared, they would be carried upwards towards the azure sky and one could see the colours of the rainbow glistening in the bubbles as they caught the rays of the sun; eventually, they burst. Dozing in the aircraft, I consciously told myself to stop thinking about work. I thought of my family and the symbolism of our offspring 'blowing bubbles of love'.

I enjoy writing prose; I do not write poetry. Thinking about our married life, our children and the family as a whole, I wrote the lines that follow on the next page:

THE BUBBLE OF LOVE
Or Reflections On A Mature Conjugal Partnership

I dream – I feel that love is like a bubble;
It dances, and laughs, in sun-kissed rays of hope.
Is it real, or illusory – clear of trouble?
Yes, it has colours of the rainbow, floats,
Shimmers in the breeze. This bubble is love.
Caressed by warm bodies in consummation
Love rests lightly on the wings of a dove;
At night a veritable constellation.
This bubble reflects only affection
Beautifully, like a myriad of stars.
Development, nourishment, attention
Steer your bubble on glittering paths.
As a maxim, strive hard for creation
Of true partnership of rock-like foundation.

Neglect your bubble? Accept the certainty
All hell will unleash; your bubble will burst
Degenerating into enmity,
First producing volatility, later, worse,
Sterility towards that loved one for whom
You once professed everlasting devotion
With glorious adoration; and which soon
Became passionately conceived perfection.
Take the advice of those in the know,
Stay true to the end and reap your harvest
Of maturing love with increasing glow
Ever plumbing new depths; till your final rest.
This is the right way to avoid trouble,
Living in love – through a radiant bubble.

In a nutshell, Emy is a role model. Emy and I are still enjoying one another. Thank God!

Fig. 15   *The Opera Ball - Vienna, 1957.*

Fig. 16   *Emy with little Emy, Carolyne and Marci - Uganda 1966.*

Fig. 17   *Emy - Montreal, 1984.*

Fig. 18   *Emy in her llama coat for the last time, before donating the coat to Croatians - 1990.*

Fig. 19   *Emy Elisabeth, 1990.*

Fig. 20   *Emy with Andrea Susanna and Carolyne Maria, 1992.*

Fig. 21   *Marceline Constance, 1993.*

Fig. 22   *The Liaison Officer's living and (on top) working accommodation - Mogadishu, 1961.*

Fig. 23   *Early morning near Moshi, Tanzania. Mount Kilimanjaro is in the background - snow capped Kibo on the left, Mawenzi on the right, with the 'Saddle' in between.*

Fig. 24   *A typical sight in East African Game Park.*

Chapter Eight

God Save the King

Working life in Kenya was quite different to that which was, of necessity, followed in Somaliland. In contrast to life in Somaliland, where one had the feeling that one was on duty virtually the whole time, one arrived at the office at 8.30 a.m. and usually left at 5.30 p.m. The working week was five and a half days; one worked until noon on Saturday.

As far as lifestyle was concerned, the difference between Hargeisa (or a bush location) and Nairobi seemed like passing from the darkness of night to the light of day. For example, one could make delightful excursions from Nairobi. If one had a week's holiday, then various game parks could be visited where there was an abundance of animals such as elephant, lion, leopard, rhino, hippopotamus, buffalo and several species of antelope. For those who liked to walk or climb, there was the possibility of walking up (or climbing) various mountains, including Mount Kenya and Mount Kilimanjaro. Emy and I walked up Mount Kilimanjaro just after we were married; I was to repeat the walk with two of our daughters when they were nine and ten years of age.

Nairobi offered a number of city facilities and the type of good restaurants which could be found there was simply unavailable in Somaliland. As far as sports' facilities were concerned, the climate was ideal for golf, tennis, squash, swimming, riding, running, soccer, rugby (mainly during the two wet seasons), hockey and cricket.

From the anti-locust work viewpoint, the perception of the locust threat at that time in such countries as Kenya, Tanzania and Uganda was quite different to the front-line feeling which existed in the countries further north. In the twenties and thirties, Kenya, in particular, had suffered from devastating locust plagues. Tremendous damage had been caused to agriculture generally; not only was catastrophic damage inflicted on crops and grassland, but thousands of coffee trees collapsed under the weight of locusts. One heard of locust swarms passing over areas continuously for up to two days; at times, the sun was totally obscured. The railway had come to a standstill; the wheels of locomotives had slipped on the heaps of corpses of locusts, as the wheels were prevented from gripping the rails.

Since the formation of the Desert Locust Control Organisation in the late forties, the anti-locust campaigns had progressively become more successful. Although invasions of swarms had occurred from time to time in Kenya, these had not been on the massive scale as had been experienced twenty years previously. The swarms constituted the escaping generation from breeding in the countries to the north and which, to the maximum extent possible, had already been decimated by control measures. Once swarms had crossed the Kenya border from the north, they would rapidly sweep southwards across Masailand and breed in the foothills of Kilimanjaro and to the south, extending across the plains towards Iringa and Dodoma.

Perhaps because of the fact that relatively few swarms had entered Kenya since the forties, there seemed to be a general feeling that the days of locust plagues had passed. In fact, this was far from the case; it was simply that the main battle against the plague was being fought in the countries to the north. Although the farmers might have indulged in a degree of complacency, within the DLC we were constantly on our guard against the possibility of a locust invasion caused by the escaping swarms from the breeding to the north.

By 1959-60 the Desert Locust Control Organisation had become, relatively speaking, significantly more technically oriented. The days of some two hundred and twenty field officers conducting vast anti-locust campaigns, using thousands of labourers, had passed. Instead, the exhaust sprayer had become the usual method of controlling locusts on the ground and, in the air, the airspray unit had already demonstrated its capacity to inflict significant damage on large locust swarms. Within two years or so, the rather large organisation which had been needed to mount anti-locust campaigns was to be reduced to some thirty-eight staff (including the administrative headquarters staff), as almost total reliance was to be placed on aerial reconnaissance followed by aerial and ground spraying.

At about 2 p.m. on a day in December 1959, a report was received that a locust swarm of significant size had crossed the border between Somalia and Kenya and was moving westwards from the Wajir area. We were surprised to receive such a report, since aerial reconnaissance was being conducted on a systematic basis throughout the area where a locust invasion might occur; apparently, we had deluded ourselves into believing that the aerial reconnaissance approach was foolproof. In this case, the swarm had invaded Kenya without having been observed.

If the swarm was to maintain its course, then we expected that it would reach the Embu area on the eastern slopes of Mount Kenya within a day or so. If the swarm was not quickly destroyed, potentially vast damage could be inflicted on the extensive coffee plantations.

We were in constant radio contact with the DLC Bases in adjacent countries, as well as with the airspray unit, which at that time was based in eastern Kenya, near Garissa. After radio consultation with the airspray unit, it was decided that I should leave at first light the following morning for the Embu area with a Land Rover and two trucks; these would carry insecticide (Acrodel (BHC) or Dieldrin), plus pumping gear which was needed to transfer the insecticide from the drums into the 100-gallon tank which was installed in the De Havilland Beaver aircraft. Once in Embu, I would ascertain whether an airstrip could be used by the airspray unit's aircraft. I would endeavour to establish radio contact with the airspray unit before sundown.

On arrival in Embu, I called on the District Officer and explained the purpose of my mission. As background, I told him that a swarm of locusts was approaching the area. I could not give its precise whereabouts, although further details would be available within a few hours, since no doubt the airspray unit would be carrying out a reconnaissance; this, in addition to pinpointing the location of the swarm, would give an estimate of its size.

Our immediate concern was to establish an airstrip as a base for aerial spraying operations. The District Officer showed understanding. He responded that there was in fact a disused airstrip in the area; the problem was that it had become overgrown with very high grass. I asked him to advise me how the grass could be cut in as short a time as possible. He responded that the best way to solve the problem would be to release the inhabitants of the local prison for work, under armed guard.

Within an hour or so, some two hundred prisoners, each armed with a scythe or slasher, were advancing steadily down the airstrip area, making short work of the grass.

At 5 p.m. I made contact with the airspray unit who informed me that the swarm had been located. It was of medium density, with dense patches, and covered an area of thirty-five square miles. The swarm had changed direction; instead of continuing its path westwards towards Embu, it was now flying south. The following day it might well continue its track southwards, in which case it would pass to the west of Garissa. The airspray unit was short of insecticide and pumping equipment; in the circumstances, it was agreed that our team would drive through the night and aim to arrive in Garissa, some three hundred and thirty miles away, at dawn the following morning. With apologies to the District Officer, thanks to the convicts and regrets to my team that we would have to endure the overnight journey on bush tracks, the radio was packed up and we departed.

The drive through the night was arduous and it seemed long. At one point, the driver went to sleep at the wheel and we crashed through a bend into the bush; at least the incident woke him up! Even though we took turns at driving, the endurance test was taking its toll; from time to time, I stopped so that we could exercise our limbs for a few minutes, which I hoped would help us to maintain consciousness.

At 6.30 a.m. we reached Garissa and drove to the campsite of the airspray unit, where the insecticide and pumping equipment were off-loaded. The swarm would soon be on the move and it was anticipated that from 7.30 a.m. it would begin to fly southwards and be in range for the aircrafts' spraying sorties.

The aerial spraying was well underway by 8 a.m. and the three spraying aircraft performed numerous spraying sorties throughout the day. Eventually, the swarm was sprayed to extinction. This may have been the first time that a swarm of significant size had been literally sprayed out of the air.

At about noon, the pilot of one of the Beaver aircraft reported that a small oil leak had become evident; the maintenance engineer had inspected the problem and had decided that the aircraft should return to the Nairobi Base for repair and maintenance. Since I had been without sleep for some thirty hours, it was suggested that the flight of the Beaver would provide an opportunity for me to return to Nairobi; I readily agreed. The Captain of the aircraft explained that he would have with him a co-pilot/engineer in the seat adjacent to his. Immediately behind them, the 100-gallon aluminium insecticide tank had been installed; behind the tank were two seats and I would occupy one of these.

When the Captain had taxied to the runway for takeoff, I heard him reduce power; looking out, I could see someone waving towards me from a Land Rover. I opened the door and a colleague shouted to me that a Kenya Police Cessna aircraft would also be returning to Nairobi. The aircraft was faster than the Beaver; it would also fly at a higher, more comfortable altitude. It was therefore suggested that I should leave the Beaver and transfer to the Cessna, which was already taxiing towards the threshold so that it could take off after the Beaver.

The flight to Nairobi was uneventful and comfortable. On arrival, I drove thirty miles to the house of the Director, Philip Stephenson, in Limuru where I was confident that I would find him, since it was a weekend. On arrival, he told me that he was pleased to see me and he was extremely satisfied with the way the aerial-spraying operation had gone. He then added that there seemed to be a problem; the Beaver which should by then have reached Nairobi had not arrived.

It was not long before the inevitable was reported. About halfway between Garissa and Nairobi, the small oil leak had suddenly increased. The windshield of the aircraft was being sprayed with black oil and the Captain, realising that the engine oil pressure would rapidly diminish and his vision would soon be totally impaired, correctly had decided to make an emergency landing. The only possibility in the hilly and stony area was to use the main road. Unfortunately, just before stalling the aircraft for the landing, a wing had hit a tree; the wing had been severed from the body of the aircraft, which had dropped to the ground. Although the Captain was hurt, he had survived; fortunately, the co-pilot/engineer was also reported to be alive.

Having been continuously involved with the operation for some forty hours, I issued various instructions so as to render any possible assistance to those involved in the accident; and then I went to sleep.

The following day the recovery of the aircraft was organised. I accompanied the recovery team and took one or two photographs of the aircraft. The propeller and front of the aircraft were smashed and distorted. As my eyes moved towards the rear, I saw that the 100-gallon aluminium tank had been pushed backwards through the seat in which I had been sitting. With hindsight, I am very grateful that the

Guardian Angel had had the foresight to intervene in such a timely way.

With the extinction of the thirty-five square mile swarm, our reconnaissance efforts were redoubled in case other swarms should cross undetected into Kenya. The essence of effective anti-locust work was to obtain an understanding of the position of locust swarms sooner, rather than later. Provided one had even a few days' notice, the necessary resources could quickly be brought to bear to attack the aggressor.

After continued, intensive reconnaissance of northern and north-eastern Kenya for about a month, we were satisfied that there were no swarms in the area. However, through our routine early morning radio dialogue, it was established that a widespread and heavy infestation of locust hoppers stretched across south-eastern Ethiopia. It was clear that the DLC resources in the area would not be sufficient to cope with the situation; it seemed likely that unless the control measures could be significantly strengthened, a large escape would take place, which would mean that the next generation would probably fly south into the crop areas of Kenya and Tanzania.

It was proposed that I should reinforce the efforts of the field officer in Southern Ethiopia. Another field officer would be diverted from his work in Somalia and would join us near a town called El Carre.

We left with two Land Rovers and, travelling in a northerly direction from Mandera in north-eastern Kenya, the road became stony and rocky. Although we endeavoured to cover as many miles as possible during the daylight hours, in fact in southern Ethiopia we never exceeded an average of ten miles per hour. At Dolo it was necessary to cross the Daua river and we found that a ferry had been constructed using oil drums with a platform above them. The river was in flood and we had problems in positioning the Land Rovers on the ferry. With considerable difficulty the crossing was completed; a separate crossing needed to be navigated for each of the vehicles.

On reaching the field officer's camp near El Carre two days later, the reports of the widespread breeding were assessed and we developed a plan of operation to control the infestation. The work began the following day and continued for a week. Progress was somewhat hindered due to the hostile attitude of the local inhabitants, who from time to time would throw themselves on to our vehicles.

Sometimes, up to ten protesting tribesmen would clamber on to a Dodge Power Wagon and try to dislocate the work. Fortunately, although many of them were armed, the tribesmen stopped short of physical aggression.

As we worked our way northwards, it became clear that the infestation extended to the north of the Webi Sciabelli river. We wished to pursue the work, but in order to achieve this we would need to ferry insecticide and sacks of locust bait across the river. With the help of some of the labourers, a ferry was constructed of drums, to which we lashed a platform. The next step was to carry a rope across the river, which would be attached to the ferry and used to pull it to and fro. We were warned not to enter the river since it was heavily infested with crocodiles. At this point, the supervisor of the labourers told us that he would send for 'the crocodile man'. The man appeared shortly afterwards and it was explained that he would cast a spell over the crocodiles; the reptiles would never harm him.

Shortly afterwards, the man entered the water with a coil of rope and soon began swimming across the river, dragging the rope with him. After he had reached the other side, the rope was duly attached to the ferry of drums, and the insecticide and bait were transported across the river, followed by gangs of labourers and ourselves. During the following few days, the work continued and the infestation was significantly controlled.

On our return to the El Carre camp, I told my colleagues that since the visa for entry into Ethiopia which I carried would expire within three days, I would either need to obtain an extension or, if this failed, I would have to return to Kenya.

We had heard that an Ethiopian District Commissioner was based in the area and we therefore visited his office for assistance. It was explained that he was away on a short excursion to shoot some birds; as he was expected back soon, perhaps we would like to wait in an ante-room. A bottle of anis was brought and we were invited to enjoy a refreshing drink.

About two hours later, the Ethiopian DC appeared. He stopped outside the office in a jeep-like vehicle; he was accompanied by two fine-looking women and in the back of the vehicle were several guinea fowl which he had shot. Shortly afterwards, I was courteously received in the office of the DC. I explained the purpose of our mission to Southern Ethiopia, what we had been doing and the results which had so far been achieved. I explained the visa problem and wondered whether my visa could be extended by one week.

The DC was dressed in a khaki drill tunic, shorts and knee-high stockings; he had placed his large pith helmet on a hook inside his door. He smiled in a charming way; of course the visa could be extended. I responded that I was most grateful for his consideration, especially as I was well aware of the time-consuming formalities which normally accompanied the renewal of an Ethiopian visa.

The DC then became serious for a moment; he explained that, while he would be pleased to arrange an extension, I should understand that my passport would need to be sent to Addis Ababa. The extension process should be completed within a week or two.

"But Sir," I responded, "As I have explained, my visa expires within three days. While my passport is in Addis Ababa, my current visa will expire. What should I do then?"

"Mr. Everard, there is really no problem. I have a prison cell exactly below my office. While you are waiting for your passport to be returned, we can keep you in the cell."

I looked at the charming DC and realised that, unfortunately, we could not claim to have a meeting of minds. I politely announced that, given the circumstances, unless there was a more appropriate alternative, I would have to leave the area within the next day or so. The DC acknowledged my position.

With a twinkle in his eye, he then announced that he would be having a party later in the evening. I and my two colleagues were invited to attend. There would be plenty to drink, the guinea fowl would be cooked and we would enjoy 'wat' and 'zigany'.

Later that evening, we were welcomed to a party of fifteen or so Ethiopians; much drink was consumed within a short period. We were then invited to eat. The 'zigany' was not simply excessively spiced; the food was laced with peppers and various other 'hot' ingredients. Within five minutes, my mouth felt as though it was on fire and I could no longer feel my lips.

The party continued apace and by 10 p.m. most of the guests were strongly intoxicated. Jokes were constantly being told (in Amharic) and each was greeted with a louder round of laughter than its predecessor.

When the party was at its height, the DC approached me. He told me that he was not only in administrative charge of the area, but he also had control of a military battalion; he was a man of power! He asked me to accompany him to a military display and, as though in haste, drove me with great confidence in the darkness along a narrow, bumpy track; eventually we reached what appeared to be a mountainous ridge. He then asked me to observe a display of force. Immediately, much firing broke out from a group of soldiers. Many of the bullets fired were tracers; together with these, what seemed to be a type of rocket illuminated the rocky hills around us. The display lasted for about a half hour, after which the DC suggested that we should return to the party. He again drove as though in extreme haste.

By now, the party was becoming somewhat rowdy; just as I was beginning to feel that we should make a courteous exit, the DC approached me, stood in front of me and placed his hands on my shoulders. He announced that he felt that we were doing excellent work and that it would be a great pity if we could not complete our task. I agreed. Suddenly, the DC smiled at me and said,

"Do you dance?"

Although taken aback, I responded that I much enjoyed dancing. The DC then said to me,

"If I play some beautiful music, will you please dance with me?"

Although the man appeared happy and harmless, and we were in public, I hesitated; I was aware that we had been invited to a party by a group of Ethiopians whose culture was different in many ways to our own. Nevertheless, why should I dance with this man? But then I would – on one condition. I thanked the DC for the invitation and said,

"That is a very nice idea, although in Europe men do not usually dance together. If you would like to dance with me, would you consider meeting one condition? I need my visa to be extended by seven days. If you can arrange tomorrow morning for the extension to be stamped in my passport on the spot, I will dance with you."

The DC was delighted. He asked me to appear at his office the following morning at 9 a.m. In the meantime, we would dance to beautiful music.

The DC asked me to wait briefly until he set his gramophone in motion. He strode across the room and leant over an ancient machine; it played only 78 r.p.m. records and it had a medium-sized 'trumpet' through which the sound would be amplified. After winding up the machine, in the poor light he peered at the label to verify the title of the old, scratched record he wished to play. He placed the record on the turntable. The arm was then lifted and, as he lowered the needle towards the edge of the record, he glanced in my direction with a triumphant smile. The sound blared out through the scratched surface.

> *God save our Gracious King,*
> *God save our Noble King,*
> *God save the King!*

The DC ran towards me and with a serene smile, said, "Shall we dance, Mr. Everard?"

We danced. I was not sure what type of step should be used for the national anthem, but experimented with hops, steps, but no jumps. The completion of the dance was greeted with loud applause.

The following morning, true to his word, the DC issued the extension. With renewed vigour, we resumed our work; we had decided to see it through to completion as quickly as possible. Although the labourers were co-operative, we again met a hostile attitude on the part of some of the local tribesmen; they sometimes threw themselves at the trucks and clambered aboard. On one of these occasions, a truck driver became alarmed. Many tribesmen had climbed on to his vehicle; they shouted and gesticulated wildly, apparently in an endeavour to dislocate our control operations.

I became anxious when I saw our Somali driver reversing his truck towards a large *acacia* tree; it seemed he had decided to try and discourage the wild tribesmen. Within a few seconds, the tribesmen began screeching as the thorns of the tree pierced their skins; some tried to avoid the thorns by grabbing branches. The driver then accelerated away, leaving at least half of his rowdy human cargo in the tree. I pleaded with the driver not to repeat the manoeuvre; if the tribesmen became angry, their hostility could translate into physical assault. He was unmoved; and angry. He wanted to teach his fellow Somalis a lesson! Fortunately, the first lesson proved to be uniquely sufficient.

After four days, it was agreed that my colleagues and I should leave the area. I left the following morning with the two Land Rovers for the return journey to Nairobi. I estimated that it would take two days or so to reach the border with Kenya, after which another two and a half days' drive should bring us back to Nairobi. At the time of leaving the area, there were a number of storms and we saw a great deal of sheet lightning at night which dramatically illuminated the mountains.

A day or so later, as we slowly progressed towards Dolo, we came to a *toug* which was in flood. One of our party waded into the flooded river-bed and, based on his report, we decided to wait an hour or so before attempting a crossing; the width of the rushing water was some twenty yards. The technique used when crossing a *toug* which was in flood was to attach a cable or rope between the two vehicles. If the first vehicle to enter the water encountered difficulties then the rear vehicle, on land, would drag the first vehicle backwards out of the water. Once the leading vehicle had traversed the strongest part of the torrent, then it would help to pull the second vehicle to dry land on the other side. Each vehicle would enter the water as though to drive upstream; as one crossed the *toug*, one would try to steer into the direction of the rushing water. If one found that the vehicle was being pushed downstream by the force of the water, then one had two options: with the help of the second vehicle dragging one backwards, either the Land Rover would be reversed, or one could accelerate and try to reach the other side before the vehicle was pushed down the river-bed.

On this occasion, we could see that there was a concrete crossing; the water was flowing over a wall which was some eight feet high. With a tow-rope attached to the vehicle behind me, I entered the water slowly, giving the wall as much berth as possible. Initially, with the steering turned into the torrent, progress was steady; however, at about the midpoint of the crossing, I felt the vehicle being pushed towards the edge of the wall. On this particular occasion, I took the decision to accelerate and hoped that the vehicle would pass through the point of the strongest torrent and continue to the other side of the *toug*. As I accelerated, I felt the vehicle move significantly towards the down-river edge of the wall. I immediately concluded that, unless the other vehicle could quickly reverse and drag my vehicle backwards, it was inevitable that the vehicle would be pushed over the wall by the force of the water.

Since I felt no pull backwards, I decided to abandon the vehicle. I intended to leave by the door on the side of the rushing water; I would climb on to the canopy and as the vehicle was washed over the wall I would jump away from the vehicle, separating myself as much as possible from it. In this way I hoped that, while being carried down the river-bed, I would be able to make my way to the edge of the rushing torrent.

I realised that my plan would need to be executed within a matter of seconds. Moving to the passenger side of the vehicle, I tried to open the door. To my dismay, I found that due to the force of the torrent which thudded against the side of the vehicle and was now beginning to spill through the perspex window, it was physically beyond my strength to open the door.

Recognising that I was trapped, I waited for the vehicle to be pushed over the wall. Whether I would then be able to escape remained to be seen. The vehicle moved inexorably towards the edge of the crossing. At any second, the Land Rover would be washed over the wall and down the river in the torrent.

Then the vehicle stopped moving. Although I was in a state of anxiety, I was perplexed. I suddenly realised that the tremendous rush of water was slightly diminishing; shortly afterwards, the force of the water had been reduced to the point where I could open the door, which I did. I clambered up to the canopy and then lowered my legs over the windscreen to the bonnet.

I could see the other members of the team waving at me and shouting, but I could not hear their voices above the noise of the rushing water. After a few minutes, a driver waded into the water and shouted to me that I should stay where I was. The rope which had been attached between our vehicles had broken. Shortly afterwards, a cable was fixed to the back of the Land Rover and the rear vehicle pulled the Land Rover which I had been driving back to the water's edge.

We waited for about an hour and watched the torrent recede; we then crossed the river-bed. We stopped and walked back in the shallow water across the concrete crossing. We wondered whether a thoughtful road engineer had constructed a ridge, or perhaps a low wall, on the edge of the crossing so as to help prevent vehicles being washed downstream. We were looking for an explanation concerning why my vehicle had stopped, literally on the brink. There was no ridge.

The slow return journey continued and at last we reached Dolo. We searched for the ferry of floating drums, but without success. After some time, we were told that the day after we had used the ferry on the outward journey, the ferry had been washed away in a flood. A new ferry was under construction, which would be ready the following day. The next afternoon we crossed the river successfully; we continued our journey southwards to Mandera in Kenya and eventually through Wajir and Isiolo to Nairobi.

During the return journey, I had given some thought to the progress made in the technical methodology of controlling locusts. I had concluded that, although anti-locust control measures on the ground were still important, aerial reconnaissance and spraying would progressively become more significant. In consultation with Philip Stephenson, I therefore decided to take a flying licence. Like hundreds of thousands of others, I found the written and practical exercises, and tests, to be interesting; the systematic study of the theory of flight, in so many aspects, was indeed an illuminating experience.

Practical instruction was delivered between 7 - 8 a.m., while theory was taught in the evenings; in this way, conflict with office hours was avoided. When I had reached the 'circuits and bumps' stage, on one occasion I made a hard landing. Conforming to instructions, I taxied the aircraft to the maintenance hangar and consulted with the engineer on duty. He told me that he had noticed the hard landing. I asked him whether he wanted to check over the aircraft? He smiled,

"Open your mouth, Colin. Do you feel all right? How about your teeth?"

"I feel fine. My teeth are still there!"

"I don't think I need to check the aircraft. But I wanted to make sure that *you* have not been shaken up too much. Go back and try to make more circuits; and when we say 'bumps', we don't mean bump. Try greasing the aircraft on to the runway. Once you've done it, it's a very nice feeling and you will probably be more comfortable that way."

As I progressed to the licence level, we made several testing cross-country flights. East Africa was ideal for such exercises. As one looked below, one might see vast areas of bush, semi-desert or, in the highlands, numerous valleys separated by mountain ridges; the problem was the appearance of sameness. Then Sven would say 'Where are we?' This was what the Americans would have described as a very good question. It was on one of those occasions that Sven taught me the importance of concentrating on the required heading, instead of becoming distracted by lengthy navigational computations; it was remarkable how one could deviate from the correct heading, while one compared the scene of confusing sameness below with the computed position on the map. By the time you had reached a conclusion (which was often wrong), the aircraft had been permitted to wander significantly from the correct heading.

Many flyers would agree that the most memorable part of their flying experience was the first solo. In my case, before taking off for that first solo circuit, the instructor crouched on the wing and repeated procedures which he had forced me to learn by heart during training. The man was a typical Scandinavian perfectionist and from the mournful expression on his face, he was evidently far more worried about the possible consequences of my flying solo than I was. I listened patiently to his monologue of repetitive instructions as though one were sitting in a church, listening to the lesson which one had heard over the years again and again. Eventually, I felt sorry for him; I patted his shoulder and tried to reassure him that I really could not see a problem in what I was about to undertake. Even if 'icing' should happen, he had time and again taught me how to overcome it; in the worst case, I could even make an emergency landing. I thoroughly enjoyed my first solo. It was not exciting; it was simply that one felt sufficiently confident to take the aircraft off the ground, to handle it in the air and to land it again. In fact, 'icing' did occur and I felt confident in clearing the problem. On the final approach, another aircraft suddenly appeared in front of me; the student pilot had not completed the circuit properly and had cut across a corner of the circuit. A Verey warning light was shot from the control tower and the air traffic controller asked me to "go round again". He then strongly rebuked the student pilot and instructed him to land forthwith.

I made my second solo circuit; again I experienced "icing" and cleared it. I made a perfect landing. The Scandinavian instructor seemed enormously relieved. This was probably because, as an experienced flyer, he knew that in fact things can go awry, especially during a first solo.

Although I had tried not to show my concern for the anxiety of the instructor, nevertheless I believe that he sensed it. With a somewhat perverted sense of humour, he took me shortly afterwards on some spinning exercises in a Tiger Moth, an aircraft which has an open cockpit. After stalling the aircraft at an altitude of several thousand feet, he applied the rudder in an almost vicious way. The aircraft responded correspondingly and I was thrown against the safety straps as the aircraft spun earthwards. The noise of the rushing wind around the ears was punctuated every few seconds by the voice of Sven,

"Do something, Colin – you don't have long to go!"

He was a hard man with a strange sense of humour; and a good instructor.

Although the intention behind my learning to fly was limited to gaining an appreciation of possibilities in controlling locusts through aerial reconnaissance and spraying, the Guardian Angel could see further ahead than my blinkered approach permitted at that particular juncture. The introduction to aviation helped to serve a useful purpose several years later.

In 1960 I was asked to return to Mogadishu as the DLC liaison officer of East Africa to Somalia. This time, I would not be a substitute for the liaison officer, who had retired; I would remain in Mogadishu for some time and this would give me the opportunity to make the maximum contribution in terms of encouraging the government's Locust Control department to become more effective.

One always looked forward to a new assignment; at the same time I had mixed feelings on this occasion. Politically, the situation in Somalia was gradually becoming unstable and I wondered what impact this might have on the effectiveness of the locust control measures. In addition, as a matter of policy, the East African governments were forging links with the United Nations Agencies. I recognised that this was a healthy development; however, I had already met one or two desert locust control 'UN experts' and had not been impressed with the quality of these men. One could only hope for the best; I for one would do my utmost to achieve the best results in what would be a changing work environment.

Chapter Nine

Say and Do

We transferred from Nairobi to Mogadishu by road; the Land Rover was followed by a truck which carried most of our household belongings. The journey lasted for about four days and an antelope (a Hartebeeste) was shot *en route* so that meat would be available for the drivers, the cook and ourselves.

As we approached Mogadishu, I thought of my first visit to the city in 1949. We had stayed at the hotel called the 'Croce del Sud'; when I had become violently ill after eating some salad, a well-meaning hotel employee had suggested that I should confront the nauseating pain with Cioffi's gin. Cioffi had made his reputation, plus a good deal of money, during the early forties by producing and selling considerable quantities of gin. In the late forties, someone had asserted that the number of Italians killed during the war had only been exceeded by those who had died as a result of drinking too much gin.

The 'Tanga Mbeele' would soon establish itself for two months in the area, when the north-east monsoon and south-east winds would meet and cast a humid calm over the city. In tropical countries, discomfort is usually caused by humidity and lack of a breeze, rather than heat; and so it was in Mogadishu. It was fashionable for the expatriate community to complain incessantly about the sweltering 'Tanga Mbeele', which was often described as suffocating! In fact, the heat and humidity were nothing compared to the conditions experienced in the Gulf of Aden, or along the Red Sea coast.

Although Mogadishu had, superficially at least, altered little since my temporary assignment there in 1957, in fact it soon became evident that fundamental changes were in progress. The majority of the Italian government advisors had departed and, to some extent at least, they had been replaced by a fairly strong contingent of United Nations personnel. The government of the young Somali Republic was exploring a number of avenues to ascertain the possibility of acquiring development assistance.

Shortly after my arrival, I visited the docks area and noticed a substantial consignment being off-loaded from a freighter. I then saw that each crate was emblazoned with the familiar sign of the flag of the United States of America; across the stars and stripes, two hands were shown locked in friendship. The moment the crate was deposited on the quay, a small group of Somalis immediately went into action; the American aid insignia was painted over in black and the crate was finally inspected to ensure that no sign would exist which would indicate that the contents were a gift of the American people.

Russian advisors began to arrive in small numbers, while some sixty foreign "school teachers" also made their presence known. Two or three evenings each week, the "school teachers" spoke in militant tones at large, loosely-organised meetings. As the evening wore on the shouting and roaring of the crowd increased; down with imperialism, down with colonialism, down with exploitation!

The early sixties in Mogadishu seemed to be a period of a free-for-all in terms of foreigners entering the country under some sort of 'aid scheme'. The foreigners concerned were not limited to those provided by governments or international organisations. For example, while one day I was clearing my office before embarking on a three-week visit to locust control field camps, I heard heavy footsteps mounting the wooden stairway outside. I was anxious to leave on schedule and had not expected a visitor. A ragged-looking man appeared in the doorway and announced that he was a Jehovah's Witness. I courteously welcomed him, but explained with regret that I had to leave the office immediately to maintain my schedule. The American sat down in front of my desk and announced that he would physically prevent me from leaving my office until I had been converted. I was in haste; so I immediately jumped to what I knew would be the end of his story. I asked him how much money he would expect a converted Jehovah's Witness to give him; the response was 100 Somalos. I responded,

"I am converted; here are 100 Somalos. Could we now both leave in peace?" He left a happy man.

The DLC liaison office of the East African governments to Somalia regularly received invitations to attend various types of diplomatic parties. We also had the pleasure of entertaining a wide spectrum of senior Somali officials and the diplomatic community. At that time, the Cold War was well underway. On one occasion we arrived at a cocktail party and, on entering the main room, a highly undiplomatic scene was being enacted. The American ambassador, an elderly man who gave the impression that his rise to the position had been achieved in a tough environment, was locked in a quarrel with the ambassador of the Soviet Union. The numerous guests who were present had resorted to dismayed silence as the allegations between the men became stronger and their voices louder; the allegations' phase gave way to threats and counter-threats, which in turn were followed by insults. The disconcerted guests began to look at one another in alarm.

The ambassadors were briefly distracted when I stood between them and wished each in turn a good evening. I then asked the American ambassador whether he was *au courant* with the locust situation. For a second he looked confused, but fortunately replied,

"Not at all; but I am in the middle of an important discussion." Ignoring the second part of what he had said, I gave both ambassadors a relatively detailed account of the position of various invading swarms of locusts and made a prognosis regarding the direction in which the swarms might fly, where rain could be expected and, most importantly, the anticipated breeding areas. After several minutes spent in delivering my monologue, I began to hear gusts of laughter in the room and realised that the distraction was probably beginning to take effect. Within a minute or two, the cocktail party atmosphere had returned to normal. Each of the ambassadors had been button-holed, and separated, by others who wished to talk to them.

Some weeks later, when we were invited to the American embassy for a reception, the ambassador welcomed me with a sincere smile and a warm handshake. He said,

"Good evening, Saviour!"

Subsequently, at another reception, I was chatting to a small group of senior Somali officials; I had met one or two of them on previous occasions. One said,

"Mr. Everard, some of us admire the way you speak so well in Somali. We were just talking about that. We live in such a poor country and you come from the west, which is so rich. You have adapted well to our country and our people. You know a lot about our tribes. You seem to know so many things about us." Then he paused; after a few seconds, he suddenly gave me a hard look, "Are you a spy?" Apart from the smile I produced in response, I instantly realised that the government was up to something that it wanted to hide. Although I had no interest in whatever it was, I could not help thinking how times had changed!

Harold Macmillan's 'wind of change' was blowing strongly across Africa. The word 'Africanisation' soon became part of a government's everyday vocabulary. It was not simply that a sensible policy had been introduced so that expatriate services should be phased-out and replaced by an indigenous capability. Regardless of the existence or otherwise of an effective infrastructure, every government job had to be 'Africanised' immediately. Qualifications for particular jobs were lightly regarded; the element of experience was ignored. The impact of the mindless sacrifice would, to a degree, become patently negative.

As far as 'Africanisation' was concerned in the Desert Locust Control Organisation, this was hardly an issue since over the years every effort had been made to train and prepare African staff for positions of responsibility. For example, the entire locust control department in Somalia was manned by Somalis. Our liaison officer in Addis Ababa was an Ethiopian. Within the world of desert locust control, there was no racial consciousness as such. Some staff had been born with black skins, some with brown and others with white; that was the beginning and end of that particular non-issue.

The blowing of the 'wind of change' not only resulted in the accelerated replacement of expatriate personnel by Africans, but led also to the review of existing institutions and organisational structures. In the case of the Desert Locust Control and Survey Organisations, those concerned at the highest level decided that, in principle, if possible the responsibility for conducting effective anti-locust control measures should be transferred to a body of the United Nations system; apparently this approach was preferred to that of forming an autonomous organisation which would have comprised those countries affected by the locust scourge. The financial aspect probably weighed heavily in favour of transference to the UN system.

From time to time, the Somali government had requested me to form part of its delegation to specialist meetings which discussed desert locust control matters. In 1961, I found myself sitting in Africa Hall in Addis Ababa. The primary subject of discussion at the meeting was the closure of the Desert Locust Control and Survey Organisations, with the proposed transfer of locust control responsibility from 1962 to the UN System. Much of the meeting was taken up with the UN spokesman explaining how future control operations would be undertaken.

The more I listened to the proposed new arrangements, the more I became convinced that the new structure would be handicapped by so-called 'controls' and bureaucracy.

During one of the coffee breaks at that meeting, I voiced some of my concerns to the senior UN spokesman. After dismissing my concerns with superficial rhetoric, the man looked at me with a grave expression on his face. Did I really believe that the meeting was about how best to control locusts?

"No Sir; we are only concerned with power!"

I told him that the meeting had the power to ensure that sensible future arrangements would be in place to control the desert locust; if the meeting did not pay attention to this fundamental requirement, then the meeting would have failed. We all had a responsibility to do our utmost to prevent losses of crops and grazing. The only way to achieve this was to be practical, realistic and to assure a soundly-structured desert locust control organisation. How could one possibly justify being party to the organised disintegration of the Desert Locust Control Organisation, without ensuring effective successor arrangements? Some seconds passed while I was subjected to a piercing stare. The senior UN official then said,

"I am not talking about the power of the meeting; I am talking about another sort of power!" He then walked away.

By the second day of the meeting, I had become convinced that not only were the newly-proposed locust control arrangements impractical; the personnel who would oversee the operations were made of the wrong stuff. Where was the knowledge, the vision or the enthusiasm to perform an important public service? These were 'little' men, their small minds preoccupied with their pathetic references to 'power'. Time would be needed for new UN bodies to develop quality. Fortunately, most managed to achieve this over the ensuing years.

In the afternoon, after there seemed to be a general (if uncomfortable) agreement regarding the proposed transfer of operations, the chairman asked if there were any final questions which any delegate might wish to raise. I asked,

"If locust swarms had reached the Somali coast from Saudi Arabia and it was decided to move a reconnaissance or spraying aircraft to

Somalia or Kenya, how long would be needed to gain approval for the re-positioning of the aircraft?"

In replying, the spokesman gave a long and detailed narration of procedures involving the transmission of a fully substantiated recommendation from the field to the headquarters, consideration at a certain level (with clarification being sought as necessary), submission in due course of the request to a Contracts Board for consideration and eventual approval (conditional or otherwise).

I commented that the current procedure was that the situation would be discussed between experienced personnel on a radio network at seven a.m. in the morning; the Director participated in the daily radio network discussions. In the type of circumstance which I had outlined in my question, the Director would normally give his approval by radio on the spot and the approval would be followed by a telegraphed message the same day. I felt this was the only, and correct, way to conduct operations. If the time-consuming new procedure was to be followed, then the aircraft would arrive at the scene of operations too late; this in turn could lead to disastrous losses of grassland and crops. I suggested that before any transfer of responsibility for locust control operations could reasonably take place, a detailed review of operational requirements should be undertaken and all necessary procedures and practices should be clearly spelled out. Otherwise the new organisation would head for certain disaster.

The chairman of the meeting thanked me for my views, asked whether there might be any more points to raise and, if there were none, suggested that the meeting forthwith endorse the proposed transfer of control operations. This was immediately agreed.

On my return to Mogadishu, I knew that the work and life to which at one point I had felt 'wedded' would soon come to an end. All of us have a 'bottom line'. Never before had I been so conscious of my personal 'bottom line'. Did I wish to be associated with a new Organisation which, I was convinced, was improperly structured and which, quite unnecessarily, could not succeed. If I had been older, perhaps more mature, I would have seen the opportunity to transfer to the new Organisation in order to help reform the ill-considered structure and work attitude. At the age of thirty-one, however, I could only see things in a clear-cut context. I had gained sufficient knowledge and experience over the previous ten years to know what, in fundamental terms, made the DLC and DLS such outstandingly successful organisations. As far as the proposed new arrangements were concerned, I recognised that the basic ingredients of success were lacking.

Did I feel hard done by or unhappy? I certainly did not feel in the slightest that I had been deprived of some sort of future in the world of desert locust control. I was not happy, but at the same time I felt relieved. I wondered how an effective transfer could be achieved, and how long it might take, in what I perceived to be a stiflingly heavy-handed bureaucratic situation. I was also conscious of feelings of sadness; the fact was that an excellent Organisation was probably to be superseded by a structure that was inappropriate. I thought of the damage which, inevitably, would be inflicted on grazing and crops. I began to think of the impending personal plight of the tribesmen and small-scale farmers.

In late 1961, I felt that before the proposed transfer took place, everything reasonably possible should be done to strengthen the Somali desert locust control department. Seminar and training sessions were organised to increase and broaden the knowledge of the Somalis about locusts and the techniques used to control them. A review was also undertaken of the organisation and management of the department and adjustments were made to overcome weaknesses. The equipment which was in use at that time by the department's staff was old and often worn out. Extra money was somehow found so that all of the department's equipment could be renewed. Apart from improving efficiency, this initiative proved to be a significant morale booster.

At the end of 1961, Emy, myself and our two children left Mogadishu. I did not feel disappointed. My ambition had been to help in combating the locust plague and, to the extent that our efforts were successful, my ambition had been realised. Untold millions of tons of grassland and crops had been saved from destruction and, through this effort, hundreds of thousands of people had been saved from hunger, even starvation. In terms of my personal position, since I had no ambition to achieve personal status, I did not feel that a career which might have led to the top had been unnecessarily cut short. I had, however, learned some lessons. One of the most important was that, in our dynamically changing world, nothing stands still; there is no such thing as permanency.

The Director of the Desert Locust Survey, Philip Stephenson, retired shortly afterwards. He became a Companion of the Order of Saint Michael and Saint George (CMG). Certainly, when in later years I compared the results of his efforts with those of others, I felt that any award offered to 'Steve' should have been at a higher level. Philip Stephenson was not only an outstanding Director, but he was a man of vision. He had been instrumental in directing and guiding an Organisation which had, after all, successfully developed techniques which had overcome a massive problem that had existed since Biblical times. He had achieved this in the most trying circumstances and with a budget which was, by today's levels, minimal. He handled himself at meetings perfectly; he was highly articulate.

At the time of my departure, Steve wrote me a typically pleasant letter. He expressed various sentiments in his letter and then stated,

"[Your task] was hard, at times very hard and even dangerous. The fact that success was achieved with increased efficiency each year was due to the senior officers in the field, including yourself, who bore the direct impact not only of the locusts but also of the local people and the impossible terrain." Steve then went on to refer to characteristics of "determination and moral courage."

After returning to England, I visited the then Anti-Locust Research Centre (ALRC) in London. One of the research officers told me that Boris Uvarov (the famous author of *Locusts and Grasshoppers*) was in his office and had expressed a wish to see me. I had met Boris Uvarov on several occasions, mainly in Somalia, and I remembered him as a man of great character and personality with firm ideas regarding how things should be run. I remembered his participation in a three-man comprehensive review mission; typically, Boris Uvarov had disagreed on certain points with the other members of the mission and had recorded his minority view in an addendum to the report.

I knocked on his door and opened it; there I saw a man who, although old, sat behind his desk like a patriarch. He did not smile; I hesitated. He said,

"Everard, close the door; come and sit down."

He did not indulge in niceties; he did not ask me how life was treating me. He blurted out,

"Everard, you have made a terrible mistake. It is such a pity you are such a young man. And so much promise. You are too young to understand that every type of organisation has its ups and its downs.

You were fortunate, and privileged, to have worked in an organisation that went up and up - and up! Now things will be different. For a time, things will go down. Just when your services were needed to stop the collapse and to help rebuild the locust control organisation, you have disassociated yourself from it. You are so young; what a pity! You are too young to know that an organisation can be cut down from one day to the next; but that it may take twenty years to rebuild it. You don't understand that with any worthwhile organisation, the most important thing is to *keep it going*. As long as it is there, the opportunity exists to improve and rejuvenate it. But if an organisation collapses, there is no opportunity to bring it back to an efficient working level. You have to start from the beginning and as I said, it could take twenty years."

Although Boris Uvarov had rebuked me, and even though I felt that his assessment of what my potential contribution might have been, was exaggerated, I did not object to his rebuke. I respected his uncomplicated, forthright honesty.

Boris Uvarov died shortly afterwards. I believe he did not live to learn of the untold devastation which subsequently occurred in eastern Ethiopia and Somalia, due to an invasion of desert locust swarms; these wrought unchecked havoc. Although efforts were made through public relations to blur the real situation, the fact was that severe losses were sustained throughout a wide area. In eastern Ethiopia, for example, there were stories of small-scale farmers who saw their crops devoured before their eyes. Some of them could not cope with the shock and were driven to the ultimate, crazed escape: rather than face certain hunger and starvation, they hanged themselves from trees.

Fortunately, after the first shocking (and unnecessary) tragedy, the locust plague abated for a few years. This should have given some time for organisational restructuring improvements to be put in place. Also, there would be an opportunity to improve on the control techniques which had already been developed. Research would lead to the possibility of biological control, for example.

As a bystander in 1962/1963, I could not avoid imagining how the DLC would have gone into easy action against the invasion of locust swarms. I recalled my excellent colleagues, such as Cliff Ashall, Adefris Bellehu, Charles Copeman, Phil Kercher, Tony Counter, George Davey, John Funnell, Diarmaid Harvey-Kelly, Ian Hay, John Lees, Ludwig Martel, Fergus McBain, Hector McMichael, Ted

Quigley, Tom Reeves, Charles Rennie, Jeremy Roffey, Jim Tunstall, 'Taffy' Saunders, Tom Spence and, of course, Steve; to name but a few. These were real men, in every sense of the word. They all had the qualities of the best one could ever expect to find in a working colleague.

But what was the point of musing? Times had changed! From my personal point of view, for good or for ill, the curtain had fallen.

A motto sometimes used by branches of the Everard family is: 'Say and Do'.

Chapter Ten

A Ugandan Interlude

Bearing in mind that I had a wife and three daughters, with hindsight the way in which I approached my state of unemployment was unusual. Perhaps the nonchalant and phlegmatic attitude I adopted was simply a function of a youngish man who, in basic terms, felt confident that the issue of future employment would be resolved without difficulty.

In any case, I suggested to my wife that we should take a holiday; a small car was purchased in England and we set off happily for a European tour which would last for several weeks. The only point I needed to bear in mind was that it would be necessary to return to East Africa, in due course, to pack up our belongings and to have final debriefing discussions.

By the early spring of 1962 we had reached Spain, where we intended to enjoy a three-week tour. In Barcelona, we located a recommended two-star hotel and the car was parked under a street light overnight in front of the hotel's main door. I asked Emy which pieces of her luggage she would need to use in the hotel; the response was that she might need everything. As far as I was concerned, I needed virtually nothing and left my suitcase and other personal belongings in the boot of the car.

The following morning, the reception called to tell me that there seemed to be a problem with our car. It was a sleepy Sunday morning and all was quiet as I passed the reception and went outside. All of my belongings had been stolen.

After a frustrating visit to the local police station where, due to a language problem, the inspector understood that I had come to admit to a theft (he was keen to arrest me), we visited the British Consulate. Her Majesty's Representative was not pleased to see me on a Sunday morning; he did not appreciate the interruption to his late breakfast of bacon and eggs. Nevertheless, through persistence and persuasion, we were eventually given a form to complete and we tried to list the various things which had been stolen.

Later that day, as we continued our journey southwards, Emy became thoughtful; she told me that I had suffered some really bad luck. Of all the things which had been stolen, which would have been the most valuable? I told Emy that most of the belongings were insured, which would mean that I would be able to replace the lost clothes. The only lost items which were of personal value to us were four four-hundred feet home-movie films. The films had been taken in Somalia and Kenya and it was a pity that some good footage had been lost.

Emy smiled and asked me whether, if the films were returned, I would pay some money to Saint Anthony. Indeed I would. However, it was my feeling that the thief would wish to destroy any evidence of his theft; if he had not already thrown the films into the sea, perhaps he would soon burn them. Emy responded that she would, nevertheless, pray to Saint Anthony.

On reaching England three weeks later, a long distance telephone call was received from the British Consulate in Barcelona. I had reported a theft; unfortunately none of my personal belongings had been traced. However, the Consulate had received a message that its representative should visit the lost property office in Barcelona and ask for four movie films. The films were subsequently sent to me by post. Accompanied by Emy, I visited the local church and happily contributed to the box which was in position below a small statue of Saint Anthony. Simple, uncomplicated faith can yield incredible results!

Shortly after, I returned to Nairobi and was happy to meet some of my former colleagues for final discussions. When these were nearing completion, I received a message that I should call on the personnel branch of the East Africa High Commission, the parent organisation of the DLC. The personnel officer welcomed me in a warm manner; to my faint surprise, he told me that the service I had given to the East Africa High Commission had been highly appreciated. The Secretary General had personally reviewed the circumstances which had led to my leaving the DLC. While the Secretary General felt the loss of my presence in the future crusade against the locust scourge was regrettable, he wondered whether I would be interested in continuing to work with the East Africa High Commission; he had in mind the position of Executive Secretary of the East African Trypanosomiasis Research Organisation (EATRO) in Tororo, Uganda. The personnel officer explained that the transfer would be on promotion to a higher level; however, appointment to the post would be subject to a positive recommendation from EATRO's Director, who had insisted that he should interview me. The personnel officer then added that three candidates for the post had already been interviewed by the Director, who had rejected them all. The personnel officer then endeavoured to reassure me; he hoped that the Director's reception to my candidacy would be positive.

The visit to Tororo by train was a delight. The Director, Dr. Russell Lumsden, had already established an international reputation in the field of trypanosomiasis research; trypanosomiasis is the deadly disease commonly known as 'sleeping sickness'. In cattle it was called 'nagana'. He was a learned man; he also had a delightful sense of humour. His main 'message' was that too many Directors became administrators; he wished to avoid this. He was looking for someone who could take over the entire responsibility for the effective administration of the East African Trypanosomiasis Research Organisation. By the end of the interview, he told me that his conclusion was that I was the right man for the job and he was pleased that he had rejected the earlier candidates. He asked me to begin work as soon as possible; my predecessor would be leaving within a month or so and if I could arrive about a week before his departure, this should mean a smooth hand-over. I readily agreed.

The *raison d'être* for EATRO was to conduct research into sleeping sickness, a disease transmitted by the trypanosome. By far the most common vector of the parasite is the tsetse fly, which is present over vast areas of Africa. Its presence strongly discourages habitation and this means that extensive areas of bush country remain virtually uninhabited. In Tanzania, in particular, one could travel a hundred miles without seeing any form of human habitation.

The control of the tsetse fly was a quite different problem to the control of the desert locust. First, tsetse fly are not found in gregarious swarms and, second, they do not roost on the top of leaves or branches, but underneath in the shade. From an aerial spraying point of view, therefore, it would be extremely difficult, virtually impossible, to devise techniques which would find the target roosting underneath the leaves of trees.

One method of controlling the encroachment of tsetse fly, which had proved to be partially successful, entailed cutting down bushes and trees to create seemingly endless swaths of naked countryside, devoid of vegetation; the shade of leaves was vital for the tsetse's survival.

Since the fly needed shade at certain known intervals, the width of the swath was gauged so that the fly would be prevented from traversing it. The problem with the method was that the rejuvenation of the vegetation occurred at amazing speed. As Winston Churchill wrote in *My African Journey* when observing the scene in Uganda: 'The soil bursts with irrepressible vegetation'. This fact meant that if the swath was to be maintained effectively as an open, bare area, a huge labour force would be needed; this, in relative terms, would be very expensive.

EATRO was not concerned with controlling the movement of tsetse fly. It concentrated on research, covering a range of disciplines which were relevant to trypanosomiasis. These included microbiology, immunology, medicine (including chemotherapy) and biochemistry.

To support the work of ten or twelve professional research staff, some three hundred and twenty additional staff were employed across a broad spectrum of activities. Since the research organisation was situated about six miles from Tororo, most of the staff were housed close by. It was, in any case, mandatory for the Director and myself to live in the vicinity. Nine senior staff houses had been built a half-mile from the research organisation; we looked out over a ranch which extended to a small river at the bottom of a shallow valley.

For the first two years of our four year stay in Uganda, we felt that we were living in a make-believe 'Shangri-La'. The serenity and tranquillity of the Ugandans extended to such a degree that it seemed unreal; these were happy, contented people. By western standards, most were relatively poor; on the other hand, they grew bananas and cash crops (like cotton or coffee) and the climate was pleasantly warm. The people showed no envy of those who were materially better off; their appearance never approached that of the wretched, poverty-stricken state of the very poor who have the misfortune to live in the slums of big cities. The missionary influence in Uganda generally was strong and, at the time that independence was declared in 1962, the country as a whole was developing steadily and well.

Several industries had been established. Tourism was a major foreign exchange earner; the Uganda Game Parks were well-run and offered wonderful opportunities to view a rich and vast array of African wildlife. The Kilembe copper mines in the foothills of the Ruwenzori (Mountains of the Moon) were highly productive; other industrial ventures based on mining showed considerable promise. Uganda cotton was an excellent cash crop and brought healthy profits, through co-operative schemes, to the growers. Plantations established for the growing and processing of tea, coffee and sugar were well-run and productive.

The foundation of good public services had also been laid. The Jinja hydro-electric scheme on the Victoria Nile (the Owen Falls Dam) was a success of far-reaching significance. Makerere University College symbolised the excellence of the educational system.

In 1963, I wrote a letter to a friend in England. I told him of the dynamic advances which had been made in various ways within Uganda. These were indeed impressive. But I tempered the account with what I saw as a reality: the situation which had been created by the progress made was, essentially, fragile. For example, I recounted that one could well be impressed with the quality of the highway between Tororo and Kampala, a drive of a hundred-and-thirty miles. But if one stopped along the way and walked into the bush, one would soon reach the conclusion that development still had some way to go, if it were to be firmly established. Away from the main towns, or the main transport arteries, rural life in the villages did not seem to have been positively touched by the benefits of development.

Two or three years later, the overall political picture was changing rapidly. The Kabaka (King Freddie) had been overthrown and had fled to England to spend his last days helping the poor in the East End of London. In order to sustain his position, Milton Obote, the Prime Minister, increasingly relied on the support of the army. The commanding officer was not prepared to give his full co-operation and he was placed under arrest and summarily dealt with. Eventually, the successor who emerged and, in fact, would later seize power was one Idi Amin.

Because of growing instability within the country as a whole, as well as the increasing frequency of breakdowns in essential services such as electricity, I felt that the day-to-day successful operation of EATRO was becoming patently more vulnerable. For example, the Organisation had established a 'bank' of trypanosomes which were stored in capillary tubes at a temperature of -70°F. The sophisticated deep-freeze equipment was operated by electricity; if the electrical supply would be interrupted for a period of six hours, the temperature in the deep-freeze system would rise and part (eventually all) of the 'bank' of trypanosomes would be lost. This event would be disastrous, since research organisations throughout the world relied on a supply of various strains of trypanosomes for experimental purposes. The stand-by diesel generator was fitted with equipment which would provide stand-by power immediately that the main power was cut. However, mechanical systems are never absolutely foolproof and this fact made us feel uneasy.

By 1965, the Organisation was virtually self-sufficient in terms of a stand-by electrical supply, water, an internal road system and maintenance of vehicles. The housing accommodation for the supporting staff was of only medium quality and we therefore took steps to upgrade the accommodation, mainly by adding rooms to those which already existed. In addition to the staff employed within the main research complex, there were others whose job it was to work in the areas infested by the tsetse fly and to net as many flies as possible (for research purposes); these men were called 'Flyboys'. When I visited their main centre of operations on the shore of Lake Victoria, I was struck by the low quality of their sleeping accommodation. During a group meeting, I suggested that we should try and find some money to build a new dormitory complex. To my surprise, the Flyboys stated that they were quite happy with the rooms at their disposal and they had no wish to see the existing accommodation replaced by a new, upgraded complex.

This was one of several examples where one found it difficult to help those who are poor. To raise the level of the poor is not an easy task, as many would believe it to be. Poor people become accustomed to their condition and they often have a tendency to suspect those who promise improvements. However compassionate one may feel towards the poor, they themselves often express a feeling of security in the condition of poverty. This seems to be illogical; but it is often the case.

In pursuing the discussion with the group of Flyboys, with some difficulty I obtained their agreement to build a new complex close to the existing one. They did not agree to move into the new accommodation; they would need to be satisfied that it was an improvement on their present condition. In fact, when the new complex was ready, the Flyboys took little time in reaching the conclusion that the new accommodation was a great improvement on the existing premises. In contrast to the older premises, the new complex was mosquito-proof and bathroom facilities were also available; none had existed in the old premises.

Before the terror overtook Uganda in 1966, we made numerous excursions to the game parks which had been established and which proved to be so popular with tourists. In addition, we walked up Mount Elgon (14,000 feet) and made several excursions to Karamoja, an area in the north eastern part of the country inhabited by distinctive tribesmen – the Karamajong.

It was during one of our weekend excursions in Karamoja that we stopped in a forest area in the foothills of Mount Elgon. We were struck by the beauty of the forest, the bird-life and the quality of the light as the sun's rays were dispersed by the leaves of the huge trees. We were surprised to suddenly hear some voices; we had thought that we were quite alone. I wandered through the dense undergrowth in the direction of the voices and, peering through the thick foliage, I saw an extraordinary sight. A group of about fifty men were being drilled in how to handle firearms. The men were dressed in semi-rags and, as they performed various parts of their drills, they made aggressive noises. I had no doubt that they were involved in an illegal activity and I felt that the sooner we could separate ourselves from them the better. What they would have done with me had they seen me, I did not know; I felt apprehensive.

The pattern of working life at EATRO was orderly in comparison with the hectic life I had followed in the DLC. Working hours were routinely followed, the workload was adequate without being onerous and, although the Tororo township was small, we were able to enjoy ourselves socially. This type of working environment permitted one to think and I began to think about my future working life.

I had already learned that, due to dynamic changes, it was foolhardy to believe that any activity would continue on a more or less permanent basis; and in Africa things were changing rapidly. It was obvious that I would not, as I had previously believed, complete my working career as an international civil servant of the East Africa High Commission (which was later to become the East African Community). Assuming that one would leave East Africa within a year or two, then where would one live and work? It did not take me long to reach the conclusion that if I were to be reasonably marketable on the international scene, I should specialise in a recognised field.

In my work in EATRO, one of the areas which I found to be in a state of serious neglect was that of logistics support. Critically important experiments had to be delayed, sometimes cancelled, because certain items of equipment were not available when required. I therefore planned and reorganised the area of logistics support for the research work which was underway; in time, the new system was recognised as successful in terms of meeting technical needs expeditiously.

In considering the matter further, I recalled the logistic problems which had arisen during my days with the DLC; in order to overcome critical shortages of equipment, sometimes disproportionate expense had been incurred to ensure the availability of equipment at the right time.

Based on my personal experience, I concluded that one of the most serious impediments to achieving work efficiency in Eastern Africa at that time, concerned the lack of an effective logistics system. With this in mind, I decided to study the field of logistics. In pursuing this goal, I read virtually the entire bibliography on logistics. In particular, I recall the excellent McGraw-Hill *Purchasing Handbook* (Aljian); I could never have foreseen that seventeen years later, I would contribute to the Fourth Edition.

In 1965, the Secretary General of the East African Community (A.L. Adu) visited EATRO and, amongst other things, I explained the new system I had introduced to assure effective logistics support for the important research work which was in progress. Subsequently, the Financial Secretary (Parmena Matemba) invited me to his office in Nairobi and told me he was interested to hear about the reformed EATRO logistics system. We discussed the matter further and I commented that in order to promote an improvement in logistics, I had just published a small book on the subject which was designed specifically for application in East Africa. Parmena Matemba was a Tanzanian who hailed from the slopes of Kilimanjaro. He was in his mid-thirties; he was a brilliant financial administrator and had already acquired a degree of wisdom which normally would have been found only in a much older man.

After about an hour, he told me that if one looked at the history of the development of the East African Community, one could see how a number of small departments had mushroomed into much larger ones; each seemed to be developing in its own way and certainly in the field of logistics, each was pursuing its own practices and procedures. Parmena Matemba felt that a review of the whole situation might prove very useful and he wondered whether I would consider transferring from Tororo to Nairobi; I would work as a member of his team in the Treasury.

I responded that I had in mind leaving the Organisation once an African successor could be found for me in Uganda. A man had in fact been under training. Unfortunately, the previous week the police had arrived and arrested him; he had been led away in handcuffs. I had not seen him since (nor would I see him again).

After some further discussion, I told Parmena Matemba that, in principle, I would be happy to fulfil the assignment. I suggested that since neither of us yet knew what was really going on in the field of logistics in the various departments, if after a review of two or three departments we found that all was reasonably in good order, then in consultation with Parmena Matemba I would make arrangements to depart. On the other hand, if we found that all was not well, then we could jointly consider an appropriate plan of action to bring the field under control. Altogether, some twenty departments were involved, located in Kenya, Tanzania and Uganda; as far as the budget was concerned, logistics' support was a multi-million pound operation.

On my return to Uganda, I found that the security situation was in a state of further degeneration. At the border crossing from Kenya into Uganda, I was mildly (although unpleasantly) manhandled and the armed immigration personnel were rude and abusive. On reaching the house which we occupied (about six miles outside Tororo), I told Emy that I was pleased that we would be transferring to Nairobi. It seemed to me that the options were either to leave Uganda as quickly as possible and return to England, or transfer to Kenya or possibly Tanzania. The domestic situation in Uganda was becoming dangerous and the last thing that I wanted was that my family should be physically vulnerable within a deteriorating security situation. If necessary, I would arrange for the family to leave Uganda before myself; I would follow as soon as I had handed over my duties to my successor.

By this time, Russell Lumsden had left EATRO to take up an appointment at the London School of Tropical Medicine and Hygiene and he had been succeeded by Dr. Ralph Onyango, an excellent man in all respects. Ralph Onyango undertook to try and expedite the arrival of a man who could work with me and take over my duties.

Meanwhile, although the EATRO staff continued to go about their business with efficiency, all were aware that the security situation was declining steadily. During the following weeks, a number of incidents reminded many of us of our physical vulnerability in the face of the worsening situation.

Some days before finally leaving Tororo, yet another incident occurred. In the East African context, it contained the ingredients of incongruous humour, irony, tragedy and, at least to me, an element of unpredictable pantomime.

We awoke one morning to a brilliantly clear day; typically, it had rained heavily the previous afternoon. From our house at the end of the row of five, we looked out across our acre of garden. The lawn was heavy with dew and glistened in the sunlight; it was surrounded by beautiful trees and shrubs. Apart from a huge fig tree and two papayas, I noticed a splash of red, which was a hibiscus bush in full flower. Looking over the expansive view which stretched below to the south-east, the definition of the shallow valley was gradually lost in a blue haze which seemed to hang over the flourishing trees along the sides of the small river. Behind the house, we looked across undulating bush land and low trees; beyond were the Sukulu hills, which were a few hundred feet high.

As I left for the office, I turned to Emy and waved; every morning of my working life Emy waved me goodbye. On this occasion, her happy smile perfectly reflected the idyllic surroundings. Although the half-mile drive was short, I could not avoid thinking about the tragedy of degradation which was beginning to overtake Uganda. The people were so contented; they did not deserve the civil unrest which was beginning to take hold in the country. An hour or so after my arrival at the office, I answered a telephone call; to my surprise, Emy was on the line. Emy said,

"Are you busy; I mean do you have time to talk for a moment?"

In view of what Emy then said, I can only comment that she was remarkably controlled and calm.

"I thought I should ring you, because our house is surrounded with soldiers."

However busy I might have been, thank goodness I had had time to talk! I ran up the corridor to the main entrance of EATRO and drove the half-mile to our house. Indeed, around our house there were soldiers crawling through the bush, crouching or running in stooped fashion from one bush to another; and they were all armed! I jumped over the garden wire fence and approached one of the crawling soldiers.

"Would you please tell me what you are doing?" I pleaded.

"We are attacking that house!"

I asked him where his commander might be and was told that the platoon commander could be found under some trees nearby, towards the Sukulu Hills. I then briefly explained that my wife and children were at home and it would be helpful if the attack could be delayed for at least an hour. The commander was soon found; he was a good-looking young lieutenant. He was sitting on a log, a sub-machine gun at his side, with a mobile radio in front of him; he seemed a little surprised to see me at that particular juncture.

I introduced myself and explained that I lived with my family in the house which was, apparently, an objective for a military attack. The young man glanced at me politely and then spoke in impeccable English; his accent was slightly affected, as though he might have attended one of the older English universities, or perhaps Sandhurst.

"My dear Mr. Everard, I am frightfully sorry that you have been inconvenienced by our military exercise. You see, my dear fellow, the present situation in Uganda is politically rather unstable; perhaps that is an understatement, don't you think, what? And we have this chap Idi Amin who seems to be throwing his weight about; well, apart from his experience as our heavyweight boxing champion, I couldn't really say whether he is ideally suited for his present job as Commander-in-Chief of the army. In any event, he is not sure at the moment whether the army will be loyal to him, especially as he has locked up the army commander, General Opolot. So you see he has spread the army to the four corners of Uganda, in fragmented fashion, just to ensure temporary military impotence until the situation becomes clearer; quite a good idea, don't you think? In any case, it gives chaps like me a problem; how do I keep my men occupied? Well, I thought why not have a field exercise and attack that house; of course if there is opposition to be overcome, this makes it that more realistic."

While he was explaining the position in cultured tones, with his sub-machine gun sweeping the air as his arms swayed back and forth,

I could not help feeling the irony of the situation. Here was a man who, apparently, had been trained in England; he and his men were armed with British firearms and the cost of their battledress was probably financed by a British taxpayers' subvention to his government. And here was an Englishman, whose house would soon be attacked, with the possibility of his family and himself being sacrificed on the altar of – what precisely? Was it irony; was it some twisted sort of revenge? I was becoming more confused by the second.

Then I had a brainwave. After thanking the young officer for explaining the situation so clearly, I told him that it could be rather dangerous for our family if the attack were pursued, but of course I fully appreciated the position and it was important that the field exercise should be properly completed! I wondered if I might make a small suggestion?

"My dear sir, in the military, we are always open to suggestions - but of course." We had a neighbour (whom I knew was on holiday with his family); might it not be possible to change the objective and attack the neighbour's house? "I must say I find that an excellent idea. We shall see how the men respond to changed orders!"

As a feeling of cautious relief began to seep into my brain, there was a blare on his field radio. The lieutenant listened intently with his hands pressed against the headset; then he said, "Wilco - out!" He looked at me and said he had just received instructions for the platoon to move immediately. I wondered what this meant and, in particular, whether he and his men would simply move to another location within the vicinity.

"Is your destination far?" I asked as quietly and innocently as possible. The lieutenant was just about to reply, but at the last second he seemed consciously to close his mouth. Then he looked at me with a look of slight distrust on his face.

"Top Secret!"

As the soldiers were being recalled, I walked back to our house. In accordance with our quickly arranged plan, my wife and children had already left for friends, where they stayed for the night just in case another military visitation occurred. I returned to the office, apologising for my absence. A colleague asked me if everything was all right.

"Yes, thank you; it was nothing much. I just had to sort out a small incident." Soon it would be time to leave and I for one would be happy to transfer to the stability of Kenya.

About a week before our departure, one evening we played what would be our last nine holes of golf at the Tororo Club. We would look back on many enjoyable competitions and friendly matches on the compact nine-hole golf course. During the week, one usually played between 5 and 6:30 p.m., since by 6:45 or so dusk fell.

We followed the usual return route to our house and shortly after we had left the main road and turned on to the dirt (murram) road which would bring us to our house, we were confronted by a road block. As I stopped and lowered my window, a Ugandan soldier approached me, a sub-machine gun hanging from his shoulder. I said,

"Good evening."

The soldier glared at me and responded, "You are a very rude man!"

I smiled gently and explained that I had simply said, good evening; perhaps I should have said: Hujambo, Bwana!

The soldier said, "You are not only a very rude man. Now you are arguing!"

It was clear that the man was in a nervous state and, as he was beginning to gesticulate with his sub-machine gun, I decided to keep quiet. I did not answer and waited for his next move. We only had to wait a few seconds. The soldier said,

"All of you; out of the car. I'm going to search it."

Emy, our children and I left the car and stood in a group close by. I turned to Emy and said,

"I am terribly sorry that this has happened. I was hoping that before there were any more incidents, we would have left the country. It is one thing for a man to take risks on his own account; but I should have arranged earlier for you and the children to have left. I am so sorry!"

After the soldier had completed his peremptory search of our car, he stood in front of me and seemed to be in a state of extreme agitation. His right hand swept his automatic weapon from side to side fairly quickly; his forefinger was outstretched, although I could not precisely see in the half-light whether his finger covered the trigger guard, or the trigger itself. His eyes flashing, he blurted out,

"You are a lucky man. Now I will let you go, but if you ever come this way again and you are rude, things will be very different!" Feeling weak, but relieved, we slowly drove home.

Our transfer to Kenya was fortunately completed without further problems. For a few months we lived in a house which was part of the complex of the East African Agriculture and Forestry Research Organisation (EAAFRO) at Muguga, about twenty miles from Nairobi. Situated at some seven thousand feet above sea level, in contrast to the climate of Tororo we grew accustomed to cool nights and, sometimes, misty mornings. Subsequently, we moved into a stone house which was a mere twelve minute drive from my office at the headquarters of the East African Community.

As far as EATRO was concerned, the inevitable happened. With the prevailing anarchy, the Organisation's work virtually came to an end. There was, however, an important sequel which, as far as I know, remained untold for many years.

In order for trypanosomiasis research to be undertaken, it was essential that trypanosomes were available for experimental purposes. I have already referred to the bank of strains of trypanosomes which were contained in capillary tubes and stored in a sophisticated deep-freeze system. The process of isolating and identifying the trypanosomes, placing them in the small capillary tubes, storing them and documenting the various strains, required considerable scientific specialised skill and was time-consuming. EATRO was recognised by the World Health Organisation for the quality of its research work and, in particular, as a designated source of trypanosomes which could be made available throughout the world for research purposes.

As the security situation in Uganda deteriorated, it was recognised that the trypanosomes, so meticulously collected and maintained in the bank, might well be put at risk. One of the research officers, a biochemist called Adriel Njogu, decided to try and transfer most of the contents of the bank to a reliable scientific environment in Nairobi.

He would pack a large vacuum flask with dry ice and insert a number of capillary tubes in the flask, which would be placed in a picnic basket. Adriel Njogu would then head for the Kenya border in his car. At the border, he would be challenged by the semi-trained young Ugandan soldiers; the explanation given was that Adriel Njogu would be meeting some friends for a picnic in Kenya. If the soldiers had examined his 'picnic', the consequences for Adriel Njogu could have been unpleasantly serious.

The picnic exercise was repeated on many occasions, until much of the collection of trypanosomes contained in the bank had been transferred to suitable deep-freeze facilities in Nairobi. Thus, trypanosomes continued to be available for research purposes world-wide. Without these efforts, research into sleeping sickness would have been severely curtailed. Mankind owes a considerable debt to the selfless, courageous action of Adriel Njogu.

Looking back on our four years' sojourn in Uganda, we remembered delightful people, a landscape which varied from the semi-desert of Karamoja to the luxuriant forest of the foothills of the Ruwenzori Mountains, the concentrations of wildlife in the parks, the warm climate (which was sometimes interrupted by dramatic electrical storms of incredible intensity), and a period of productive work. The work aspect seemed to be a period of personal re-adjustment, in preparation for a change of career orientation.

We also would never forget those isolated unpleasant incidents; these had harshly reminded us that we were living in a country which had gradually degenerated until it would become savagely ravaged as a result of the crazed actions of a handful of misguided, selfish, anarchic political leaders. That so many owed so much misery to so few, represents one of the worst blots on what should have been (without their efforts) one of the most successful stories of social and industrial development in recent African history.

Our Guardian Angel had never failed to step in at critical moments during the Ugandan interlude; perhaps sometimes he might have felt that the dangerous circumstances in which we had found ourselves, had created excessive demands on his powers of positive intervention on our behalf. In any case, now that we were in Kenya, we hoped the Guardian Angel would be able to take some well-earned rest. And we were right.

Chapter Eleven

The Party

The first few weeks of my new assignment in the Treasury of the East African Community were spent in formulating a plan of operation for the logistics review I was to undertake. As necessary, consultations were held with the Secretary of the Treasury (Parmena Matemba), some of his colleagues and one or two departmental Directors.

Just as the work programme was about to commence, I received a telephone call from the Secretary General's office; Dunstan Omari wanted to see me. In his office, over a coffee, he explained that for several years East Africa had pursued the aim of concluding a Treaty of Association with the European Economic Community (EEC). Since the East African governments had not been able to negotiate terms which they regarded as minimally acceptable, the various rounds of negotiations had been broken off without a conclusive result.

Recently, the East African governments had made an overture to the EEC, suggesting that another attempt be made to negotiate terms for a Treaty of Association. To the surprise of the East Africans, the EEC had conveyed a message that it saw little point in trying to negotiate further; in effect, as far as the East Africans were concerned, the EEC door had been politely closed.

Dunstan Omari then said that the East Africans wanted to convince the Europeans that they meant business. Apart from having expressed their serious intentions in a letter, Dunstan Omari felt that some action was now necessary. He had received endorsement from the East African governments for a proposal that an East African Mission to the European Economic Community should be established in Brussels.

In his charming way, Dunstan Omari then went on to explain that he had held discussions with his colleagues regarding a suitable official who could be relied upon to find appropriate premises, negotiate an agreement to rent the accommodation, staff, equip the offices and bring the Mission into being. He told me that the consensus which had emerged was that I would be the best choice for the assignment. He explained that the primary consideration in reaching the conclusion was that I was a European, albeit an Englishman! Dunstan Omari explained that just as it would be difficult for me to travel to Pygmyland and negotiate with the Pygmies, so the East Africans felt that they might encounter difficulties in successfully performing the assignment in Brussels. Dunstan Omari stated that he had fully consulted Parmena Matemba, who had kindly agreed to release me for the assignment for three or four months, naturally subject to my own agreement.

In Brussels, I established my base in the Park Hotel, which was a short distance from the headquarters' buildings of the EEC. The assignment lasted some three and a half months and was completed in stages. My daily routine was to rise at six a.m., deal with correspondence and office matters until about 8.30 a.m. when, after a quick breakfast, I would leave for the first appointment. The work proved to be arduous, especially since property (real estate) representatives often preferred to meet in the evenings. On several occasions, I returned to the hotel at about two a.m., which meant that my sleep was reduced to some four hours.

Apart from dealing with the considerable volume of work associated with the specific assignment, I spent some time with representatives of the EEC in an endeavour to explain the sincerity of the East African position, which was that the East African governments seriously wished to pursue their goal of entering into a Treaty of Association. After some weeks, the discussions bore fruit, in the sense that the EEC invited the East Africans at Ministerial level to attend meetings in Brussels; the hope was that it would be possible finally to reach an agreement on the Treaty of Association.

Before the arrival of three Ministers from East Africa, a contingent of bureaucrats arrived from the East African Community whose job it was to have preliminary discussions. I knew most of the officials and we had an easy relationship. One evening, while we were discussing the progress so far achieved, it was suggested that after dinner a visit should be paid to a night-club in Brussels. I announced that, unfortunately, since I had been reduced to about four hours nightly sleep for some days, I felt extremely tired and would therefore go to bed. The group vociferously lamented my attitude and pleaded with me to accompany them; they told me that they enjoyed my company, even if I were sleepy. The important thing was that I should be present. I reluctantly agreed to go, but cautioned them that they might well find themselves with one sleeping member of their group; my statement was greeted with ringing laughter.

On arrival at the night-club, I tried to enter into the lively mood of the visit, but unfortunately my body was weaker than the spirit. I fell asleep. I was awoken by a loud round of applause and, on opening my eyes, could see a strip-tease artiste removing the last scanty shred of her transparent underwear. The girl was rather short, slightly plump, not very pretty and devoid of poise. My neighbour turned to me and said enthusiastically,

"Colin, what do you think of that?"

I blinked once or twice and responded, "Not much; my wife is so much more beautiful!" I then immediately fell back into a deep slumber.

My peaceful sleep was interrupted a second time, on this occasion by some persistent tapping on my shoulder. On opening my eyes, I found a middle-aged man's face close to mine; he looked distinctly annoyed. He said,

"I am the proprietor. You are bad for my business. Please leave immediately."

I apologised to my colleagues, explaining that I had warned them that I was fatigued; it would have been more comfortable if they had agreed to let me go to bed in the hotel. In any case, that was exactly what I would do then.

On the work front, things continued to progress well and eventually the group of Ministers arrived. The Kenya Minister, Mr. Kibaki, excelled himself during the negotiations and clearly impressed the Europeans with his knowledge and negotiating skill. After two or three days, it was clear that the Treaty of Association would almost certainly become a reality.

As we were leaving the meeting room, Mr. Kibaki and the Tanzanian Minister (Sheikh Babu) asked me to join them for a moment. In a courteous manner, Mr. Kibaki told me that the East African delegation had greatly appreciated the behind-the-scenes groundwork which I had been undertaking. They understood also that the East African Mission premises had not only been rented, but were already equipped and staffed. I confirmed that this was so. Mr. Kibaki then turned to me and explained that he and his colleagues felt that it would be appropriate to have a cocktail party at the new premises; this should finally convince the Europeans that the East

Africans were sincere, in the sense that when the Europeans actually saw the Mission, they would believe in the seriousness of the East Africans. He appreciated that I was busy on a number of matters; he had also seen the terms of reference for my work. Although the Ministers realised that I was overworked and what was now to be proposed had no relation to my duties as such, nevertheless, since I was already a familiar figure to a number of the EEC senior officials, he wondered whether I would be so kind and organise the party. I agreed. A date and time were also agreed upon and I told Mr. Kibaki that I would be consulting him within a day regarding the invitation list, organisation and costs. Two days later, the invitations were delivered. I was used to large-scale entertaining and envisaged no particular problems.

On my return to the Park Hotel, I spoke with the chief receptionist and asked Robert if he could provide me with a team of waiters to assist at the reception, which would be held in a few days; in addition, we would need a wide choice of succulent cocktail snacks. The matter was discussed at some length and all the requirements were then listed, including such items as glasses, plates, wine-coolers, ice and so forth. When the list of needs had been agreed, we both signed and dated the list, which Robert stated would be regarded as an order on the hotel.

On the appointed day of the party, I slipped out of the meeting about a half hour early; I wanted to return to the hotel so that I could pick up some of the waiters and transport the food and glasses to the newly-established Mission, which was located about four kilometres from the Park Hotel.

As I entered the lobby of the hotel, Robert smiled in his usual way, wished me a good afternoon and commented that I seemed to be a little earlier than usual. Indeed I was; I had come to start preparations for the large party which had been organised. Robert would have the list; we would check that everything was present. Robert looked at me in a strange, slightly confused, way. I repeated that I had come to prepare for the party and we should check that all the items ordered were present. A look of horror crossed the face of Robert; with consternation, he said,

"I am very sorry sir, I have completely forgotten about the party. There are no waiters, no glasses, no ice – and no food!"

Although my metabolism normally prevents me from becoming excited, on this occasion I briefly lost my self-control. My two hands struck the counter behind which he was standing; Robert flushed visibly and looked as though he wanted to take cover, but I fixed him with a stare,

"You must be joking, Robert. Yesterday and today I mentioned to you that I was sure everything would be perfectly arranged by you. You have faithfully agreed to make the food. Everything is in writing, signed by you and me. I think you will have to start moving very, very quickly, Robert!"

Initially, Robert's reaction was that it was so late that the hotel could do absolutely nothing. However, after my remonstrations, and after I had pulled him into the kitchen and instructed him to personally start working on the agreed requirements, some hopeful signs began to emerge. After an hour or so a number of trays of snacks were ready and many glasses had been produced; most importantly, two waiters had been found. I then persuaded the two waiters to find two others, which they did. One of the men unilaterally assumed the role of head waiter and insisted on calling me 'Son Excellence'.

We left the hotel about an hour later than I had planned; however, I felt that if we were lucky enough not to be delayed by a traffic jam, we should reach the office ahead of the first arrival of guests. In fact, we found ourselves in dense traffic and my heart sank when I noticed that some fifteen minutes after our departure, we had only reached the back of the hotel as we drove in a one-way system around the block.

The first guest to appear arrived in a Mercedes 600 car. The arrival of the Mercedes 600 coincided with the off-loading of crates of bottles from the office car. I welcomed the guest, who shortly afterwards was followed by numerous others. Although the champagne and wine were not as cold as they should have been, the party commenced in an orderly manner; at least, I hoped that this would be the impression created.

The planned cocktail party was typically a 6-8 p.m. affair. By seven p.m., however, it was clear to me that the real party was just getting underway. The participants were evidently enjoying themselves tremendously; there were frequent congratulatory exchanges, as well as much joking. I realised that since the party would extend well beyond 8 p.m., the wine and other liquor would be insufficient. I therefore called for the chauffeur of the office car, so that I could dispatch him to the hotel with a request to provide us with some more wine. He could not be found. I had firmly let it be known that no chauffeur was to enter the building; under no circumstances did we wish to risk any case of driving after drinking. I was mystified regarding the whereabouts of the chauffeur and we needed the man urgently.

I decided to search the house. In the communications room on the third floor, I discovered the chauffeur in an amorous embrace with an economics assistant whom I had recruited from Paris. I rebuked both of them and suggested that, instead of 'necking', they could do their duty by coming downstairs and assisting in entertaining the guests. The chauffeur should in any case immediately return to the office car as I needed his services urgently. The young woman looked shaken and stunned. Then she said,

"He told me he was a film star! I thought he looked like a film star. Now you tell me he is the chauffeur!"

With a new supply of wine about to arrive, and with the party in full swing, at last I could begin to relax and to chat with various guests. In one group, a Minister was instructing an East African ambassador to return home; the man stubbornly refused. Eventually, another member of the group explained to me that the ambassador knew that he was wanted by the police on corruption charges; the ambassador would therefore steadfastly continue to refuse to go home to East Africa. The last we heard of him was that he had contrived to obtain an instruction from East Africa that he should become a roving ambassador; he was apparently enjoying the assignment.

My feeling of relaxation was short-lived. Sheikh Babu approached me and told me that he felt that this was one of the most wonderful parties he had ever attended. But where was the photographer to record the historic event? I responded that I had given that particular aspect some thought. I had concluded that the business of agreeing the Treaty of Association would be concluded officially in the meeting room, not at a cocktail party. On balance, I had decided not to arrange for the attendance of a photographer.

Sheikh Babu was a man who not only had an infectious sense of humour, but he gave the impression that he had boundless physical energy at his disposal. He also had an awesome political reputation. He let out a huge laugh; then he began jumping up and down. After a few seconds, he paused and looked at me with serious intensity,

"Mr. Everard, please arrange to have a photographer here within fifteen minutes, at the latest!"

I withdrew and called the Hotel Metropole, who explained that the hotel retained the services of a photographer; unfortunately, the man was fully engaged that evening. However, he probably had an assistant and this man should be present with us very shortly.

When the man appeared, he was encouraged to take a number of photographs; I estimated that he probably took about one hundred. Although Sheikh Babu wished him to take some more, I quietly informed the photographer that I was sure that he had taken enough. As our meeting would be concluded within the following two days, in order to select some good photographs I wondered whether some proofs might be available the following day. The photographer looked slightly confused; turning to me he said,

"All of the photographs will be ready tomorrow and you will buy all of them."

I responded that this seemed to be a rather unreasonable approach; it really depended on how well the photographs would please the Ministers and senior officials who were present at the party. I hoped they would order many photographs, but one could not be sure. There was no question of immediately giving a *carte blanche* to buy all of the photographs.

The man looked at me with fury on his face.

"You are a *filthy* Englishman! I hate you! You think you can play with me! In that case, I will not sell you one photo."

Without further ado, the man packed his camera in its case, put his coat on and strode towards the inner glass door in the lobby of the premises. He swung the door open, rushed out and slammed the door with such furious force that the glass shattered with a loud crack – and fell to the floor. The photographer looked at me through the jagged remains and shouted a torrent of abuse in my direction. After he had heavily closed the front door, I gained small comfort that the door had withstood his angry strength.

Although the departing commotion made by the man was considerable, the party had fortunately reached such momentum that there was merely a few seconds' pause while heads were turned towards the source of the noise. Once the participants' eyes had fallen on the broken glass, all had been explained; and the party continued.

It was after midnight before the last guests departed. As one of them stumbled towards a waiting car, I helped to open the door and the hefty body fell through the gap; since the legs were apparently unwilling to follow the body into the car, I lifted them and pushed them inside so that the door could be closed.

Before locking up the new premises, which had just been the subject of an extraordinary baptism, I felt I should quickly check the various rooms. Starting on the third floor, again I found the economics assistant in the deep embrace of the chauffeur. I reminded her that this time she knew that the man was a chauffeur; and even though he was good-looking, he was certainly no film star. I reproached her and hoped that she would show better judgement when undertaking her economic analyses!

The following day, I made my peace with the photographer and a number of good photographs were ordered. As I shook his hand and said *au revoir*, he kissed me on the cheek; he hoped that we would meet again! At least he received a non-committal smile in response.

Two days later, the Treaty of Association was duly initialled. The Ministers and their entourage of officials returned to East Africa. I followed two weeks later, leaving the new Mission to fulfil its functions.

About two years later, one Saturday afternoon, Emy and I were buying some carnations at a shopping centre in Nairobi. As we walked back to our car, I noticed Mr. Kibaki walking towards us. At that time, he was Minister of Economic Affairs and excelled in his work; he was later to become Deputy Prime Minister. As he approached us, his face broke into a broad smile. Shaking hands, he said,

"My dear Everard. What a pleasure to see you again. How are you? Yes, we signed the Treaty of Association with the Europeans. But, you know, during that visit of mine to Brussels, there is one particular thing that stands out clearly and vividly in my memory; it was that *amazing* party – unforgettable!"

Chapter Twelve

Preparation for Take-Off

It was only on my return to East Africa from the Brussels assignment that I realised how mentally fatigued I had become. For the first week or two after my return, I had difficulty in dealing with day-to-day tasks. I was convinced that others must have noticed the sudden problem which confronted me. On the one hand, it irked me that no reference was made to my lack of productivity; I was sure that this must have impinged on the work output of others. On the other hand, I was relieved that others did not seem to take my condition seriously; which I did. I did not feel stressed in the slightest; I simply could not produce a normal day's work. With hindsight, this was the only period of my working life when the level of my work productivity fell below a reasonable norm. Fortunately, within a week or two, my working life returned to its normal tempo.

During the period 1966-67, with the assistance of colleagues the established plan of operation was pursued and the logistics situation in a number of departments, spread throughout Kenya, Tanzania and Uganda, was systematically reviewed; the largest of the departments was that which dealt with civil aviation.

Although I had paid special attention to ensuring that the various departmental Directors were well informed about the purpose and thrust of my work, in fact I received little co-operation and encouragement during the various review visits. I also found that the staff who were involved with logistics management often adopted an unprofessional approach; in consequence, their overall status was low. Although I felt disappointed concerning the lack of a positive reaction to my work, I knew that I had the personal support of the Financial Secretary (Parmena Matemba) and I found this sustaining and strengthening.

One aspect of the work which emerged during the reviews was unexpected. There had never been an intention that I would incorporate an audit element into my task; however, if one checks a multi-million pound inventory and significant (and valuable) discrepancies come to light, even if one is not auditing as such, what does one do? For example, I shall never forget the expression on a storekeeper's face when I asked him whether he could explain what had happened to one and a half miles of copper wire. From the contrived, artificial look of astonishment which he produced, he gave an instant impression that he knew precisely what had happened to the copper wire! In such cases, I felt the only correct course of action was to record the apparent discrepancy in a short report to the Financial Secretary, who presumably in turn would refer the matter for further investigation to the audit department.

Some eighteen months after I had commenced the logistics review, I felt that we had learned a great deal of the various ways in which logistics support was being handled and managed in the various departments. Based on the knowledge gained, I decided to write a report summarising the work carried out and, based on the findings, formulate a number of recommendations. If the recommendations were adopted, the entire logistics system of the East African Community would be reformed.

While working on the summary report, the planned work continued and, eventually, all of the departments of the East African Community, plus some of the main regional offices, were reviewed throughout Kenya, Tanzania and Uganda.

One of these visits involved a review of the department in Zanzibar, where I arrived shortly after the government had been overthrown. I stayed in a guest house which was run by a former government Minister. He recounted to me in vivid terms the violent nature of the overthrow of the previous government. He talked of the 'People's Court', which had been responsible for the 'trial' of many Zanzibari citizens; some had been condemned to death, while others were sentenced to long terms of imprisonment. In his case, since he had been a member of the government, he had expected to be executed. The People's Court had rejected his evidence, as well as his pleas for mercy. He had been marched to a tree and was to be hanged. Suddenly, a voice from the crowd of onlookers vehemently explained that, in fact, the man had conducted himself well in his government duties and he had never been guilty of crimes against the people. Apparently, some other individuals in the crowd had supported the favourable report on the man. The People's Court ordered the man to return to them for a review of his case. The outcome had been that, since he had served in the government, he would be stripped of all personal possessions, including land (his plantation of cloves had been confiscated), property and money. As an act of mercy and special leniency, he would spend the rest of his days administering the guest house where I was staying.

Within ten minutes of settling into my room, I was again downstairs with my host. Did he know that we had company in the house?

"I think I know what you are talking about," he commented, "You mean the rats!"

"Yes, I know that running the house is not really your profession; why not employ some cats? They should be able to do the job."

My host looked at me with an expression which seemed to be gravely sad,

"In theory, you are quite right, but in practice it is impossible. You see, we have a Chinese presence here. It has been reported that they have eaten all the cats."

The following evening I was invited to a dinner; the Director of the department had kindly invited about fifteen guests. During the dinner, I was asked whether I was married; did I have children? Did I enjoy my married life, or had I found that married life was not always 'plain sailing'? It is on occasions such as these that one enjoys the fascination of observing human nature at first hand. These questions were put to me against a background of the continuously oscillating hum of dinner conversation. I responded,

"Yes, I am married and I have children; but I have in fact always regretted an intractable problem in my marriage."

At that moment, all of the different conversations in progress around the table stopped; although those involved in discussion were no doubt concentrating on their various subjects, at the same time an ear was constantly open to catch another item of particular interest. I broke the pregnant silence,

"As I was saying, in answer to your question I have experienced only one real problem in my marriage." My questioner said,

"As you must realise from the expectant silence, we are all ears. Tell us about the problem."

"The problem is quite simple. When I met my wife she was twenty-five years of age and I married her the following year, when she was twenty-six. Although I have enjoyed being married to her enormously, I have often thought how nice it would have been if I had met her sooner and had married her, perhaps, when she was twenty-two or twenty-three; that way I would have enjoyed her for three or four more years. But that is now history; there is nothing that can be done to overcome the problem of having been married a few years later."

The silence continued for a few more seconds. When I looked around the table, the faces of the guests seemed to be concealing slight disappointment; their looks seemed to say, 'What sort of a 'problem' was that? We were expecting a juicy morsel!'

On completion of the review in Zanzibar, before leaving the island I made enquiries about the possibility of buying a Zanzibari chest. Typically, a Zanzibari chest has its origins in one of the Arab Gulf States and finds its way to Zanzibar on an Arab dhow; the dhow is a sturdy boat which is used for freight purposes between the Gulf and Zanzibar. The dhows usually arrive in Zanzibar toward the end of the year, their sails being driven by the north-east monsoon wind; the dhows return to the Gulf in the early spring on the south-east wind.

During the late afternoon on the day before I departed, I was invited to tea on the third floor of an old Arab house. The intention was that during the tea I would be shown an Arab chest; if I liked it, then the purchase would be negotiated. Three women welcomed me at tea-time and the chest was displayed; unfortunately it was not of the type I had in mind.

While we were discussing the merits of the chest, we could hear a child shouting; sometimes there were screams. The noise gradually became louder, until suddenly a woman appeared in the doorway of the room and threw the child to the ground. The young boy was obviously in a state of distress and lay weeping on the floor. I was moved to ask,

"Surely you do not normally treat your children in this way?"

One of the women responded, "Mister Everard, you must have heard that there has been a revolution in Zanzibar. Do you know that seven thousand men have been murdered during the revolution? The result is that the women who are left have to look after the children; in our family, we have no fathers any more, but we look after twelve children. This boy is in trouble because he has not learned the verses of the Koran properly today. He must learn them like the other children. You see, we must have discipline. It may seem hard to you, but unless this boy understands quickly how to learn properly and behave in a disciplined manner, he will cause total chaos. Do you understand?"

I looked at the pathetic youngster who was lying on the floor; his panting body cast forth a sob every now and then. I wondered how Emy would feel if we were to adopt the boy. I asked the women whether, since there was such an overload of children, offers had come forward to adopt some of the children. My question was met with a sullen silence; then the women explained that the new government had stated that no member of the population was permitted to leave the island, regardless of age. Such is the stuff of revolution!

On my return to Nairobi, I completed the main report. Although I was determined to ensure that the substance was properly supported by analyses and that the recommendations would be well-based, I had to resist a distraction from several of my colleagues. While they recognised the value of the work which I had undertaken, all were convinced that the compilation of the comprehensive report was a sheer waste of time. They insisted that the report would never be read by key senior officials; they would never have the time, nor inclination, to do so. In spite of the discouragement, I persisted with my task until I was satisfied that the report was convincingly complete. I then submitted the report under an appropriate letter to the Financial Secretary, Parmena Matemba.

As I continued with the residual reviews, from time to time my colleagues would jokingly ask me whether I had received any reaction to the comprehensive report which I had submitted; for several weeks the answer was 'No'. At last, I received a call from Parmena Matemba's secretary who asked me whether I would be available to meet with the Financial Secretary during the afternoon.

As I entered Parmena Matemba's office, he made a few jovial comments and gestured to me to sit down. He looked tired and overworked, then he said,

"I am sorry to have kept you waiting with a reaction to your report. The problem for me these days is that I have too much to do. I started reading the report about a month ago, but only finished it on the 'plane last night. I have just arrived from London where we had some financing discussions. I have read the whole report and I have done my best to study the analyses. I agree with your findings and I accept the recommendations. So now we have to reform the entire logistics system throughout the East African Community. There will need to be restructuring and, if the Supplies Branch is to be truly effective, there will need to be a great deal of training, as you have recommended. My question to you today is simple: Assuming that the Secretary General agrees that we accept your recommendations, if we can obtain the endorsement of the three Presidents to reform the logistics system, would you be prepared to serve as our first Chief Supplies Officer?"

I responded that I appreciated the time and thought which Parmena Matemba had given to the subject. I felt that a good deal of progress had already been made in the field of logistics because, during the various reviews, where it had been possible to do so, improvements had been introduced and unprofessional practices had been reformed. With the continued personal support of Parmena Matemba, plus my own efforts, I would certainly be prepared to transform the recommendations into reality. Parmena Matemba promised to be in touch again on the subject as soon as possible.

In 1968 I was appointed as the East African Community's first Chief Supplies Officer and, with the support of colleagues, went to work. In consultation with the British Institute of Purchasing and Supply, various training courses were established and, over the following two years, sixty staff were trained in the main elements of logistics, as well as in the detailed practices and procedures which were now to be incorporated into a uniform system. A computerised supplies vocabulary and numbering system was also introduced. Frequent consultations were held with the various departmental Directors and, as the newly-structured system came into effect, not only was the level of logistics support generally enhanced, but the working attitude of the staff was transformed to one of confidence based on knowledge; and their status was significantly raised.

Although the professional aspect of life in East Africa was positive, unfortunately there were also underlying negative forces at work. For example, after the departure of most of the expatriate civil servants, there seemed to be much scheming and manoeuvring by many of their successors. During a routine discussion with Parmena Matemba, he explained that he might not be able to complete a certain task, "because, you know, I have to spend about fifty per cent of my time in ensuring my own survival!"

On another occasion, during a courtesy call on a senior official whom I had known for some five years, during our discussion I heard the click of a switch. The official then smilingly told me that he had heard that I had made some abusive statements about one of his colleagues. I told him that, as a matter of principle, not only was I unfailingly courteous to colleagues; he had known me long enough not to waste time in discussing a patent falsehood. We should talk about more constructive matters. The official repeated what he had said, although on this occasion he framed his statement in such a way that I need not have corrected him; he spoke as though he was referring to a fact. Again, I clearly corrected him. Then I heard the second click of the switch.

A few weeks later I was passing the man's office and, on the spur of the moment, decided to enquire if he might be free to discuss a small point. I entered the ante-room and asked the secretary whether the official might be free. The secretary responded that the official had left the Organisation and had been appointed by his President as the country's chief of secret police. I briefly wondered how many tape recordings he had taken with him.

Another negative factor which began to impact on our daily lives was the level of violence which seemed to be steadily increasing, especially in the cities. The violence was not only directed towards Europeans, but also involved inter-tribal rivalries. Because of the number of reports of violent break-ins and the physical assault which often accompanied theft, we felt it was essential to have an Alsatian dog to help protect our house and ourselves. During the periods when I needed to work away from home, we asked our gardener to sleep during the day and guard the house at night. Jecton was tall and muscular and, although a man of few words, proved to be totally reliable. When he was on guard, Emy would lend Jecton her red Aquascutum coat, which he draped over his shoulders. In his right hand he would hold a large *panga*, which is a broad-bladed cutting instrument. During the period in Nairobi, Jecton served us well and fortunately we were never attacked.

Our three children seemed to have a special relationship with Jecton. Although he spoke little, the children felt at home with him and from time to time one would find them talking happily with Jecton. One evening, our third daughter, Carolyne, opened the door to the veranda. Carolyne was three-and-a-half years old and enjoyed her easy relationship with Jecton.

"I don't know why you sit on the veranda, Jecton. You seem to be happy sitting there with the dog and with the *panga* in your hand and with Mummy's red coat on your shoulders. You look very strong. But why do you sit there, Jecton; and what are you doing?"

Jecton did not often smile, but he would look down at these small children with patience and benevolence.

"I am a watchman; you understand? A watchman."

Carolyne's face lit up with expectancy and she briefly tugged at the red coat,

"Oh, I see. You are a watchman. Please, Jecton, it is much warmer inside. Come and watch the television!"

The backdrop against which local incidents of violence occurred was not encouraging. In Uganda, for example, the terror of the Amin years was at its height. Many Ugandans had fled the country; most of these were from the central and western areas. Some had settled in Nairobi and tried to live *incognito* amongst the Nairobi population; this was not always achieved. The Uganda secret police tried to keep track of these individuals. A knock on the door at 2 o'clock in the depth of night, almost always meant the successful detection of a refugee. Within a day or two, yet another report in the press would relate how the Kenya border authorities had opened the boot of a car, only to discover the severed remains of one or two Ugandans. In order for the promised reward to be paid, identifiable limbs had to be available for inspection.

Emy and I began to discuss the future of our family. On the one hand, things were generally progressing well from both the professional and personal aspects. On the other, however, although we were not alarmed by the personal security situation, sometimes we felt anxious. Inevitably, a question which arose was whether we wished our children to be brought up in such a way that, in later life, they might well find it difficult to convert from the open and easy East African lifestyle to that, for example, of Europe or North America. Another consideration was my age; I was thirty-eight years old. If we were to make a move, perhaps we should consider doing this before I reached the age of forty, rather than later.

Although we felt we were living good, productive lives, on balance we decided that we should aim to leave East Africa; if possible, this should be done in a planned way. We would certainly not be amongst those who, having left the East African environment, sometimes spent a year or two travelling around the world looking for a substitute that would bear similarities to East Africa; these people almost invariably became disappointed.

Our severance from the East African Community and departure from East Africa need not to precipitous. I would give the East African Community two years' notice; we would either buy a house (or have one built) in England and about a year before our departure from East Africa, I would explore the market in terms of alternative employment.

The two years' notice was duly given, with an appeal that a successor should be found for my post about a year before my departure in order that I could train him for the work I would relinquish. As far as our new house was concerned, after making a number of enquiries, it was decided that I should travel to England to inspect a development site in Surrey which seemed suitable for the construction of our house.

I was to leave one Saturday evening. During the afternoon, Emy and I played a round of golf with two Kenyan club members; one explained that he was an auditor and the other told us he was a lawyer. We had an excellent match and after nine holes we were all square. At that point, we suddenly saw the manager of the club running towards us; he seemed to be in a state of distress. He told us that a leading politician called Tom Mboya had just been murdered in Nairobi; he had been shot down in broad daylight in the street. Remembering Tom Mboya as an active and colourful politician, Emy and I felt shocked; I developed a feeling of nausea. Emy and I felt, as relative outsiders, that if we were shocked then almost certainly our companions would not wish to play the second nine holes. We therefore expressed condolences on the loss of one of East Africa's foremost young politicians and told the players that we would quite understand if they wished to discontinue our match. Each looked questioningly at the other; one said,

"Yes, it's a pity; we can't afford to lose too many good men. Anyway, it's happened; let's get on with the game."

For the rest of the match, as Emy and I meditated on the instability of the political situation, our opponents went from strength to strength in their golf and easily won the match.

A few weeks later, the defence counsel for the assassin was announced; it was the lawyer who had been our golf opponent. Within a day or two the assassin had 'escaped' and nothing further was heard in connection with prosecuting the murderer.

Some months before I was due to depart from East Africa, a letter of appreciation was received from Parmena Matemba. In the letter he explained that our Minister (Hon. R.J. Ouko) had been discussing progress in the field of logistics; resulting from this, the Minister had requested Parmena Matemba to write to me. Mr. Ouko was one of those rare birds who was perfect for his job. He was highly educated, although he (probably unconsciously) showed this only through succinctly expressed valuable comments, which invariably were entirely to the point under discussion. He was of a balanced disposition, always well turned-out and intervened in matters with informed diplomatic skill. As chairman of meetings or as a representative of East Africa in international fora, one could feel proud of his style and his grasp of a wide range of subjects; here was a man who really did his homework and never shirked his responsibilities.

I eventually lost contact with Mr. Ouko. At one stage, it was mentioned that he had become an ambassador to the United Nations. His name subsequently came to the fore in the early nineties when, sadly, one read in the press that under great pressure from the people, the government of Kenya had asked Scotland Yard of the United Kingdom to investigate the death of this man. It was alleged that he had been thrown from a light aircraft near Kakamega.

One of the tragedies which too often characterises the developing world, is the frequent loss of those who could serve their countries more effectively than most. It is often through politics and in-fighting that they become casualties, losing at least their jobs – and sometimes their lives.

Although I had sent one or two reminders regarding my departure from East Africa, some three months before I was due to leave my successor had still not been appointed. I therefore called personally on the head of personnel to plead that someone should be found to take over my work.

The following day, the head of personnel telephoned me; he told me that the Minister who was in overall charge of administrative and financial matters wished to see me. The head of personnel and myself should call on the Minister in the afternoon. On entering the Minister's office, he shook me amicably by the hand and offered the head of personnel and myself a cup of tea. The Minister was a polished politician who spoke easily and clearly; at various points he would pause and smile warmly. When offering a second cup of tea the Minister said,

"Incidentally, Mr. Everard, what is all this we hear about you wanting to leave us. We would like you to stay with us for many years to come, you know. What is this sudden announcement about? You are not really serious about leaving, are you? I mean, have we done something that has offended you?" I responded,

"Excellency, I gave the East African Community notice of my departure almost two years ago. Nobody has offended me in any respect. It is simply that I am leaving."

The Minister looked perplexed; he simply could not understand why I should wish to leave. He said,

"Yes, I had heard that you had given notice; but we thought you were bluffing." I retorted,

"Well, Minister, I can only say that there really would have been no point in my bluffing about anything; there is nothing to bluff about. You know, if I were to stay, one day I might meet a problem trying to keep people on the rails; and I may well end up on the losing end. Don't you think it is much nicer that we say goodbye to one another on good terms, with a feeling that I could always return some time to see old friends, than risk overstaying my welcome and leaving in a way which, perhaps, would not be pleasant?"

We shook hands and I said goodbye.

Like many expatriates before me, I was duly seen off the premises with a pleasant farewell party. By the time of my departure, the Supplies Branch was functioning fully and effectively. One of my colleagues mentioned at the party that to have had a European at the head of the Supplies Branch had been a great advantage. All of the staff had been treated according to the same, fair criteria. He was concerned that on my departure, depending on my successor, tribal bias would become apparent and certain staff would disappear, while others would be promoted ahead of their time.

A year before we were due to leave East Africa, I had started investigating the market for my future employment. Although our house in Surrey would be ready by the end of 1970, and although it would have been logical to have worked in England, in fact the responses which I received to various enquiries were disappointing; apparently, the knowledge that I had gained in logistics and the management experience I had acquired were not regarded as suitable in the English context. I therefore considered the international scene. By then, I had had the opportunity of seeing various international agencies in action. Within the United Nations System, there were two which impressed me. The World Health Organisation (WHO) was one of these; I had met a number of WHO professional staff and I had formed a favourable impression of the way in which the Agency was operating. The other Agency was the International Civil Aviation Organisation (ICAO), which was based in Montreal, Canada; I felt that ICAO (pronounced ee-kay-o) was in a class of its own. The professional staff of the organisation whom I had met were thoroughly knowledgeable, dedicated and produced a great deal of work. Having studied various elements within the field of civil aviation, especially during the period when I had held a flying licence, I had enjoyed contact with some of the excellent staff of ICAO.

When I was completing various reports at the headquarters of the East Africa Community in Nairobi one day, the Deputy Director of Civil Aviation walked into my office and, handing me a document, suggested I might like to read it. The document was headed: 'Vacancy Notice – International Civil Aviation Organisation'. ICAO was looking for someone to head a section in the Organisation's Technical Assistance Bureau; the person appointed would organise the purchase and delivery of technical equipment to various projects in the Third World. Essentially, the work involved logistics support to the projects and, inherent in the work, there would be a significant element of broad management. From the enunciated terms of reference it seemed to me that, in certain respects, the type of work would be quite similar to what I was already doing in East Africa; one of the main differences, however, was that instead of working in developing countries themselves, one would be operating in the environment of the developed world, albeit for the benefit of the Third World.

I applied to fill the vacancy. Although I had learned that British professional staff within ICAO were 'over-represented', which meant that the Organisation would have preferred to fill posts from other nationalities, I saw no reason in becoming discouraged. In my work in East Africa, I had already experienced discouragement from well-meaning colleagues. What I had learned was that, ultimately, the only opinion which counts is the opinion at the top. If, through knowledge and experience, I was judged to be the right man to fill the vacancy, then I felt that I would be selected, regardless of various negative factors which are always present in any given situation. And so it was. I agreed to travel to Montreal on 9 January 1971 to take up my position in ICAO.

A few months before our departure from East Africa a major event occurred when our fourth daughter was born in June 1970. Although we adored our daughters and were grateful that each baby arrived in the world in good shape physically and mentally, we had hoped that one of our children would be a boy. Before the arrival of each of the four babies, Emy and I had had long discussions concerning the Christian names of the expected child. Invariably, we had prepared ourselves for a 'Michael'. When the last chance occurred for Emy to give birth to the long-awaited 'Michael', again we subsequently found ourselves locked in discussion to find suitable names for the baby girl who had just arrived. After various compromises, we eventually agreed to call her 'Andrea Susanna Maria Marcelline'. Although throughout our lives we always endeavoured to treat our children on an equal basis, inevitably the newly-arrived angel received an exceptional degree of attention from her parents and her adoring sisters; she was eleven years younger than her eldest sister. As she sometimes lay helplessly on our bed during the first few weeks of her life, one could only feel love for the small creature who was our latest 'tadpole'.

During the first week of December 1970, we found ourselves sitting in a VC-10 aircraft on Nairobi Airport, ready to take off to England. The intention was that I would stay with the family in England for about a month to help arrange things in our new house; I would then travel to Canada alone to start my new work. Emy would follow with the children once I had found suitable accommodation in Montreal.

On entering the aircraft, we were courteously conducted into the first-class compartment. Although we were booked to travel in the economy class, in fact some of my former colleagues had thoughtfully arranged the upgrading.

As we took off into the night sky, how did I feel? To use an old cliché, we left East Africa with mixed feelings. On the one hand, we had enjoyed our experiences in the Somali Republic, Ethiopia (including the country of Eritrea), Uganda, Tanzania and, above all, Kenya.

With the help of the Guardian Angel, we had not only survived but we had led lives which were rich in exotic experiences. On the other hand, I did not feel comfortable regarding the future of foreigners in Africa who, as in my case, might be employed in an executive capacity by the East African governments; even those who were not close to the government had to pay in some way for their presence to be tolerated. Ideally, we should live in non-racial societies; I know of no area in the world where the idealism is matched by reality. At that time, mainly for historical and cultural reasons the concept of non-racialism was beyond the reach of the East African governments and the people they were supposed to serve. Although I was well integrated within the East African scene, and had demonstrated that I could adjust to unstable conditions, I would never be regarded in the same light as the local people; our backgrounds and cultures did not correspond. In my case, for example, it had seemed only a question of time before some discriminatory action would be taken against me, aimed at forcing me to the conclusion that I should leave the area. There was no doubt in my mind that we had adopted the right course of action. Leaving East Africa at the time we chose meant that we maintained friendship and good relations with the local society; and the inevitable future confrontation was avoided.

As the aircraft climbed into the darkness, we looked back on our life in Kenya. We had lived in a small, but pleasant, stone house which was surrounded by a large garden. Life had been very good to us. Our children had attended the Loretto Convent School and had received a high level of elementary education from the dedicated nuns. We had made excursions to the main game parks of East Africa, including Amboselli, Tsavo, the Serengeti and the Ngorongoro Crater. We had walked up and down Mount Kilimanjaro on two occasions; the second time, I had undertaken the five-day walk with our two older children (Emy and Marci) so that they might remember the endeavour for the rest of their lives.

I recalled a scene in the top hut, at 16,000 feet above sea level, on Kilimanjaro; on being awoken at two in the morning for the final scramble up the last three thousand feet, we were told that the outside temperature was well below freezing point.

Apart from keeping their pyjamas on, the children pulled on layer upon layer of clothing to keep themselves warm. Before leaving the hut, little Emy held up the flickering lantern, struck a somewhat impressive pose and turned to her younger sister,

"How do I look, Marci?"

Marci surveyed the figure in front of her, a figure which had been somewhat inflated by the several layers of clothing. The response was quick and to the point; with a look of slightly affected boredom, the nine-year old said to the ten-year old,

"Since you asked me, Emy, I must say you look pregnant!"

Various scenes, each full of colour, continued to pass through the mind. I became absorbed in memories of the Kenya coast and the idyllic holidays we had spent there with our children, including a fishing expedition that we had undertaken in the warm waters of the Indian Ocean. I thought of the Makondi carvers I had met and their marvellously imaginative carvings; some were Picasso-like. My reverie was interrupted by the opening of the cockpit door. The Captain asked me whether I could spare him a moment in the cockpit. He asked me whether I might have any ideas regarding a warning light which was glowing; I told him that, unfortunately, I could not be of assistance. We did not have to wait long for the problem to make itself known. The passenger compartment was losing pressure; on examination, it was found that a door had opened one stage. The Captain requested area control's permission to reduce altitude; in any case, within about forty minutes he was scheduled to land at Entebbe to take on passengers.

At Entebbe, some engineering ground staff tried to adjust the door-locking mechanism and solid efforts were made to close the door effectively. After take-off, near the top of his climb, the condition repeated itself. The Captain then announced his decision that, given the circumstances, the correct action to take was to return to Nairobi. He also announced that it would be necessary to reduce altitude. He hoped the passengers would not suffer too much discomfort on the return leg to Nairobi.

We flew through the Rift Valley; this is a giant cleavage in the earth's surface, several thousand feet deep, which begins with the Red Sea and continues through the vast lakes southwards through Ethiopia,

Uganda, Kenya, Tanzania and beyond. The conditions suddenly became turbulent; looking out one could see that we had entered a dramatically intense electric storm. At times, the sheet lightning illuminated large areas; on one particular occasion I remember seeing clearly the roofs of a farm homestead. We were indeed flying at a low altitude!

On landing in Nairobi, the Captain and his crew left the cockpit. Each looked pale and worn-out; I heard one of them mention that he had 'had it'. The Captain requested the passengers to remain seated until buses could be brought to off-load the passengers from the aircraft which had been parked on the apron, some way from the terminal building.

We waited patiently; but no buses appeared. After a few weakly-expressed protests, the passengers realised that something had gone awry in the airport's organisation. It was already 3 a.m. and most passengers dozed into a slumber.

When we were eventually discovered, the sun was already shining brightly; arrangements were made to collect us from the aircraft and we were given something to eat. The airline then announced that another aircraft would fly us to London non-stop. I wondered whether, on this occasion, we would finally depart from East Africa; or would some invisible hand bring us back yet again?

After an uneventful flight, we arrived in London. We soon moved into our house and began to furnish it. The month of December in England tends to be gloomy; however, that particular December was memorable due to the incessant strikes which plagued the country, often converting the gloom to darkness. Due to strike action, the electrical power supply was unreliable. It seemed that just at the time when we needed some light to be thrown on a particular subject, the power would be withdrawn. Our bedroom furniture was chosen by candlelight; at one point I struck a match to increase the illumination.

To an outsider such as myself, the inherent civilisation and patience of the British people seemed hopelessly misguided. The post-war socialist revolution was turning full circle. Although the revolution was noteworthy in the sense that it had occurred without bloodshed, the majority of the population were being held helplessly to ransom by an anarchic minority. And, it seemed, the government was virtually impotent.

On 9 January 1971, I boarded an aircraft for Montreal, Canada. For Emy and myself, one of the perceived advantages of moving to Canada was that we would not be tempted to compare the country and conditions to those to which we had grown accustomed in East Africa. The contrast between East Africa and Canada was such that it denied comparison. There would therefore be no risk that we might be tempted to say or think that certain things were better or worse in East Africa compared with what we would find in Canada; we had no wish to be counted amongst those who hankered after the past.

On arrival in Montreal I found myself one of a large crowd attempting to pass through the Immigration at Dorval Airport. Trying to take in the scene around me, I concluded that most of the individuals in the noisy, jostling crowd were poor immigrants; some seemed to be from the Balkans or Eastern Europe. Although I was used to travelling in foreign countries, I was surprised to find myself amongst such a totally alien group of people.

The hotel where I spent the first night was located in the centre of Montreal, about two hundred yards from the then headquarters of ICAO. My first full day in Canada was a Sunday and I decided to walk the two hundred yards from the hotel to the ICAO headquarters' building. Within three minutes of leaving the hotel I realised that I had entered a type of environment which was outside my experience, The temperature was approximately -22°C, and a strong wind attacked my face, which was numb. When I had covered a hundred yards, half-way to ICAO, I recognised that the moment of decision had arrived; reluctantly I decided to retreat. I ran back to the hotel and felt relieved to re-enter the environment of well-regulated central heating.

Based on my abortive brief excursion into the Canadian winter conditions, I realised that I would have much to learn about surviving and living in Canada. And so it proved to be.

PART TWO

WIDER HORIZONS

Chapter Thirteen

A New World

For someone who had been brought up in England and had spent his working life in Africa, the experience of being thrust into a Montreal winter in early January 1971 was nothing less than a physical, and mental, shock. I had grown accustomed to the hostile environment of, for example, the Horn of Africa; I had learned how to cope with heat, humidity, hot winds and blowing dust or sand. But many of the conditions I experienced during my first Montreal winter were simply outside my experience. The only physically abrasive condition I had experienced in Africa was a burning of my feet and ankles as we walked through hot, soft sand. For those first weeks in Montreal, it seemed that I was, in contrast, continuously subjected to cold, the intensity of which defied description; when the wind blew, the radio meteorologist would happily inform his listeners that the 'chill factor' would equate to $-40°C$. If you needed to walk for fifteen or twenty minutes, then you would have to accept that, after two or three minutes, exposed areas of your skin would lose the normal feeling of circulation. If your protective clothing was not adequate to cope with the temperature, the cold would strike your body.

After arriving in Montreal, sitting in the bus which transported me from the airport to the hotel late at night, I would peer from time to time into the darkness outside; there often seemed to be high banks on either side of the road, their irregular crests silhouetted against the night sky. It was not until the following day that I realised that what I had been looking at was snow. Banks or piles of snow became part of the day-to-day winter landscape. In the city, after a significant storm, the snow would be removed and transported to dumps during an efficiently organised and executed operation. Outside the city, the ploughs would heap up the snow banks and they would remain there until finally disappearing during the spring in the second half of May.

A personal task which needed early attention was to find living accommodation. Within two weeks of my arrival in Montreal, several colleagues had already given me some recommendations about where to live. Unfortunately, there was little consistency in these ideas. Some people felt that the closer one lived to one's place of work in the centre of Montreal, the better. Others convincingly recounted the benefits (especially in the summer) of living in the Lakeshore area, some ten miles from the centre of the city. Yet others favoured a compromise. They suggested that by far the best approach would be to live in one of the suburban townships which now form part of the city of Montreal; such names as Hampstead, Outremont, the Town of Mount Royal, Westmount and Côte-des-Neiges were mentioned.

Although confused on the subject, I decided that it would make sense to look at various districts on a systematic basis and, with the help of a colleague, listed specific areas to be visited. If the area seemed to be pleasant, then I would make enquiries about the availability of rental living accommodation. The (so-called) downtown area was dealt with quite quickly, due to its close proximity. Visits to suburban areas proved to take up a good deal of time, especially as I had to rely on public transport.

One Sunday morning, I took a commuter train to a township in the Lakeshore area. Leaving the station at my destination, I followed my pre-set course and, as I began to feel the cold air piercing my limbs (my face had already lost its feeling), I quickened my pace. I did my best to form an impression of the area as I passed the neat houses; except for the garage drives, the gardens were covered with snow. Because I felt colder by the minute, the brisk walking pace became faster until I was almost trotting. As I continued, I wondered why I had not seen another soul in the area. Perhaps the residents were sleeping-in on a Sunday morning; or could it be too cold, even for them?

Within the next minute or so, I had come to realise that I was so cold that almost certainly I would not be able to complete my planned walk. Apart from the lack of feeling in my face and the shafts of cold which pierced my body at increasingly frequent intervals, there was no feeling in my feet. I decided to turn around and run back to the station, where I would take the next train to the city. About halfway to the station, I was forced to the conclusion that I might not be able to reach the station. In plain language, I was frozen stiff. A wind had begun to blow and the gusts of intensely cold air seemed to cut straight through my body. I had now been exposed to those wintry morning's elements for about forty-five minutes; and I was asking myself how much longer I might be able to endure the conditions.

Although I was in a built-up area, the loneliness of the street was astonishing. I had still seen no one.

As I ran on, I noticed that a small door which had been inset into a large garage door was open. In a desperate attempt to find some shelter where I might be able to warm myself, just a little, I ran through the door and rested against a wall. Partly supported by the wall, I slipped into a state of light slumber.

I was woken gently by a hand on my shoulder; as I opened my eyes, I saw a thick-set, pleasant-looking man who, understandably, asked me what I was doing in his garage. I explained that I had recently arrived in the country; mistakenly, I had decided to take a walk in the area. Apparently, the degree of cold was too much for my endurance.

The man asked me to follow him into his house and we sat in his living room for about a half hour. He showed interest in the fact that I thought that I could simply walk around residential areas of Greater Montreal during the winter. He told me that no Canadian in his right mind would do such a thing. One might drive through areas and, if essential, walk for a minute or two to check on a particular point. But one would never deliberately walk in very cold conditions for a protracted period, as I had intended.

Apart from giving me this advice, he suggested that I should invest in proper clothing, designed to withstand the intensely cold conditions. Effective protection against real cold does not depend on how many layers of clothing cocoon the body; the scientific design of the clothing itself is of much greater significance.

During the early part of February 1971, after I had visited several residential areas of Montreal, I had singled out three possible houses which seemed to be suitable for the family. Rather than take a unilateral decision on one of them, I decided to ask Emy to visit Montreal so that we could jointly decide on our future accommodation. Because England continued to be plagued by 'industrial action', there was no reasonable expectation that a letter written by me would be delivered to Emy in our house in England; we had no telephone in our new house and had been told that we would probably have to wait two years for its installation. I therefore arranged for an airline to inform Emy, through its London office, that I had purchased a ticket for her.

Some days later, on my return to the apartment hotel into which I had moved, as usual I was thinking about some problems, problems which I should have left behind in my new office. My musing was disturbed as I entered the lobby; I was told that the telephone had just rung and someone wished to talk to me.

"Hello", I said, "Colin Everard speaking."

"Hello Colin Everard, how are you? You don't sound too far away."

"My darling Emy! How wonderful to hear your voice! I have just got back from the office. Where are you speaking from?"

"Well, it is nice that you recognise my voice. I am sitting in Dorval airport. Do you remember that you sent me a ticket?"

"Oh! I am terribly sorry! I thought you were coming tomorrow. I will come straightaway and pick you up. Please be patient, as I have to take the bus."

On my arrival at Dorval airport, I rushed into the arrival hall and immediately saw my wife sitting on a chair, suitcase at her side, reading Vogue magazine. Under the circumstances, I found my wife to be remarkably relaxed!

As time permitted (which was mainly during the weekends), I showed Emy the houses I had thought might be suitable as family accommodation. As always, each had various advantages and disadvantages.

On one occasion, as a house agent was kindly driving us to look over a house, plus one or two others the agent felt might be worth considering, we suddenly found ourselves in the middle of what Emy and I thought was a snowstorm. About fifteen minutes later, the tyres were spinning in the snow and the car came to a halt. After rocking the car backwards and forwards, it was persuaded to leave the hole which the spinning tyres were progressively digging; with a hefty push we continued on our way. The visits to the houses were completed with difficulty in the snowy conditions. Eventually, as we said a thankful goodbye to the house agent, it was explained that the snow conditions were very mild and the inconvenience of the car grinding to a halt in the snow had been caused by a passing 'flurry'; by Montreal standards, this was certainly no snowstorm!

A few days later, the weather forecaster explained that the Montreal average annual snow accumulation is one hundred inches (250 cms); he went on to say that the winter of 1970-71 was, in relative terms, severe and the snowfall average would be well exceeded, perhaps by fifty percent. Up to the end of February, Montreal had already experienced four major snowstorms; the fifth was expected to reach Montreal within a day or so.

And so it did! We awoke to steady snow, a sight to which I had already become accustomed. As I left for the office, I noticed that there were quite strong gusts of wind and at times one would have to lean forward into the wind, with one's head a little bowed towards one's feet, to avoid the driving snow hurting one's eyes. As usual, the office was hectic and one had no time to glance out of the window to view the weather conditions. At about 3 p.m. a message was received that all staff should stop work and return to their homes, as the snowfall which had commenced in the early hours of the morning was expected to intensify into a major storm.

As I left the office, I contrasted the early morning scene with that which now confronted my eyes. The depth of the snow on the pavement was about eight inches and, although many pedestrians were walking briskly (some were running) through the snow, every step seemed to need a special plodding effort if one were to maintain some sort of momentum. Every now and then someone would slip and fall; the other pedestrians would immediately gather round to help and support the fallen one.

In the road, the overall traffic scene was one of chaos. Some vehicles had already come to a standstill; their owners had deserted their cars, apparently deciding that they would stand a better chance either travelling home by train or possibly staying overnight in an hotel. The cars which were moving progressed with difficulty, the drivers peering through windscreens which were the subject of an incessant onslaught of snow of increasing intensity. Some drivers demonstrated a charging type of mentality and gave the impression that, at all costs, they would maintain momentum through the deepening snow; they would soon be disappointed. Others tried to drive with care through the traffic; sometimes, the rear of the vehicles would slew to one side or the other. Eventually, all the traffic would come to a standstill.

As I resolutely plodded my way to the apartment hotel, I became conscious of the difference between a snow fall and a storm. At times the wind roared, howled and gusted so that thick clouds of snow enveloped all animate and inanimate objects in its path. I was indeed relieved to reach the apartment hotel; as I entered the door, I felt that I was escaping the clutches of an uncontrollable giant whose strength was increasing by the minute.

When we awoke the following morning, we had expected the storm to have passed. We had hoped to see a calm scene of a deep blanket of snow with the sun shining from a cloudless azure. But our hope was forlorn; it did not begin to resemble the reality. The intensity of the wind was such that the snow no longer seemed to fall; with the raging wind the flakes were blown horizontally. The streets were strewn with vehicles, all of which were deserted. Not one pedestrian disturbed the white blanket.

Turning on the radio, the main headline of the news was the great storm which had hit the city of Montreal. A city with a population of three million was in a state of paralysis. And it was still snowing.

At mid-morning, the mayor of Montreal (Mr. Jean Drapeau) appealed to everyone to stay inside, wherever they were; this was, even by Montreal standards, an 'historic snowstorm'. Where were the people whom the mayor addressed? Fortunately, most had had the good sense to stay at home; they would indeed stay there. But some were sitting or lying in hotel lobbies; since the hotels were full, the overflow of people had taken refuge in the lobbies. Some were stranded at the airport. Others were slumped in their cars. These individuals had stayed in their cars hoping to absorb some of the warmth from the car heater; as the level of the snow rose and covered exhaust pipes, cars would fill with carbon monoxide fumes, killing some of the drivers.

This was not the only winter storm of 1971, but it was by far the most severe. The officially recorded snowfall of seventeen inches (itself very high for a single, continuous snowfall) seemed to bear little relationship to the scene which confronted Montreal's inhabitants when, at last, the storm had passed. Due to the strong wind, drifting snow seemed to meet one's eyes in all directions. Whole doorways and the lower sections of buildings were totally obscured by vast amounts of drifting snow. Even though Montrealers were used to long winters with heavy falls of snow, no one seemed quite able to take the 'historic snowstorm' in his stride.

A few days later, over a glass of wine in a cosy bar, Emy and I felt we should reach a conclusion about our future living accommodation. After our recent, and new, snow experience we agreed that we should not live far from the city centre; we simply did not wish to survive the Montreal winters in what seemed to be a state of relative isolation. We then took what was for us an unusual decision; we decided that until we had more time at our disposal to find ideal accommodation, we would live in an apartment. And so it was; we rented an apartment.

About a week after Emy's return to England, I looked up one day in my office at an unusual sight; a thick-set young man with long, untidy hair was peering at me intently through horn-rimmed glasses. While I was wondering whom he might be, he quickly turned to the door and strode away, along the corridor. I followed him and, as I caught up with him, I asked him if I could assist in some way. The man ignored me. As he approached the lift I tugged at his ragged, somewhat dirty, jacket and repeated my enquiry. The man stopped, turned to me and said,

"It doesn't matter; I was looking for a man called Everard. But it doesn't matter any more."

I responded, "You have found him. Who are you?"

"I am a friend of your wife!" he happily replied.

Slightly perplexed, I persuaded the ragged-looking creature to accompany me back to my office and to explain who he was. Nigel told me that he had met Emy in the aircraft on her recent visit to Montreal. Emy had told him that if he should ever visit Montreal, then he should make contact with me.

Nigel explained that he had responded to an advertisement for an assistant to a horse-trainer in eastern Canada. On his arrival from England, he had been put to work in the stables, apparently with unlimited working hours. He told me that he would rise at 5 a.m. each morning and often he worked until late in the evening, occasionally until midnight.

After he had worked at the stables for a few weeks, he had been invited by a middle-aged woman to tea one Sunday afternoon. He had asked whether he could accept the invitation, but had been told that his job was for seven days a week; the permission was withheld. Nigel had persisted with his request and eventually decided that, as a matter of principle, he should accept the invitation. He returned to the stables in the early Sunday evening. At the gate he had found his suitcase and coat. Attached to the coat was a note stating that he had violated his contract; this had resulted in his summary dismissal. He had then made his way to Montreal.

I told Nigel that I had just moved into the small apartment which Emy and I had decided to rent. Although the furnishings were basic, until he found himself a job he was welcome to stay in the apartment. There was however one condition: he should have his hair cut and generally clean himself and his clothes.

My invitation to help Nigel during his transition period was what Emy would typically describe as 'rewarded virtue'. Whereas I had no knowledge of cooking, Nigel was an expert. Over the next few weeks, while he searched for employment, the only other demand on his time was to cook breakfast and dinner for the two of us. Instead of being alone (I was too busy to feel lonely) each evening, as I entered the apartment Nigel would soon appear.

"You do look awfully tired; let me pour you a whisky and soda. I have cooked a fantastic dinner and the pudding is one of my secrets!" And so it went on. Fortunately, shortly before Emy arrived with our children in June, Nigel had found himself a job with another horse-trainer. By that time, I had been well-fed and, as they say, I was strong as a horse!

Shortly before the family arrived, I called Bell Canada to request a telephone installation. My request was met with an apologetic tone of voice,

"We are so sorry, sir, our usual level of service is not available. Instead of installing your telephone tomorrow, would it be in order if we did it the following day? We do sincerely regret the inconvenience, sir!"

Having experienced telephone service of many types in innumerable countries, I have never experienced all-round service which matched the levels attained by Bell Canada. Most others, whether in the developed or developing worlds, paled by comparison.

The family was reunited in June. Life in our apartment, however, was in strong contrast to the type of life which we had led in East Africa. The apartment had two bedrooms. The main bedroom was used by the children. Two children slept in bunk beds against one of the walls and two children each had a bed against the two remaining walls; the fourth side of the room comprised a 'picture' window. Emy and I slept in the smaller bedroom. The remaining room was L-shaped and consisted of a living area and a dining alcove. In the summer months we had the use of a small balcony.

For our second winter, I felt reasonably well prepared. For the sake of exercise, I suggested that we should all learn to ice-skate. In one of the courtyards of the apartment building complex, a quadrangle of ice was regularly groomed for those who wished to skate. Clad in heavy clothing, I would spend forty-five minutes each evening trying to learn the art of skating. This did not come easily to a man of forty-one. My ability to balance was only average and I lacked the courage to launch myself at reasonable speed across the ice; because of my lack of basic technique, I fell relatively frequently. But I persevered.

On one occasion, as I left the ice and entered the apartment building, I met Emy who was standing inside the door; apparently she had been looking through the glass at my pathetic efforts. She told me that when she had arrived at the door, she had met a man; as he stood peering through the glass, he turned to Emy and said,

"I can hardly speak because I keep bursting out laughing. But it really cheers me up to watch that creature out there on the ice. Look, there he goes again – down!"

He let out a howl of laughter. Emy watched me through the glass; then turning to the amused onlooker, she said,

"That is my husband."

After we had lived in the apartment for some sixteen months, I took stock of our situation. Although my salary level was not good, I concluded that we could live reasonably well on our disposable income. I also felt that in the office I was making headway, which in time I hoped would be recognised. During the summer, we had made a number of pleasantly interesting excursions. However, to some extent at least, we felt that we had a tendency to find some reason to leave our apartment, simply because of the feeling of confinement which its smallness generated in us. Again, I hoped that if my salary level were raised in time, then we would be in a position to rent a larger apartment.

But there was one overriding consideration that could not be ignored. Although Emy had never complained in any way concerning our changed circumstances and lifestyle, the fact was that this dedicated, eternally happy, intelligently provocative, amusing wife had become a quiet person who seemed to live her life from day to day, perhaps not wishing to speculate on how she would feel in a year's time. When Emy had arrived in Canada, she had struck me as a strong and happy flame; now her being seemed to be reduced to a flicker.

I told Emy that there seemed to be little sense in living in Canada in a small apartment, when we had at our disposal in England a reasonably-sized house. Unless we would resolve our accommodation problem within the next few months, then I would certainly be willing to return to England.

Fortunately, within a few months, we found a fine 'estate' house. Everyone to whom I spoke advised me against buying the house. The October Crisis of 1970 was fresh in the minds of Montrealers, who had practically no experience of physical violence. The kidnapping of the British Trade Commissioner and the murdering of a Quebec government Minister had sent a signal of fear through Montreal. Many inhabitants concluded that Montreal was not a safe place in which to live; and they left. The result was that many houses were available for purchase at prices which, by normal standards, were low.

As I looked one day over the city of Montreal and the magnificent St. Lawrence River, I concluded that it would take much more than the violence which had recently been experienced to bring a great city such as Montreal to its knees. Whereas the Montrealers felt that they lived in a city of violence, for someone such as myself, it was by far the most peaceful city I had lived in during the entire period of my working life. I saw no reason to hesitate in buying our house, which I did.

In September 1972, we moved into our house, a house built of stone by a Scotsman. There was much to do to bring the house into good condition and I would have to learn how to repair and paint the house; and the garden would need some attention. However, the main thing was that we were installed. We were happy and the flickering flame would quickly recover.

A few months after we had moved into our house, the City of Montreal sent the annual assessment of taxes; these were to be paid in two instalments. For the sake of explanation, in North America the taxes generally equate to English rates. The assessment was accompanied by a description of the main elements which were included in the taxes. It was also stated that if a house owner wished to appeal against the amount assessed, he or she should give early written notice; in the meantime, the amount shown on the assessment should be paid. Because the price of the house we had purchased was below the assessed evaluation, I submitted a notice of appeal.

Later, I received a form letter from the City of Montreal stating that my case would be heard in Court Number 1 at 9.30 a.m. on a certain day. Before attending the court, for my own reference, I had itemised the main elements of my plea on the back of a large brown envelope. I referred to the actual price which I had paid, which was lower than the evaluation; I also made mention of the poor condition of the house, plus peripheral considerations such as noise, pollution and so forth.

Armed with my envelope, and dressed in my best suit, I left in good time to avoid any risk that I might be late for my appearance in Court Number 1. Although I realised that there was no direct connection between the municipal law and tennis, an onlooker that morning who might have been watching my jaunty step, would have been forgiven for concluding that I was heading for the equivalent of Wimbledon's Number One Court.

In my ignorance, I had vaguely imagined that those involved in hearing my case would have little else to do that morning than to prepare themselves for my plea. However, on arrival in the area of the court, I found the reality to be far removed from what I had expected. I joined a crowd of citizens, all of whom for some reason seemed to be in a state of agitation. There were several courts and I had difficulty forcing my way through the bustling, noisy crowd. When I reached the large, imposing door of Court Number 1, I found that it was locked. My neighbour explained that the door would only be opened just before the first case was to be heard; at that moment, the door was in fact opened and three lawyers immediately entered the court and began to spread a huge amount of documentation across a large table. When their briefcases had been emptied, they commenced an intense oral consultation. They seemed to ignore the noisy environment; they were in a world of their own.

After further enquiries, I found the office of the Clerk of the Court. The Clerk was a small, pale, elderly man of slight build, dressed in a black suit; he wore pince-nez. His appearance struck me as a Pickwickian caricature. I introduced myself and stated that I was ready to make my plea at the appointed time. The Clerk of the Court shuffled through some papers until he eventually found my name. He then said that there would be a long delay before my case would be heard, since the case before mine involved an apartment building and this would be a complex hearing; depending on the detail which might be required by the President of the Court, the case might well last for two days.

I was slightly shocked, but tried to maintain a calm countenance. I explained to the Clerk that we had invited my mother-in-law from Europe to stay with us in Canada and she would be arriving at the airport at 11 a.m. I had specially taken a half day's leave from my office so that the morning hours could be used for my case to be heard, after which I would meet my mother-in-law at the airport. In the circumstances, I wondered whether the Clerk could give me some advice? The small man looked up at me with a serious expression on his face; but I could see that he was sympathetic. He told me that he would have a word with the President of the Court; perhaps my case could be heard first. In the meantime, I should stand near the door inside the court.

As I stood against the wall near the door, I looked around me. The three lawyers had apparently finished their consultation and, rather like sprinters at the beginning of a race, were standing in a state of readiness at the table behind their heaps of documentation. In addition to these men, there were three or four other individuals who were sitting on both sides of the court. Outside, the noise of the crowd seemed to have abated; apparently, most people had made their various ways to the courts and other offices to attend to their particular business.

Suddenly, a loud, ringing voice said, "Stand up!" Those in the courtroom stood up. The President, flanked by two Members, entered the court from the side and mounted some steps before sitting behind a high bench. Below the bench, the Clerk of the Court was arranging some papers; I saw him scribble a note on one of the papers, which he passed above his head to the President. The President briefly annotated the document and handed it down to the Clerk. Another voice rang out,

"First case is the City of Montreal versus Mr. Colin Everard. Will the appellant please come forward."

The three lawyers immediately in front of me looked at one another in consternation. One of them said, "Mr. President, we are first."

The President looked grimly at the lawyer and responded, "I will not hear your case first, please leave the court. Where is the appellant?"

With this cue, I stepped forward. With a mock look of impatience, I asked the lawyers to quickly remove all of the documentation from the table as I did not wish my case to be spoiled by a distraction! The frustrated lawyers were evidently furious; at the same time they were powerless. They gathered up the documentation and with their arms bulging from their loads, retreated.

The President looked at me and asked me to confirm that I was Colin Everard; I was.

"Would you please name your lawyer?"

Taken aback, I responded, "Mr. President, I do not have a lawyer."

"Mr. Everard, please name your secretary."

The response: "Mr. President, I regret I do not have a secretary."

The President then explained that a recent rule had been introduced to the effect that all appellants should be represented by a lawyer and a secretary; however, he would take into account the fact that the law was only recently introduced and he would show understanding that I was not familiar with the law. He then instructed the Clerk of the Court as follows,

"This court deems that Mr. Everard has a lawyer and a secretary."

After these preliminary exchanges, I was beginning to sense that I was out of my depth. I was not a lawyer and I had no knowledge of court procedure. Also lurking in the back of my mind was that I should not be late in meeting my mother-in-law who would be arriving at the airport from Vienna.

In a mistaken endeavour to move things along, and holding my large brown envelope so that I could read the substance of my plea, I said in a strong voice,

"Mr. President, may I please now make my plea?"

From his elevated position, the President looked at me unsmilingly for some seconds; then he said, "Be quiet!"

He turned his head to one side of the court and asked for the assessor's report. One of the men stood up and recounted that he had inspected the house and had done his best to place a value on it; unfortunately, he had not been able to inspect the whole of the interior, although he had looked through the windows. My memory immediately 'clicked'. A few weeks before, my second daughter (Marci) had explained that a strange man had appeared in the doorway of the house and had told her that he wanted to inspect the rooms; while he was talking he had walked through the front door and into the hall. As he had begun to look into the dining room, Marci had concluded that the man was an imposter. Although Marci was a girl of only thirteen years of age, she had somehow forced the 'criminal' to leave. This was the man who was now giving the President his report.

When the assessor had completed his oral report, the President asked for further information about the residential area. Another man stood up and made an oral report. I felt frustrated; perhaps at last I would now be permitted to make my plea.

When the second man had sat down, I cleared my throat in readiness to speak. However, the President looked at me and said,

"I have heard the case. If the court were to reduce the valuation of your house by eight thousand dollars, would you consider accepting the new valuation as reasonable?"

I was now in a state of total confusion. I had given no evidence; in fact, I had taken no part in the proceedings at all. Although a feeling of inner weakness was beginning to take hold, I resolutely held my brown envelope in front of me and announced that I would like to explain the main points of my plea. The expression on the face of the President of the Court became more severe; in firm tones he said,

"Stop talking! I repeat, I have heard the case. If the court were to propose a reduction in value of eight thousand dollars, would you accept?"

The President was using the conditional tense; he did not appear to be making a firm proposal. Was I suddenly involved in a negotiation; or would the President dismiss the case if I began to argue?

I responded,

"Mr. President, if the court were to consider lowering the valuation by eight thousand dollars I would consider this to be reasonable. But since I understand the court has not made a decision, I think I should reserve my position."

The President's face became grim; he raised his arm and pointed his index finger directly at me, "This is your last chance. Do you accept?"

I looked at the pointed finger and my eyes moved to a face which reminded me of thunder, except that at that moment all was silent. My response was weak and to the point,

"Yes, I accept."

The finger was withdrawn and the look of thunder left the face; there was a rustling of papers and then I heard a voice say,

"Case heard. Next!"

I stood in the court for a few more seconds, my envelope at my side. What had happened? I was not quite sure; but I understood that my appeal had somehow been dealt with. To help expedite my departure from the court, I heard a voice say,

"Please leave the court immediately, Mr. Everard."

My mind was dulled by the strange happenings of the court. As I reached the door, however, I was jerked back to reality; the lawyers I had displaced had gathered around me and seemed to be bubbling with excitement. One said,

"Congratulations Sir! You are a genius! What a tactician. It was like a pantomime. You gave the perfect impersonation of a helpless person who had not the slightest idea what he was doing. And the court fell for it. If you had tried to argue in a logical manner, you would never have got that size of a reduction. It was wonderful to watch you!"

I looked at the lawyers and found myself practically speechless; I said, "Thank you. If you will kindly excuse me, I must meet my mother-in-law at the airport; she will shortly arrive from Vienna. Good luck with your case." As I passed a waste bin, I folded the large envelope and duly deposited it.

A few days later, a letter was received from the City of Montreal which formally confirmed that the value of our house had been reduced by eight thousand dollars; in consequence, the annual tax bill would be reduced. At least for a year or two, the reduction would significantly contribute to an affordable lifestyle.

Now there was no looking back. We had come to stay in Canada and North America. And we would enjoy our New World.

Chapter Fourteen

The Third (Developing) World and ICAO

In 1944, when the end of the Second World War was in sight, representatives of fifty-two countries attended a conference in Chicago to consider the ramifications of civil air transport once the war had ended. The impact of civil aviation growth had already been experienced during the first part of the century, especially between the wars. For example, the United States Post Office had opted for air mail, a decision which not only drastically reduced the delivery time for mail, but also led to the establishment of air routes and ground facilities to enable aircraft to land and take-off safely.

After the Second World War, aviation was to become one of the most spectacular developments of the twentieth century. In the 1940s, governments could already foresee to some extent that this would be the case; they recognised that unless some degree of order was introduced into the development process of civil aviation, not only would chaos ensue but safety standards would be compromised.

The substance of the long and complex deliberations which took place in Chicago is not the subject of this book. Suffice it to record that, eventually, the main points to be included in 'The Convention On International Civil Aviation' were agreed. On 4 April 1947, the Convention came into force. The preamble to the Convention reads as follows:

> WHEREAS the future development of international civil aviation can greatly help to create and preserve friendship and understanding among the nations and peoples of the world, yet its abuse can become a threat to the general security; and

> WHEREAS it is desirable to avoid friction and to promote that co-operation between nations and peoples upon which the peace of the world depends;

> THEREFORE, the undersigned governments having agreed on certain principles and arrangements in order that international civil aviation may be developed in a safe and orderly manner

and that international air transport services may be established on the basis of equality of opportunity and operated soundly and economically;

Have accordingly concluded this Convention to that end.

The intent of the Convention on International Civil Aviation was to encourage the adoption of an internationally accepted air transport system, supported by unified standards of safety and related procedures. To give effect to this huge undertaking, the governments agreed that an Organisation would be needed to tackle the vast amount of technical, economic, legal and administrative work which would become a pre-requisite for the attainment of the overall objective. The International Civil Aviation Organisation (ICAO) thus came into being in the late forties; initially it was established on a provisional basis, but permanency quickly followed.

In the late forties and fifties, much of the time of the Regular Programme of ICAO was taken up with the development of Annexes to the Convention. These would cover such vital areas as Personnel Licensing, Rules of the Air, Operation of Aircraft, Airworthiness, Aeronautical Telecommunications, Air Traffic Services, Search and Rescue, Aerodromes, Aviation Security and several other definable aviation subjects. As necessary, the Annexes would be supported by Manuals, which would explain the intent of the Standards and Recommended Practices contained in the Annexes. In the legal and economics' fields, work was directed to reaching international consensus on Protocols and Agreements.

Although the approach adopted to introducing some order in the development of international air transport was sound, there was no doubt that complex challenges would have to be faced, especially with respect to achieving effective co-ordination between certain countries. Not only would political differences emerge as barriers to successful co-ordination, but there would be wide discrepancies in the relative stages of development of various countries and this fact would also need to be taken into account.

When governments supported the introduction of a United Nations Special Fund to assist developing countries and, later, the United Nations Development Programme (UNDP), the opportunity would be taken by ICAO to enter into a relationship with the UN System. As an Agency of the United Nations, funding could be made available to support a project which would aim to upgrade an area of weakness in its air transport sector, provided the government of a developing country would accord the matter the required priority.

Although ICAO would tend to be preoccupied with the relatively major air transport problems of the developed countries, the Organisation could not ignore the gap (sometimes a gulf) which existed in terms of each country's development capability as applied to the effective installation and operation of aeronautical facilities. In general, Australasia, Europe, Japan and North America have the financial and human resources to meet the challenge of assuring the safe and orderly operation of air transport. The developing world (often referred to as the Third World) frequently meets problems; first, financing may not be available at the required level and second, even if a budget is adequate, there is often a lack of effective human resources to implement what is needed to assure aviation safety.

In the late forties and early fifties, ICAO recognised the challenge of bringing the developing countries into the mainstream of the development of international civil aviation. There would be little point in having a wide range of minimum standards of safety in various fields, if the developing countries of the Third World found themselves in a position where they could not implement these basic standards. As far as ICAO was concerned, the possibility of co-operating with the Special Fund and, subsequently, the UNDP would mean that ICAO, acting as an Agency of the UN System, would be in a position to assist directly countries of the developing world.

Structurally, ICAO is divided into Bureaux (Divisions). Under the management of the Secretary General, these Bureaux cover: Air Navigation (Ground and Flight), Air Transport (Economics and Statistics), Legal and Administration. In addition to the ICAO Secretariat in Montreal, the Organisation finances the operation of seven regional offices. The permanent political body which oversees the day-to-day work of the Organisation is the ICAO Council. The Council is elected every three years by a gathering (the Assembly) of all the Member States; these number about one hundred and eighty.

In the early fifties, recognising the importance of helping to bridge the gap between the developed and developing world, ICAO established another Bureau; this would cover Technical Assistance, later termed Technical Co-operation. Although the Technical

Co-operation Bureau would, from a structural point of view, be included in the overall secretariat, there was an important difference in the financing of the operations of the new Bureau. The Council of ICAO did not wish to see an expansion of the budget which was established to finance the activities of the other Bureaux; these constituted the Regular Programme which had been created to carry out the special activities needed to support the aims of The Convention On International Civil Aviation. Since the nature of the work of the new Bureau would not include regulatory matters, it was decided in principle that the newly-established Bureau should endeavour to finance its operations from the fees it would receive, acting on behalf of the Organisation in its role as an Executing Agency.

The decision reached by the ICAO Council that the financing arrangements for technical co-operation should be separate from the financing basis of the Regular Programme was logical. Just as it is sometimes said that, typically, the proverbial camel (with all its strange bodily disadvantages) was probably a logical product of a committee, so the decision to separate the activities of the newly-established Bureau and the Regular Programme was one which emanated from a committee, in this case the Council of ICAO.

It was inevitable that, although the staff who worked in the field of technical co-operation would be recruited on the same terms and conditions as the staff of the Regular Programme, the technical co-operation staff would be regarded as 'different'. In fact, to some extent, this was true. Although at all times the standard of the work of the technical co-operation staff had to reach the highest possible technical levels, since the staff were employed on an Agency basis there was an element of entrepreneurial flair in their work; this was absent in the case of the Regular Programme. The perceived difference did not end there. During periods of high activity, when the Technical Co-operation Bureau showed a surplus of income above its overhead costs, the staff of the Bureau were regarded as a professional group who at the drop of a hat and, in contrast with the staff on the 'other' side of the house, could decide to leave for an extensive monitoring tour of, say, Asia. Again, if the surplus became substantial, there were always those outside the Bureau who had good ideas on how to dispose of the surplus funds; these 'planners' ignored the concept of maintaining a contingency reserve for times which would not be so healthy from the financial aspect. Hard times fall, sometimes heavily, on all of us and the Technical Co-operation Bureau would be no exception to this general rule. And when the inevitable hard times were to overtake the Bureau, the halo of affluence was transformed into an image of the 'poor cousin'. As far as the Council members were concerned, the financial problems of the Bureau were bothersome. For a Council in anguish over the financing of the Organisation's activities, it was one thing to declare its strong support not only for the Regular Programme but also for the Technical Co-operation Bureau; it was quite another, however, to financially support these activities.

Personally, I welcomed the discussion on the relative importance of technical co-operation. Although one would hear that air navigation fields should constitute the primary focal point for the Organisation's work programme, there was also recognition of the fact that, unless the Third World could participate fully in the advances being made in civil aviation, there would be a danger that ICAO would become the island sanctuary of the latest knowledge which would be circulated from the proverbial 'ivory tower'; without proper preparation, how could this knowledge be used by the developing world? How, for example, would the transitional jump to the most modern civil aviation technologies be organised (with all the related complex issues involved) and financed in poor countries, especially when some of them had in place, and continued to use, technologies of thirty years previously? And if the developed countries already had the capability to implement advanced civil aviation technologies, then what, precisely, would be the function of ICAO *vis-à-vis* these technologies? After the establishment of the various Annexes, was a full-time Work Programme really justified to amend and polish this documentation to reflect technological developments? Or could the money be better spent by stronger, intensified efforts to bridge the gulf between the developed and developing world? If civil aviation depends for its safety and efficiency on a global system, then surely it would be sensible to direct supporting efforts to the weakest links in the chain. Or again, with so many 'hot spots' in our world, what degree of risk is involved in operating an aeroplane (which may have cost US$100 million), fully loaded with passengers, when it is known that the aviation security measures in a certain developing country do not meet the minimum ICAO Standards and Recommended Practices?

These types of questions pre-occupied the ICAO Council for years. They would never be resolved to the satisfaction of all the States because of the divergent interests of the various countries. The fact that a compromise was invariably reached not only speaks well for the efforts of the Council and its President Assad Kotaite; it was a triumph for the international community. The compromise achieved recognised that it was illogical to name one field as pre-eminent amongst several; otherwise civil aviation development could be likened to the heart surgeon who keeps a heart beating, but ignores the health of the rest of the body. Each field of endeavour in civil aviation development complements efforts in related fields; and the work performed in each specialisation has an impact on complementary efforts. The quest, and riddle, for the decision-makers is to find the right balance; as conditions change over the years, the balance may well need adjustment.

In accepting an appointment with ICAO, apart from my exposure to flying and the considerable experience I had already gained with respect to logistics' problems encountered in developing countries, did I feel that I would be maintaining my original objective of contributing to the development of some aspect of humanity, however humble? My response was decidedly positive.

Although the developed world takes safe civil aviation for granted, in the developing world this is certainly not the case. As the demand for the air transport mode of transportation expands, developing countries increasingly experience infrastructural problems. Depending on the country concerned, the availability of technical expertise and air transport managerial competence falls short, sometimes severely so, of the basic infrastructure needs.

In terms of a country's development, civil aviation often plays a key role. A number of island countries rely on tourism as a major revenue-earning industry; however, in order for the tourists to arrive at and leave their destination, safe aviation is vital. Again, in a land-locked country (such as Nepal for example) the main generator of foreign exchange is tourism; for the industry to develop, safe aviation is of crucial importance.

Without safe civil aviation, the development process in any country will be seriously impeded simply because, for the development process to take place at all, it is essential that people and goods can be brought to the area to be developed safely and with reasonable speed;

it is aviation that has proven to be the most appropriate mode of transportation in countless cases. If we consider the much-needed development of Irian Jaya in eastern Indonesia, for example, the utilisation of aviation to open up the area initially can be achieved relatively quickly; and at far lesser cost than constructing a road network.

The siting of a number of industries has depended on the availability of safe and efficiently-operated civil air transport services. For example, perishables and light industries producing consumer goods (such as electronics) rely almost totally on civil aviation to bring their goods to the market place. As another example, every day of the week at least one wide-bodied freighter leaves Nairobi in Kenya loaded with flowers and dairy produce, bound for European markets.

To the extent that civil aviation can be operated safely and efficiently, industries such as tourism will use air transport and the revenue derived from these industries, especially foreign exchange, is available to increase the relative wealth of the country concerned. Furthermore, apart from the direct impact of assisting in the development of specialised skills and expertise in the field of civil aviation, through the multiplier effect additional industrial activity is generated, which in turn means employment.

Since civil aviation has a strongly positive impact on development, whether through the training and upgrading of human resources, providing employment or generating profits, the ultimate result should lead to an improvement in the human condition within the overall context of development.

When I arrived in ICAO on a cold morning in January 1971, I was soon shown to my office and I had a few introductory exchanges with the members of the staff of the section which I had been appointed to oversee. As with any new job, initially I concentrated on reading and learning the various practices and procedures which were then in force. I soon discovered that there was a considerable backlog of work and, as I came to grips with the substance of our work, from the historical aspect several 'skeletons' seemed to fall out of the dark past and on to my desk. Systematically, I tried to resolve various outstanding problems which I had inherited, often with little or no vital information at my disposal.

After a week or so, the branch chief asked me to visit him. After a cursory welcome, he told me that the section that I had come to lead had a poor reputation in terms of efficiency. He had organised the departure of my predecessor some nine months earlier; during the interim period, the man who had acted as chief of section had shown himself to be ineffectual. I was then firmly told that a significant improvement in the operation of the section was expected within a short period; the poor level of the section's operation was adversely affecting ICAO's efforts as a whole in the field of technical co-operation. If I was not able to upgrade the performance of the section quickly, then I might well consider making arrangements for my own departure! It was hoped that I would do better than my predecessor; however, if this should not prove to be the case, then I would pay the price.

Although by any standard the initial interview which I had suffered was hard, in fact it made little negative impact upon me. First, I recognised that the man who was supposed to be managing my activities was not practised in the art of management; I recognised this as his problem and one which, unless he learned fairly quickly, would lead to his sidelining (which in fact it did). Second, I had learned a great deal about the theory and practice of logistics and I was confident that in virtually any situation which might arise within the field, due to the level of my knowledge and experience I would act properly and give the right professional advice. Third, with some eighteen years of experience of life in the developing world, my confidence level in terms of dealing with those in the Third World was high.

During the period of work which I spent with ICAO (twenty years) my colleagues and I often worked long hours; this is simply an observation. To work long hours is not necessarily meritorious; in fact, there are those who need to work long hours simply to maintain an average standard. But we were not in that category. We could have been average-type employees; but I, for one, always wished to achieve the highest possible professional standards and because of the nature of our work, there was ample scope to produce relatively more. And one had to 'think through' complex issues if good, defensible decisions were to be made. Many of these took into account not only the current position, but our appreciation of what would develop in any given situation over the ensuing months; in this sense, many of the decisions which needed to be taken were judgement decisions.

When coming to grips with my work, I needed to understand why a country is categorised as a 'developing' country, or a country of the Third World. In perhaps vague terms, when we think of a developing country we see an image of Bangladesh, Cambodia or the poor of Africa. Indeed, these examples are part of the developing world; however, they are representative of the poorer countries with the lowest average incomes. But there are many other countries of the Third World where, although incomes are relatively low, the country in general terms is progressing towards the status of a developed country. For example, countries such as Chile, Ecuador, Egypt or Nigeria quickly come to mind. During the last few years, a number of developing countries have progressed to such an extent that the relative well-being of their populations, and their economic indicators, demonstrate many of the characteristics of fully developed countries; for example, Indonesia, the Republic of Korea, Malaysia, Singapore and Thailand have already reached this stage and the UN has given them a special designation: Newly Industrialised Countries (NICs). So what we learn from these facts is that it rarely makes sense to refer simply to the 'Third World'; we need to be more specific and we need to recognise that every country in the world is in a state of development which is singular to itself.

During those first few months with ICAO, I spent much time and effort in seeing the backlog of work eliminated. From a management viewpoint, I felt it was essential for the morale of my colleagues to be substantially raised. Once they felt that they were up-to-date and on top of their work, which would soon be the case, they would feel professionally uplifted.

During the process of dealing with the considerable backlog of work, in consultation with my colleagues I performed an analysis of the main reasons for delays. Arising from this, a Suppliers and Equipment Information Retrieval System (SEIRS) was designed and brought into operation. The computerised/microfilm system was described in some articles which were published in professional journals. A description of the system was also included in McGraw Hill's *Purchasing Handbook* textbook, an earlier edition of which I had studied with such dedication in Uganda. The system resulted in many advantages, one of which was to reduce the time spent in locating suitable suppliers and equipment on a world-wide basis.

Six weeks after assuming my new job, the chief of projects for South America met with me in my office for a consultation. He had just received approval for a regional project involving four countries in South America; under the project, financing had been included for a complex Very High Frequency Extended Range Aeronautical Telecommunications System. ICAO, in consultation with the countries involved, was to specify the system, contract for its purchase and installation and administer the contract up to completion. My visitor wanted to know how we should approach this part of the project, how did I see the logistics element, how long would it take to complete the competitive bidding process and issue the contract; and were we geared to start the process immediately? Dealing with the last part first, I responded that we could start immediately; I then gave him complete information on his remaining questions.

Four months later, the contract had been issued. The text of the contract was complex, since not only were we purchasing the best equipment at the lowest possible price, but full account needed to be taken of spare parts, technicians' training and support to the various installations once the equipment had been installed, tested and commissioned for operation.

When the contractor visited Montreal for final discussions which would lead to finalisation of the contract text, he asked whether he could be given a photocopy of the agreed contract, since this would enable him to commence company work on the contract without delay. I asked the contractor's representative whether he would be staying the night in Montreal; when he told me that he would be departing the following day at lunchtime, I asked him to visit my office at noon. By the time he reappeared, not only had ICAO's Legal Bureau cleared the contract text, but I had called the Secretary General's office to enquire whether the Secretary General would be able to sign the contract on behalf of ICAO straightaway. As soon as the Legal Bureau had cleared the contract, the Secretary General's office called me and invited me to bring the contract to Dr. Assad Kotaite; the Secretary General already knew the circumstances of the award of contract, since under ICAO's rules, above a certain value threshold the Secretary General's approval is required before entering into negotiations with a contractor. After satisfying a few questions posed by Dr. Kotaite, the contract was signed which was then dated and stamped on behalf of ICAO.

On re-visiting my office, the contractor was impressed that ICAO was organised in such a way that not only could decisions be taken quickly, but a matter such as an important contract could be dealt with so expeditiously. The contractor's representative was authorised to sign on behalf of his company; he took his copy of the contract with him.

As with all contracts, the activities of the contractor were closely monitored and periodic payments were released only after systematic technical inspections. The contract was executed well and the systems were duly installed and commissioned. Safety of flight in South America was significantly raised as a result of that particular project.

The speed, professional teamwork and general efficiency of the contractual work I have just described impressed me. I reflected on how long would have been needed in East Africa before such an operation could have been brought to fruition. I recalled the endless discussions in East Africa which had so often ended inconclusively; I remembered those who had been instructed to initiate some action, but who had done either very little or nothing. I remembered the effort and perseverance needed to achieve a minimum degree of progress as one groped through the bureaucracy of government.

And here was ICAO, with professional efficiency and ease, moving ahead and taking decisions, each member of the team knowing what was expected of her or him and acting accordingly. I felt that what ICAO had achieved in four months might well have taken three to five years to have happened in East Africa, if at all. I realised that this was what I had been missing and what I had hoped would become for me a reality; I felt privileged to be a member of a team which would make things happen not only speedily, but in a professionally correct way. I retained that feeling during the whole of the period during which I worked with ICAO.

In contrast to many governments in the developed world, ICAO had few traditions, if any; this was because the Organisation was simply too young. By 1994 only fifty years had elapsed since the year of the signing of the Convention On International Civil Aviation. The lack of tradition was, in certain respects, an advantage. It meant we had virtually no respect for 'traditional' practices and procedures; in turn, this meant that if a procedure was not working as well as it should have been, then it was improved. Inefficiency could be dealt with quickly. We were never inhibited nor impeded by time-honoured traditions, as is so frequently the case in national governments.

In the spring of 1971 there was a change in the Directorship of the then Technical Assistance Bureau. Jack Vivian was appointed as the new Director. He had excellent credentials for the job and led the Bureau successfully until his retirement several years later. During the period 1971-1980, the funding level for the ICAO inputs into projects which were implemented in developing countries rose from an annual level of US$7 million to US$85 million. The administrative overhead derived from these projects, although established at an unreasonably low level, enabled the Bureau to maintain a healthy financial reserve, which itself earned interest. Unfortunately, during the eighties the picture was reversed; in relative terms, governments adopted a lower priority for civil aviation development, which led to a reduction in the level of project activity in which ICAO was involved. It seemed that however much one reduced the actual overhead cost of the Bureau's activities, because of the lack of volume of project work linked with the cost of maintaining a medium to long-term planning capability, it was impossible to balance the budget; especially in a field such as civil aviation, from the technical viewpoint there was an irreducible minimum which had to be respected, if the technical integrity of the projects was to be maintained.

Shortly after the change in Directorship, Jack Vivian asked each of us to consider how we could contribute to a positive development in the field of technical assistance. My contribution was to plan and see established the ICAO Civil Aviation Purchasing Service (CAPS).

Based on my work in developing countries, I recognised the great difficulty experienced by most countries in specifying the correct aeronautical equipment to meet their requirements. Once the specification had been established, then how could one be sure that one was in contact with the best manufacturers to obtain international bids (tenders)? The Suppliers and Equipment Information Retrieval System (SEIRS) was already developed, which meant that some twenty-five thousand items of civil aviation equipment had been categorised in the system; retrieval of potential needs, supported by microfilm data, could be achieved within a matter of seconds. In establishing the Civil Aviation Purchasing Service, ICAO would specify the required need, implement international competitive bidding procedures and, in consultation with the government Agency or department involved, award the contract. The recipient government would finance the contract, sometimes using ICAO's good offices to obtain financing; the covering funds would be transferred to ICAO, where the money was held in a country trust fund account. It was also clear that if we could generate a good level of interest in the scheme, in certain cases this would lead to the purchase of similar requirements for two or three countries at the same time, which in turn would lead to a negotiated price reduction; the savings would be passed on to the countries involved.

Although I planned the scheme in considerable detail, initially my colleagues were not wholly enthusiastic with regard to CAPS. Some of them did not understand its significance in terms of the help it would give those in developing countries. However, I had personally observed some of the problems associated with equipment acquisition in eastern Africa and I was convinced the situation was typical of many developing countries. My colleagues in ICAO were also busy people professionally, each trying to achieve the highest professional standards in his or her work; perhaps they found the challenge of a possible broadening of our work to be onerous.

Jack Vivian then suggested that we should write to the various civil aviation administrations of developing countries, outline the concept of CAPS and endeavour to ascertain whether the countries would use such a service. Within three months we had received fifty-two responses; all were positive in various degrees of enthusiasm. This was the signal to proceed. The scheme was presented to the Council of ICAO, which approved CAPS for implementation. After the Council meeting, the then representative of the United Kingdom walked across to me and shook me by the hand,

"You have given to the developing world something which they have needed for many years. The more CAPS develops, the greater you will find the challenges. I am sure ICAO will succeed with CAPS, but no one will recognise what you have done; and no one will thank you. But *I* know what you have done and I am sure you are the sort of person who will never become discouraged."

During the period of my tenure of the post of Chief of Procurement, I took the primary responsibility for the issuance of over 12,000 contracts and purchase orders utilising 2,500 firms in many countries. The equipment or services were provided in some one hundred countries. My aim, on behalf of ICAO, was to establish

ICAO's reputation within the field of procurement and logistics at the highest possible level in the civil aviation industry. During a period of eight years' work, we received four complaints from contractors or suppliers who felt they had deserved a certain award of contract; I invited each of them to ICAO headquarters to discuss the complaint. Three of the four accepted that our decision had been correct; the fourth was a man who seemed to have a nature which prevented him from participating in rational discussion and reaching a balanced decision.

By the end of the 1970s, the complex field of technical co-operation had reached such a stage of development that it could well be defined as a specialised field. Gone was the amateurish approach which had been woolly and undefined; and which so often had, mistakenly, contained a strong thread of sentimentality. Now the approach was properly structured and businesslike. One element in project work which I welcomed was that the project was defined, in basic terms, as a project of the government. If the project was to receive some financing support through, for example, UNDP then the government would have to demonstrate its willingness to contribute a certain percentage of the overall cost of the project, whether in cash or kind; typically, the contribution level was pitched at fifty per cent. I felt that, in human terms, this type of arrangement gave some dignity to the project. We would not be involved in some mindless 'give away' project, under which high-value foreign resources would be sent to assist a government as some misapplied 'gift'. As far as UNDP-funded projects were concerned, a government need not only simply pay lip service to accepting a project; it had also to contribute funding, staff, equipment and premises. In other words, before entering into a project with a government, UNDP wished to be convinced of the government's serious commitment.

What do such terms as 'technical co-operation', 'development co-operation' or 'technical assistance practitioner' mean? The UN System produces vast amounts of documentation on the subject. In order to properly understand the substance of the endless stream of papers, one needs to learn the UN jargon. For example, reference to a UN 'expert' simply refers to a professional staff member; in the true sense of the term, the staff member is unlikely to be amongst the small élite of this world who may be really expert in a particular field. Again, when the UN System refers to its representative offices which are maintained in well over a hundred developing countries, these offices are referred to as 'the field' or 'field offices'!

Some years ago, while I was attending a meeting devoted to discussing civil aviation development projects, informally I was asked whether I would care to try and succinctly define, in the civil aviation context, the meaning of technical co-operation. My response was the following:

> Within the wider social and economic development context, the pursuit of the achievement of civil aviation minimum (ICAO) safety standards on a sustainable, and preferably financially viable, basis by countries which are referred to (under UN criteria) as 'developing countries'.

Typically, a technical co-operation project would contain three main elements: Professional Personnel, Training Fellowships and Equipment. The overall project would be defined in comprehensive and specific terms; the three elements referred to would comprise the foreign inputs required to support the planned project. In the case of civil aviation, projects often involved the establishment or development of civil aviation training centres; for these, ICAO would provide specialised instructors in, for example, air traffic services, telecommunications or aviation security. Funding would be provided for the national instructors to be sent abroad to be trained, or upgraded, in their specialised instructional duties. As necessary, equipment to support in-country training would be supplied.

Generally speaking, the projects in which ICAO became involved were successful. The main problem which was encountered was that, due to the rapidly expanding situation in civil aviation in many developing countries, the staff trained under various projects would soon be promoted or transferred, which weakened the long-term impact of the project.

The strength of the system was that within ICAO there existed a high concentration of virtually every civil aviation specialisation; the degree of specialisation, linked with its breadth, was (and continues to be) unequalled in the world in its sheer concentration. Great emphasis was placed on day-to-day support, and monitoring missions were regularly undertaken to assess the progress of project activities. Eventually, the government, UNDP and ICAO would be involved in a detailed evaluation of the project; the fact that the project participants knew that the evaluation would take place, was itself an incentive to achieve the maximum degree of success.

After some eight years during which I headed the technical co-operation section dealing with equipment and logistics, I consulted Jack Vivian. I told him that I had overseen the section for several years. The demoralised group of staff to whom I had been introduced in January 1971 were now proud of their professional achievements; each looked forward to the latest challenge with enthusiasm. I believed it was generally recognised that for a person to spend five years in a post should normally suffice in terms of the person's career development. During the five year period, either the person concerned should have contributed to the enhancement of the work or, if no contribution had been made, then none would be forthcoming. In a nutshell, five years was enough. In this case, in terms of financial volume, the value of contractual work had increased over the years by twenty times. The section's staff had trebled in number. ICAO now had SEIRS and CAPS. After eight years, it seemed to me unlikely that I would contribute more in this particular area. It was time for a new mind to take over the work. I would like to stay within the field of technical co-operation; but I needed a change.

Shortly afterwards, I was appointed as chief of field operations for Asia and Pacific. I held the post for twelve years. During this period, in spite of a general reduction of development financing, in Asia and Pacific the level of annual funding for ICAO inputs into projects increased from US$5 million to US$25 million annually. For technical co-operation purposes, the Asia/Pacific area stretched from Iran in the west through the Pacific in the east; and from Mongolia in the north to the Maldive Islands in the south. Some eighty projects to support civil aviation safety were developed in the countries geographically spread within these limits.

The technical integrity of these projects was not the only essential ingredient. If a project was to be undertaken, the external ICAO inputs would need to be financed. This was where the entrepreneurial aspect came into its own; and where the talent for 'selling' ideas would make the difference between the granting of financing, or its withholding. We all know that money does not 'grow on trees'. If a project was to be financed, strongly convincing arguments had to be in place, sometimes over a period of three to five years. Within the limited financial resources at its disposal, a government would need to decide on the primary thrusts of its external development requirements. In the context of planning, financing support for civil aviation development would need to compete with such fields as agriculture, health and education, to name but a few; arguments to convince a government to support civil aviation safety projects, at the cost of excluding projects in more 'obvious' fields, often seemed to be in the nature of the contest fought between David and Goliath. Fortunately, many governments recognised technology transfer as an important element in their overall development aspirations. Over the years, civil aviation officials within their governments, ICAO colleagues and myself, were directly associated with financing discussions which resulted in the release of US$250 million for civil aviation project work, much of it in support of human resources' development. This sum financed only the external inputs through ICAO; these formed part of the much larger overall projects' financing.

As far as the national part of the effort was concerned, we were fortunate that the Directors General of Civil Aviation in various countries were men of the highest calibre and members of the aviation community who commanded respect in exercising their critically important responsibilities. They needed no convincing of the merit of a development assistance project. They were men with a mission; they recognised the crucial importance of providing safe facilities and services within an overall situation under which, in many respects, Asia would lead the world in civil aviation development.

In the seventies and eighties, the rate of growth of Asian civil aviation often equated to twenty per cent annually. Whereas in the late sixties, the annual share of international tonne-kilometres performed by airlines of Asia and the Pacific was of the order of sixteen per cent of the global international traffic carried, by 1988 the percentage had jumped to twenty-eight per cent; and it would continue to increase. As far as the freight picture was concerned, in 1975 the international portion of the global freight traffic of Asia and Pacific airlines equated to eighteen per cent. Ten years later this share had grown to twenty-nine per cent; and ICAO was forecasting that the share would rise to forty per cent. By any standard, these figures were impressive. But to support this expansion, great strain was placed on the civil aviation administrations to ensure safety. The

Directors General welcomed co-operation with ICAO, including ICAO's intervention in supporting their requests for project financing, whether within their own governments or when discussing needs with external funding organisations; typically, the latter would include the Development and Regional Banks, the Arab Funds, the OPEC Fund and UNDP.

Our constructive and healthy working relationship with UNDP was of particular importance. The UNDP Bureau which dealt with financing support for civil aviation infrastructure development projects in Asia and the Pacific was of special significance. This Bureau, ably led by Andrew Joseph, constituted a fine group of truly constructive, knowledgeable, responsive and dedicated professionals.

When looking back on ICAO, I would always remember the Organisation with deep affection. ICAO would never be perfect; no organisational entity is ever perfect and it would be a misrepresentation to assert that ICAO was an exception to this rule. But it always strove to be perfect and, supported by a superb staff, always looked for better ways to realise the aims of the Convention On International Civil Aviation. Through ICAO, I was able to give of my best to the field of civil aviation development co-operation; as far as I was concerned, to have been presented with the opportunity to do so was a privilege. At the same time, over those exhilaratingly active years, I had developed a deep respect for the civil aviation community worldwide.

When the time came for me to retire from ICAO, at the age of sixty-one, I left a happy man. Although the 'loss of really competent, trusted and intellectually able people such as yourself' was for some a subject of regret, I had always maintained the view that, certainly in the developed world, no one should be regarded as indispensable. I was confident that others would continue to fulfil the thoroughly worthwhile mission of ICAO in developing countries.

Chapter Fifteen

How to Build an Airport – By Really Trying

Many of us have seen a series of books which claim to enable the reader to master a subject 'without really trying'. Within the field of civil aviation, nothing is achieved without trying very hard indeed. Especially with respect to endeavours in the developing world, an array of infrastructural and physical problems confront those who become involved in major projects.

Within the International Civil Aviation Organisation (ICAO), in addition to the day-to-day work associated with the establishment of Standards and Recommended Practices, the Organisation also has the responsibility for compiling Regional Air Navigation Plans. These plans are developed in consultation with the countries of various regions. ICAO maintains offices for the regions in Bangkok, Cairo, Dakar, Lima, Mexico City, Nairobi and Paris. The Air Navigation Plans set out the air navigation facilities which should be made available by the countries of the various regions; these facilities and services typically include air traffic services, aeronautical communications (including radio navigation aids), rescue and fire fighting, aeronautical meteorological services, search and rescue and aerodromes. All of the facilities to be provided are regarded as essential for the safe and orderly operation of international civil aviation; and the required facilities and services should adhere to ICAO's minimum Standards and Recommended Practices. Where a country is unable to meet the stipulated requirements, then the country should submit a notice to ICAO to this effect.

In the mid-seventies, arriving one morning in my office, I leafed through the stapled set of messages from around the world; typically, some seventy messages would have been received overnight. Many of these would be handled by others; concerning the messages which would be dealt with by my section colleagues or myself, these would be annotated by me regarding action to be taken. If one particular message was regarded as of particular importance, I would detach it and retain it on my desk. Of the many messages received that morning, one seemed to be of special importance; it was duly detached so that I could deal with it personally.

One of the smaller Arab countries had received information regarding the establishment of ICAO's Civil Aviation Purchasing Service (CAPS). The message in question referred with pleasure to the establishment of the service and the government wished immediately to take advantage of it. The ICAO Regional Air Navigation Plan indicated that a certain city in the country should operate an airport for international traffic. The message recorded that the airport did not yet exist, although ICAO had previously overseen the compilation of a master plan for its development. The government therefore now wished to 'purchase' an airport.

A week or two later I found myself *en route* to the country. There was no direct air route from Europe to the country's capital city. I had arrived at an airport where I should connect with another flight which would carry me to my destination. Although I had made enquiries at the airport transit desk regarding the onward flight, after two hours I had made no progress in obtaining firm information. Amongst those who were waiting patiently in the airport transit lounge, I noticed a young woman who occasionally exchanged comments with her neighbour. Since I had overheard a few English words, I introduced myself and commented that I was waiting for a flight to enable me to reach my destination. The young woman, who seemed to be fatigued, responded that she also was heading in the same direction.

"I have already been waiting here for two hours, how long have you been here?" I asked.

"A week."

The young woman explained that she was a nurse by profession. When it had become clear that there would be a long delay in connecting with her flight, she had asked whether she could stay in an hotel. The response had been that the aircraft was expected "very shortly"; with regret, the airport staff had asked her to stay at the airport.

Four hours later, to the astonished disbelief of the nurse, we were asked to board our connecting flight and we arrived at our destination at dawn. After completing a number of formalities, we waited patiently for our luggage. At last, it came into view. Near the parked aircraft we could see some labourers struggling with two-wheeled carts, each of which was piled high with suitcases; in the warmth of the early morning sun, the carts were slowly pulled towards the small terminal building where we were waiting. Suddenly, the first cart appeared through a hole in the wall and, with a final push, the handle was raised and the heap of luggage was deposited on the floor; the operation was repeated two or three times before all of the luggage had arrived. We were then informed that the luggage was available for collection. The passengers jostled for position as they searched for their suitcases in the large heap. Fortunately, my suitcase was soon discovered and the ICAO project manager, whom I soon learned was often called 'the Captain' by his Arab counterparts, drove me to his office.

Without delay, various discussions ensued regarding the construction of the new airport. In the afternoon, I was introduced to the Minister who was responsible for the development of civil aviation in his country. The Minister explained that he had obtained the government's agreement that an airport should be constructed in accordance with ICAO's Regional Air Navigation Plan. He was pleased that ICAO had arranged for my visit. He and his colleagues would be available for necessary discussions on how to proceed. As a first step, he asked that the project manager should drive with me to the site of the proposed new airport the following day; since the drive would take five hours, we should stay overnight near the site of the proposed airport. On our return, we should again call on the Minister for further discussions, during which he hoped that all arrangements would be finalised so that ICAO could work with the government up to the successful achievement of the project.

At five a.m. the following morning, I was picked up at the hotel. Because I was not used to the local food, my stomach had involved me in a physical revolution. It seemed that during each hour of the night yet another stomach explosion was imminent. As was to happen on several occasions, within twenty-four hours of arrival in the country I was laid low.

The initial part of our journey was relatively pleasant. My physical condition, however, was rather poor. I had also developed bouts of nausea, which I found difficult to ignore. We were travelling fast and, on two or three occasions, I asked the project manager to explain to the driver that, if he persisted in speeding, as the heat of the sun warmed the surface of the road, the danger of a blow-out would increase. On receiving this information, the driver would slow down for a few minutes; soon, however, he would again be speeding.

After about three hours of driving, there was a bang and the vehicle slewed to a halt. One of the front tyres had blown out; the spare wheel was fitted in its place and we set off again. The driver again ignored my advice on the danger of speeding and, within half an hour, the second blow-out occurred. The driver explained that he did not have a second spare tyre and this meant that our journey had come to its end. There was a certain fatality and indeed banality inherent in his statement.

That morning we had only seen one other vehicle on the road; so we concluded that the chances of obtaining assistance were remote. We had come to a standstill on a large desert plain; the sandy waste supported sparse, low scrub. It was hot.

My initial reaction was simply to rest, hoping that my condition might improve after a sleep. However, after fifteen minutes I woke up and suggested to the project manager that we should walk to our destination; the distance was estimated at twenty-five to thirty miles. The Captain looked slightly taken aback and wondered whether this was the right thing to do, given my condition. I responded that we would soon find out. We should start without delay.

Because the hot sun would beat down on us for several hours, we pulled down the sleeves of our shirts and covered our skin as much as possible; although our faces were protected from the direct rays of the sun, the effect of the heat which was reflected from the road was similar to that which is felt when one opens the door of a hot oven.

After an hour and a half, the noise of a vehicle could be heard behind us. The Captain stopped and stood at the side of the road with his arm in the 'stop' position. A low truck approached us at high speed and, with a screaming of brakes, came to a sudden standstill. As though he had full knowledge of our situation, the driver opened the doors of the rear of the vehicle, which was enclosed by panels. On opening the two doors, four men burst out of the rear of the truck and lay gasping on the road. Looking inside the back of the vehicle, I could see at least four other sardine-like creatures crouching in the cabin; the roof was low and they travelled in a permanently bent posture.

After a consultation between the Captain and the driver, I was invited to enter the rear cabin; there were no seats and it would be necessary to stand in the low vehicle, with my head and body inclined. Two of the passengers were told that there was no longer any room for them; they would have to walk to the next town. I protested to the Captain that we should not displace the passengers. His response was short and to the point,

"Please! Remember that you are not in North America or Europe. Our customs our different. You need not concern yourself with anything!" And so the discussion ended.

I then had the audacity to raise the question of our own driver, who was marooned in the desert with his vehicle; once we had arrived at our destination, should we send him assistance to replace the blown out tyres? Again, I was firmly put in my place. I was in a foreign country and need not concern myself with such matters; they would take care of themselves.

On arrival at our destination, we went to work and continued to discuss the project until sundown. The following morning, feeling slightly stronger and more stable, I hesitatingly made my way towards a breakfast table where I tentatively selected a piece of dry bread, as experimental food. Shortly afterwards, I was joined by the Captain who was in good spirits. We glanced through the window of the dining room and, to my surprise at least if not the Captain's, saw our driver standing next to our car. Full of curiosity, I immediately went outside and asked him how he had managed to have the car repaired.

"In this country we are all brothers. Yesterday evening one of my brothers stopped when he saw that I had a problem. He transferred the wheels from his car to this car; and I gave him the two wheels with the burst tyres in exchange. Then I drove more slowly. Now I am here."

I was impressed. "And where is your brother now?" I asked.

"I left him in the middle of the desert."

As arranged, on our return we again called on the Minister. By this time, I had drafted an outline proposal which covered the arrangements for the establishment of the design and specifications for the airport, the calling of international bids, their evaluation, award of contract and supervision of the construction work up to completion. Before my departure for Montreal, all foreseen arrangements were agreed.

The ICAO execution of this project should be seen in the context of providing logistics support to projects in about one hundred countries. As far as the government was concerned, certainly this project would be regarded as one of the highest national importance.

While ICAO shared the government's sentiments, it was inevitable that only so much time could be allocated by ICAO to the project, simply because we were also involved with supporting projects in some ninety-nine other countries.

Although the available technical resources within ICAO were formidable, in this case we decided to supplement our available expertise by retaining the services of a consultancy group which would work under ICAO's supervision. The sheer volume of the work warranted this decision. As far as my own position was concerned, bearing in mind the high volume of day-to-day work involving so many countries, for the next two years I would designate many weekends as 'an airport weekend'; by adopting this approach, I hoped to keep abreast of developments and to remain sufficiently in touch to enable me to take balanced decisions, in consultation with ICAO technical specialists. With respect to the more important decisions (and there were several), then I would advise on these matters to the level which would be responsible for declaring ICAO's decision, typically a Director or the Secretary General.

In consultation with the government, once we had obtained the proposals for the construction of the airport, we appointed an ICAO resident engineer who, working with the ICAO technical staff and our consultants, would be responsible for undertaking the required technical evaluation of bids, prior to our making a presentation to the government on the subject. The evaluation work would take some three months.

When the evaluation work had been virtually completed, I again found myself sitting before the Minister to explain the work which had been undertaken. The government had asked each of the companies which had made a proposal to make a presentation to the government to explain how each would tackle the construction. Separately, the ICAO technical experts commented on each of the proposals. In consultation with government officials, we then analysed the commercial elements. The overall evaluation was then completed and the best contractor selected.

Once this stage had been reached, accompanied by the Captain, I consulted further with the Minister. I summarised the sequence of events which had occurred up to that point. The arrangements which had been put in place to give effect to the government's desire to construct the airport had worked well. All essential steps leading to the final evaluation and selection of a contractor had been properly carried out within the time-frame originally envisaged. The Minister agreed.

I then explained that the next step would be that the government should issue a Letter of Intent to the selected contractor. The letter could be a qualified Letter of Intent, in the sense that although it would state the government's intention to utilise the services of the successful contractor, a contract would be entered into only provided that certain points were first resolved.

The Minister was a wise man and conducted himself admirably. He frequently expressed confidence in the government's relationship with ICAO and seemed to have implicit faith in our technical and managerial ability to ensure that the government would achieve its goal. While I awaited the Minister's response, he began to look somewhat uncomfortable; he had certainly heard my suggestion that the Letter of Intent should be issued, but for some reason he seemed to be disengaging himself from the discussion. He turned his head and stared out of the window.

"Excellency," I repeated. "If the government now wishes to proceed with the construction of the airport, then the next step is for the government to issue a Letter of Intent."

The Minister turned his head and looked at me with an expression of embarrassment,

"Mr. Everard, the government has deeply appreciated all of the good work which ICAO has done. Unfortunately, we have a problem. We have no money to build the airport."

A silence ensued; the Captain and myself were speechless. The Minister then explained that his country had hoped that by then the financing would be available; although funding had been promised from one or two quarters, in fact it had not so far been made available. He stated that one of the richer countries had shown considerable interest in the project but, at the last moment, what had seemed to have been positive discussions had suddenly collapsed. It was the Minister's view that if the country was again approached, provided ICAO would be represented at the meeting, this would give the project enhanced credibility. It would then be likely that a gift or loan would be forthcoming.

The Minister then asked whether ICAO would be prepared to assist the government during the proposed re-opening of financing discussions. I responded that I would strongly recommend ICAO's involvement; however, I was not in a position to give a decision, which would soon be advised.

"Excellency," I asked, "May I ask when you would anticipate that the financing discussions would be held?"

"Tomorrow. I have already booked your seat on the flight."

I explained to the Minister that before I would be in a position to travel for the financing discussions, I would need to obtain approval from ICAO headquarters. I pleaded with the Minister to understand that the government's project in which we had become involved was one of many which ICAO was supporting throughout the Third World. I was expected to return to Montreal on a certain day; unless a serious and unexpected problem were to arise, there would be no justification for a delay in my return. The Minister smiled,

"So you would like me to create a serious problem?"

The Minister promised to call ICAO by telephone within the next few hours; I should in any case prepare to depart the following morning. The Minister would follow some twenty-four hours later.

Early the following morning, as I was packing my suitcase, a message was received that *en route* to the airport I should call on the Minister. The Minister told me that the financing discussions were extremely important. He felt that they could not succeed without effective intervention from ICAO; he looked to me to assist the government by injecting a high level of credibility into the project. He then added that,

"When you arrive, you may not be received very well. Some of the highest officials have been rather rude to us. If they treat you badly, I know that you will not become upset; you will continue to work to help us. I felt I should warn you because I do not want you to receive a shock at the moment you arrive."

In fact, I had already received a shock, although of a different kind; I had become ill. Because of a high fever, the previous day a doctor had been called. Before endeavouring to treat me he had explained that, although qualified in his country, he had lost his certificates; I should understand this. I weakly asked him what alternative medical assistance was available; he explained there was none. He then stated that, in his opinion, I was probably suffering from one of three possibilities; he would treat me for all three. I immediately slipped into a deep slumber.

Moving through the arrival hall at my destination, I felt as weak as a leaf in a breeze. As I tottered towards the immigration, bearing in mind the Minister's advice, I was prepared for the worst; however, the officials were helpful and charming. As I left the customs area, a good-looking young man approached me, smartly dressed in a dark suit. With a pleasant smile he said,

"You are probably Mr. Everard of ICAO. I am the Minister's personal representative. We have two cars for you, each with a chauffeur. The black car is for use during the day between your hotel and the meeting room; the white car is in case you would like to visit some of our night spots in the evenings." Was this the shock for which I should prepare?

The financing discussions commenced and within three days there was overall agreement on the terms and conditions under which the recipient government would be provided with the financing for the airport. Bearing in mind that I was long delayed in returning to ICAO headquarters in Montreal, I informed the Minister that since the main discussions had been successfully concluded, with his permission I would take my leave. Since the financing was now in place, if the government would agree to issue the Letter of Intent, ICAO could commence negotiations on the government's behalf with the contractor. There were a number of technical issues which needed to be clarified. Assuming that these would be resolved, the commercial terms of the contract would need to be discussed in detail and agreed. To the extent that any residual issues might remain which would impinge on the government's position, the Minister could rest assured that ICAO would refer such matters to the government for final resolution. The Minister agreed with this approach and signed the Letter of Intent.

Shortly after my return to Montreal, a message was received from the government to the effect that the financing country wished to receive the finally agreed details of all of the work to be undertaken; the specifications for the airport design comprised some four heavy volumes of documentation. The government noted that the Paris Air Show would shortly be held and proposed that representatives of the government, the consultants and ICAO should meet in Paris. Once the final statement of work had been produced, the government's representative would hand-carry two copies to the financing country.

On arrival in Paris, I made contact with the consultants and the government's representative, who was referred to as the 'Deputy Director'. The Captain was also present. When the statement of work was almost ready, I heard the Captain talking in firm tones to the Deputy Director. He said,

"You know what your function is, don't you? You are to hand-carry two copies of the statement of work to the financing country. Once you have handed over the two copies, just wait until your colleagues arrive to give any clarification. If you are asked questions, explain that you have no knowledge of the work; your job is to deliver the documentation. That is all."

The Captain then turned to me and explained that, although the Deputy Director had an excellent command of English, unfortunately the Deputy Director often misunderstood matters, regardless of language. The Captain did not want things to go wrong at this late stage due to any misunderstandings. He quietly mused on the problems resulting from what he termed, 'political appointments'.

That evening I answered a telephone call. The hotel switchboard explained that a caller from an Arab country was on the line; he wished to speak with someone called the 'Deputy Director.' I gave the switchboard the number of the man's room and asked the switchboard to transfer the call. I was told that this was an impossibility; the system in use by the hotel did not enable the switchboard to transfer the call. The hotel operator also stated that the caller had been trying to get through for two or three hours and the risk of cutting off the call should be avoided. Would I please try and bring the Deputy Director to my room to answer the call.

Bearing in mind that the Deputy Director's room was three floors above my own, I decided to try and call him from another room. I knocked on the door of the room next to my own; there was no response. I then noticed a man standing in the doorway of the following room; apparently he had heard the knocking. The thick-set man was dressed in an undervest and underpants. I asked him whether I could briefly use his telephone. Since he did not respond to my question in English, French or German, I apologetically slipped between his broad form and the doorpost and called the room of the Deputy Director. The man advanced towards me like a large, white bear; it later transpired he was in fact a Russian. Although the telephone was ringing, the Deputy Director was not answering.

I rushed from the room and took the lift to the level of the Deputy Director's room. The door was half open; I knocked and walked in. The man was asleep in an armchair. Gently taking his arm, I explained that there was a call from his country and he should take it in my room. With my arm through his, he accompanied me to my room; he seemed to be sleep-walking.

Fortunately, the call was still open. The Deputy Director spoke and immediately assumed the air of someone who was wide awake. He commenced an agitated discussion and seemed to be constantly interrupting the speaker to obtain clarification. While the heated telephone discussion was in progress, a messenger delivered a note to the effect that one of the consultants wished to see me in the hotel lobby. Since there was no sign of the telephone discussion abating, I asked if the consultant would kindly visit me in my room.

During the following hour, the consultant and myself consumed many of the hard and soft drinks which were available in the room mini-bar. Although neither of us spoke Arabic, by now we had reached the conclusion that an occurrence of major significance had overtaken the country; the caller seemed to be engaged in giving endless explanations. Perhaps there had been a natural catastrophe; it might well be that the country had been plunged into chaos through revolution.

At last the receiver was replaced. There was a grave look on the face of the Deputy Director. The consultant and myself looked at one another; perhaps something had happened which would affect the construction of the airport? As the Deputy Director moved towards the door I said,

"Deputy Director, we hope that everything in your country is progressing well. Do you have any special news?"

"No."

"Deputy Director, you have been on the telephone for a long time. The call must have been very costly. Perhaps something of great importance has happened. You were probably speaking with a senior colleague?"

The Deputy Director looked mildly surprised; he seemed to be returning to his sleep-walking state. As he left the room he briefly turned in the doorway and said,

"That was my wife."

The following day, the consultants escorted the Deputy Director, the Captain and myself to the Paris Air Show. I for one was singularly impressed with the quality of the display of aviation equipment and systems. As we returned to our hotel, one of the consultants explained that the previous day, a pair of trousers belonging to the Deputy Director had been delivered for cleaning and if it was agreed, a small detour would be made to pick up the cleaned trousers. A half-hour later, the Deputy Director seemed to be happy with the result of the cleaning process.

That evening the statement of work was produced in its final form and two copies were handed to the Deputy Director. He would be leaving the following morning to deliver the documentation to the financing country.

Early next day the Captain and I had breakfast with the Deputy Director. The Captain repeated that the Deputy Director had a very important duty to deliver the two copies of the statement of work; again, the Captain emphasised that the Deputy Director should not respond to any questions on the subject.

While we were awaiting a taxi which would deliver the Deputy Director to the airport, I asked him whether he had all his belongings; usually, when we are travelling the most important of these are ticket, passport and money. Yes, the Deputy Director checked the three items and confirmed that all were in order. Were all his belongings packed? He thought so.

"And the two copies, Deputy Director. You definitely have them with you, don't you?"

The Deputy Director looked slightly vague; he seemed to have slipped again into his sleepy state. After a long pause, he hesitatingly announced that he had the two copies.

Because he had responded in such a way that he did not seem to be totally sure, I said,

"Deputy Director, you know it is extremely important that you have the two copies with you and that they are delivered to the right office at the other end. Please excuse me making this request, but would you be so kind and show us the two copies?"

The Deputy Director was a polite man; he stated that he did not mind my request. He would now show us the two copies. He opened his suitcase, pulled out the just-cleaned trousers and triumphantly held the trousers in the air. With a look of self-satisfaction on his face, he turned to the Captain and myself and, looking at the two suspended trouser legs, he said,

"Now you should be happy. As you can see, there are two."

Although the nature of the misunderstanding was potentially serious, for a few moments the enormity of the misunderstanding was placed on one side. The immediate problem was how to avoid becoming convulsed in laughter. The situation was saved by the arrival of the taxi. Our return to reality was instantaneous. After all, a great deal of work had gone into the project and the future financing should not be jeopardised due to a hopeless misunderstanding. Where were the two copies of the statement of work? After further rummaging, the Deputy Director produced the genuine article. Although we felt that, normally, such valuable documentation would be safer in a hand-carried briefcase rather than in a suitcase which would become checked baggage, the fact was that the circumstances were not normal. On balance, we felt that it made little difference. The most important thing was to emphasise that the documentation should be delivered, without any comment, to the correct office.

A few days later we were relieved to hear that the government's appointee had faithfully performed his duty. What was also of importance was that he had refused to provide some requested clarification, commenting that technical staff would soon be available to explain matters.

With the financing agreement in place, the contract negotiations continued. Within a month, the stage had been reached where there remained four points which could only be resolved with the full participation of the government. Shortly after, on behalf of ICAO, I found myself in discussion with the Minister and his colleagues so that I could explain the salient aspects of each of the points to be resolved.

In the conference room where the final negotiation of the contract was to take place, the Minister sat at one end of a table, flanked by his senior officials and the Captain; the contractor, represented by three senior technical and commercial representatives, sat at the other end. I positioned myself on the side of the table between the two potential parties to the contract. The final negotiation commenced on a Wednesday morning and it was agreed that, at the latest, the contract should be agreed by 10 a.m. on Friday morning, when the government representatives would leave for prayers. If agreement could not be reached by 10 a.m. on Friday, then the negotiation would have failed and the government would enter into a negotiation with the next contractor, in order of merit.

Three points were resolved during the first day and a half of discussions. The final point proved to be complex and, as the clock ticked, resolution of the issue appeared somewhat doubtful. The matter came to a head early on Friday morning, when the Minister made a long, poetic statement. In a nutshell he had appreciated the efforts of the contractor to reach agreement, but unfortunately the government was not able to meet the contractor's demands on that particular point. The negotiation should therefore be considered closed, unless the contractor wished to revise his position. In his turn, the contractor made a relatively short statement, explaining that he had tried to meet the government's position; he accepted that the gap remained. At this point the contractor and one of his colleagues stood up; the Minister and his officials also stood up. Each party walked slowly towards the door.

For a few seconds, as I sat at the table, vivid scenes flashed through my mind in quick succession: the initial site survey, the agreement with the government on how to proceed, the vast amount of work involved in establishing the design and specifications for the airport, the financing discussions, the negotiations with the Contractor - and now things would come to a halt. How long would a negotiation with another Contractor take? Perhaps the entire project would lose its momentum and come to a standstill.

I jumped up and reached the door at the same time as the two groups. I took hold of the large key which enticingly protruded from the door and turned it in the lock; the key was then placed in my pocket. I smiled at the surprised Minister,

"Gentlemen, you have come a long way and you are almost there. Would you be so kind as to sit down again for five minutes."

Five minutes later, both parties had been persuaded to accept a compromise and after I had written the essence of the finally agreed point on a piece of paper, I asked each side to read and initial what I had written. I then announced that all points had been resolved and ICAO would prepare the contract for final signature; I estimated that this would take about two weeks.

The heat and stuffiness of the room were relieved when I unlocked the door. I heard the senior member of the contractor's group asking one of his colleagues whether he knew what "solidarity" meant?

When the representative of the contractor had signified his agreement to the end of the negotiations by walking towards the door with the intention of leaving the room with his group, one member had remained seated at the table. Why had this happened? The seated man looked humbled; then he said,

"Do you remember what happened to me when I walked out of a negotiation in Africa? I was put in jail for a week! I didn't want to risk that sort of situation again!"

After we had left the meeting room, walking up a corridor, the Minister seemed happy; he jovially asked me,

"What is the next step, Mr. Everard?"

I responded, "Excellency, your government will now achieve its goal. The next step is the construction of the airport."

I continued walking, expecting to hear a comment of satisfaction from the Minister at my side. Since there was silence I turned my head and was surprised that he was no longer there; I was walking alone. I stopped and looked back. The Minister had stopped in his tracks. He was looking at me with concern on his face. I walked back to him and enquired if something was wrong.

The Minister said, "Did you say that the next step is that the airport will be built?"

"Yes, Your Excellency. As you know, you have just initialled the final point of the final negotiation. As I stated, ICAO will finalise the contract text for your signature."

The Minister responded, "Why did you not inform me that this was the final negotiation? I did not realise that the negotiation had come to an end. You should have explained this to me in a proper way. You know how I love to negotiate; now it is all over!"

My flight would leave at 3 a.m. the following morning. I returned to the hotel, packed my suitcase and paid the hotel bill. A message was received that the Minister wished to hold a dinner late in the evening. Senior representatives of the government would be present, plus the group representing the contractor. The Minister expressed the wish that the Captain and I should attend his dinner, which we did with pleasure. I would then be taken directly from the dinner to the airport for my departure.

At midnight the dinner was drawing to a close. The festivity had been a great success and much had been eaten. I noticed that the Minister's chair at the head of our table was vacant. A messenger's voice in my ear whispered that the Minister wished to see me immediately and I should follow the messenger. I was led away from the festivities, along a corridor; as a red velvet curtain was held to one side, I entered a small room. The messenger left the room and I stood before the Minister.

He explained that we had travelled a long and difficult road together. At the outset, he had gained his President's agreement to his suggestion that the government should rely on ICAO's support in the planning and subsequent construction of the international airport. His speech was eloquent and poetic. He recalled the meetings on the financing of the project; on one occasion he had rebuked me for insisting that a certain point should be recorded in writing in the financing agreement. At the time, he had been concerned that my insistence might have jeopardised the agreement itself. It was only later that he had come to understand that ICAO was protecting his government's position. He was sorry that he had rebuked me; he hoped that I would understand that in the heat of the moment he may have thoughtlessly said something which may have been out of place.

A tear of emotion slowly trickled its way over the contours of the Minister's cheek.

The Minister then explained that, traditionally, in the Arab world one should show not only hospitality but appreciation. If I would indicate some special wish, the Minister would make any necessary arrangements to ensure that my wish would be met. The country would always remember the contribution of ICAO through myself. The government would like to recognise the contribution.

I thanked the Minister for his kind words. As for the rebuke, although I remembered it, at the same time I knew it had been made in the heat of the moment. Concerning some sort of reward, the Western system was different to the way things worked in Arab countries. I received a monthly salary and this was the reward for doing my job. I had done nothing special in terms of my own profession; I had simply tried to perform to the best of my ability.

The Minister looked somewhat frustrated. If I did not wish to discuss something of significance, at least the government should pay my hotel bill. I explained that I had already settled it. I thanked His Excellency for the highly enjoyable evening; and took my leave. As I passed through the velvet curtain, I turned and bowed slightly. Then I said "Goodnight, Excellency." I was suddenly struck by the loneliness of this man and the tremendous responsibility that he carried within his government. Silently, I vowed that we would give him all the support possible; whatever the circumstances, he should always feel that he could rely on us.

The contract was duly prepared and signed. The work then commenced and with a number of trials and tribulations along the way, the airport was completed within twenty-one months and within the originally agreed cost.

Although the role of ICAO had been fully explained to the Minister and his colleagues on a number of occasions, the concept of ICAO overseeing the work with objectivity and impartiality was not easily understood. In the view of some in the government, since the government had met the cost of the ICAO effort, then all decisions of ICAO relating to contentious matters should have favoured the government.

One of the progress meetings which was held after about a year proved to be particularly difficult in terms of making financial allowances for delays on the part of not only the contractor but also the government. It was understandable that the exchanges on various matters between representatives of the contractor and the government should sometimes be forceful and noisy. Depending on the outcome of contentious issues, which would be notified by ICAO, considerable sums of money were at stake with respect to both the contractor and the government.

At the height of the work, the contractor had some forty engineers on the construction site; they were supported by a workforce of hundreds of skilled, semi-skilled and administrative staff. In many areas, claims and counter-claims were made by both parties to the contract. From ICAO's point of view, we felt that to have various contentious claims outstanding for long periods would lead to an unhealthy work atmosphere. We therefore organised regular progress meetings so that we could use our good offices either to see issues resolved or, if necessary, pass judgement ourselves on the issues, a judgement which would be accepted by both the government and the contractor.

On arrival for one of the site meetings, I chatted with the ICAO resident engineer. Amongst other things, I asked him whether his domestic accommodation was satisfactory; especially during the summer months I knew the weather was trying, with heat and blowing dust. The resident engineer responded that the accommodation he had obtained was of a low standard, but it was the best which was available. Unfortunately, during some municipal road works the main electrical power cable had been cut; the resident engineer and his wife had lived without electrical power for some six weeks. He had told the municipal authorities about the situation; he had also written a letter to the Governor of the area on the subject, but without result. He smiled gently,

"It just means that we go to bed early; in any case, I get up at 4.30 each morning. I have to maintain a good relationship with the local people, so I don't want to make a fuss."

Later that morning, I was to call on the Governor of the area. I had met him during a previous visit. The Governor was an impressively dignified man; his white beard and the attentive look he would accord his visitor seemed to enhance his dignity and authority. He had invited Kenneth Wilde (ICAO's Chief of Airports) and myself to a dinner, which had been preceded by the offering of tea in a room which was furnished with brightly coloured cushions. The Governor had sat on a cushion at one end of the room and was host to those who sat cross-legged on the cushions, which extended in lines on either side. The room, spotlessly white, was cool; there were two small windows set in the thick walls which, in addition to allowing sufficient light to enter, provided welcome ventilation.

After an hour or so, it was suggested that we should leave the cushioned room and enjoy a dinner with the Governor. Soon, with many other local delicacies, a sizzling whole sheep had been placed on our table and the servants had sliced off juicy morsels, using long, sharp knives for the operation. In addition to these succulent pieces of meat, I had been offered an eye of the sheep as a special delicacy.

As we approached the Governor's small palace that morning, I remembered the earlier hospitality and the exotic ambience which had surrounded it and which had been in such pleasant contrast to the generally harsh environment which existed outside.

Shortly before our arrival at the palace, looking through the car window, I noticed that we had some company. A truck was following our car. In the back of the vehicle six heavily-armed soldiers were, apparently, escorting us. The militia wore normal Arab clothing; however, each man was weighed down with belts of bullets.

As I opened the door of the car, the leader of the armed group stepped forward and motioned that I should mount a stairway. The militia members noisily followed me up the stairs; at the top, their leader escorted me to a large doorway. I then walked the length of a long room until I found myself standing in front of the Governor; from his imposing, carved wooden chair he gestured to me to sit on his right. The Captain sat opposite me and prepared to assist with translation.

The Governor appeared to be in serious mood; as he watched me intensely, he uttered a few words of welcome and then invited me to raise any points I might wish.

I explained that, with his permission, I would like to raise four points. However, before embarking on these, I wished to draw the Governor's attention to the fact that the house rented by the ICAO resident engineer was without electricity; unfortunately, the main power cable had been accidentally severed. The lack of power had persisted for weeks and I would appreciate it if His Excellency would kindly give an assurance that the necessary steps would be taken to ensure that the power was restored within the next several days.

The intensity of the Governor's expression heightened. For a minute or so he simply looked at me. For my part, I did my best to maintain a pleasant countenance. Then the Governor said,

"I am surprised you have raised this matter with me. At my level, I have no involvement with such matters. My only interest is the construction of the airport. As Governor of this area, our power and prestige will be increased once the airport is ready for use. If there are any matters which require my intervention, then let us discuss these."

"Thank you, Excellency. The ICAO resident engineer has an extremely important function. He has to monitor all of the work which the contractor is performing to build the airport. On the advice of the ICAO resident engineer, we shall bring to bear whatever resources may be required to ensure that all of the work undertaken is properly supervised and tested for quality. The resident engineer may well need to work in his house during the evenings. We also regard it as important that the resident engineer has a reasonable degree of comfort; he cannot function properly without the availability of electrical power. If he is to give of his best in terms of his highly important supervisory duties, which in turn will ensure the best possible quality in the construction of the airport, then the electrical power will need to be restored, please."

It was clear that the Governor had no wish to continue any discussion on the point. He dismissed my explanation with a stroke of the hand. He would not become involved in the matter. Were there other questions to raise?

For my part, I expressed disappointment that such a straightforward matter could, apparently, not be dealt with. As for the remaining questions, I was sure that they would be resolved during the progress meeting which was scheduled to start the following morning. I thanked the Governor for having received me, stood up, shook his hand and bowed my head slightly in respect, after which I then began the long walk down the centre of the room; I was sorry that the unfortunate exchange had occurred and hoped the Governor would not harbour feelings of annoyance or, perhaps, anger.

As I hesitated at the top of the stairway, I was conscious that a degree of tension had been created, resulting from the exchanges between the Governor and myself. Initially, as I had walked up the centre of the room I had been impressed by the quietude of my surroundings; except for the sound of my shoes making contact with the wooden floor, all was still. As I continued walking, I suddenly noticed a young messenger who, barefoot, seemed to glide as he passed me; when he reached the top of the stairs he placed a note in the hand of one of the militia. The man read the note and, as I approached the top of the stairway, he fixed his eyes on me.

As I prepared to leave, the clanking of the militia's bullet belts disturbed the relative silence. Standing with the militia at the top of the stairway, I turned to the leader and gestured that he should go first. My gesture was met by a grim response; the man's eyes narrowed and he directed that I should be the first to go down. I was suddenly beginning to feel uncomfortable; I wanted to follow the militia, rather than precede them.

The discussion ended abruptly as the leader took my arm and half-pulled me down the top step. I slowly descended; after a few steps, I could hear the noise of the militia behind me as they heavily descended. When I was about half-way down the stairway, I heard a sound which was similar to the cocking of a rifle; I wondered why one of the militia should be positioning a bullet in the breach of his firearm as he descended the stairway. I stopped and turned around.

The militia stopped. I found myself looking at several expressionless faces; I lowered my eyes and looked into the barrels of their short rifles. The faces above stared at me. I continued my descent and felt relieved to reach the bottom of the stairway and the waiting car.

We were escorted on our departure in the same way as had been the case on our arrival. The militia accompanied us in their vehicle for about a half mile; then they had disappeared.

The following morning, the important progress meeting was scheduled to start at 8 a.m. We were all in good time for the meeting. On the arrival of the resident engineer, I wished him a good morning; it was indeed a good morning for him. He explained that the previous afternoon the electrical power had been restored to his house. Now he could function again fully.

After a particularly difficult week of discussions, negotiations and the passing of judgement on many complex issues, I left the hotel with my valued ICAO colleague, Kenneth Wilde, whose airport engineering expertise had proved to be of inestimable value. As we were driven to the airport at dawn, I confessed that we had indeed been trying to walk a tight-rope over the previous several days; a thin line had frequently divided the position held by the government and the situation as seen by the contractor. For ICAO to resolve various matters by giving the correct decision in each case had been a difficult test. Unfortunately, several of the decisions had not been in favour of the government; and we had said so. I still lacked confidence in the government's understanding of ICAO's role in ensuring fair judgement and consequent financial reward, or penalty, for the government or the contractor.

At last we found ourselves sitting in the aircraft, taxiing towards the runway threshold. We heard the roar of the engines as the Captain began to apply power for take-off; suddenly, he reduced power and returned to the parking apron. The Captain explained that he had been instructed by the control tower to return to the apron and await further instructions. I turned to Kenneth Wilde and wondered what had prevented us departing. The passengers silently waited for the next development.

As we heard the door open, we turned our heads and saw a man in a dark suit enter the aircraft. Immediately behind him were two soldiers; the shoulders of each supported a belt of cartridges in a diagonal position between the shoulder and the waist. The group made its way along the aisle of the aircraft and when they reached the mid-point, the man in the dark suit said,

"We are looking for two men; one is called Wilde and the other is called Everard."

I thought of the events of the previous week. I knew that certain personalities on the sides of both the contractor and the government had not been pleased with the outcome of discussions and the ensuing judgements which had been delivered on the part of ICAO. I had already been concerned with this fact when we were leaving the hotel and during our journey to the airport. Now, it seemed that the first results were beginning to show. There was certainly no reason to delay the departure of our fellow passengers; without hesitation we raised our arms to identify ourselves.

The small group made its way towards us; I wondered whether we should leave our seats to be taken off the aircraft. The man in the dark suit gestured to us to remain seated. Behind him stood the soldiers. The man with the dark suit smiled,

"Gentlemen, the Minister deeply regrets that due to the early departure of the aircraft, he was unable personally to say farewell to you at the airport. The Minister considers that each of you has been of great service to our country. As a token of our appreciation, the Minister wishes me to present to each of you, in accordance with our custom, one kilogram of coffee. Thank you gentlemen. The aircraft may now leave."

En route to Montreal, I stopped over in England for one night; I wanted to take the opportunity to see my father who was nearing the end of his life. I travelled by train to a country inn in a small town. Because I felt tired and mentally exhausted, I decided to try and sleep. The following morning, I would see my father. As I unpacked my suitcase in the small, rather cool room, a thought struck me; although I had been well fed on the flight, before going to bed it would be pleasant to drink a pint of bitter beer. I entered the bar of the hotel,

"A pint of bitter, please." The barman replied,

"Certainly, sir. As you can see, we have four brands of bitter here. Which do you prefer?"

I was not prepared for the question; my mental reaction was,

"Oh no! Not another decision!" The barman was looking at me questioningly; how could he know that I had participated in so many decisions over the previous week that I had reached the end of my span. After a few seconds I muttered,

"You decide. Thank you."

As the main elements of the airport were completed, each was subjected to rigorous acceptance testing. For example, before the runway was finally accepted, Kenneth Wilde slowly walked the entire length of the three thousand metre runway with technical counterparts of the government and the contractor; every apparent blemish was recorded and would later be rectified. In spite of the harsh environment, which included heat, humidity and blowing dust, the goal was to achieve a level of construction that would equate as near as possible to perfection.

About nine months before the completion of the airport, we in ICAO discussed with the government the requirements for the operation of the airport. The matter had been thoroughly studied some two years previously and all the main requirements had been itemised and explained. A development plan had been formulated and a meeting was held to assess the progress made under the plan. Most infrastructural developments were in place and progress was satisfactory. However, one area which appeared to have been neglected was that which concerned rescue and fire-fighting facilities. This need was therefore given emphasis during our discussions and a proposal was submitted to the government under which ICAO's CAPS would purchase the equipment and assist in the specialised training of the staff.

Two or three months before the formal opening of the airport, the Minister was discussing with me the government's invitation list for the opening. In the case of ICAO, invitations to attend the formal opening would be extended to the President and Secretary General. I asked the Minister whether the rescue and fire-fighting facilities would be in place. I was sure he would appreciate that without such facilities the airport opening should not take place. Should the government decide nevertheless to proceed with the opening without adequate facilities, then the government should be aware that ICAO was unlikely to be represented. For ICAO to have been associated with an airport which had inadequate rescue and fire-fighting services would simply have been a contradiction in terms.

From the exaggerated reaction which ensued, it seemed clear that little action had been taken to organise the airport's rescue and fire-fighting facilities. The government made immediate arrangements for the purchase and supply of several fire-fighting vehicles, including those capable of 'rapid intervention'; urgent arrangements were made to train the staff to operate these specialised vehicles.

The formal opening took place on schedule and a number of visiting dignitaries arrived and departed safely by air, with the required rescue and fire-fighting facilities in place.

Some months later, a turbo jet passenger aircraft was commencing its take-off from the country *en route* to Europe. One of the engines caught fire, causing the Captain to abort his take-off. By the time the aircraft had been brought to a standstill, the wing was on fire and it seemed that the aircraft, full of passengers, would soon be engulfed. The airport rescue and fire-fighting teams were, however, highly-trained and at the ready. The fire-fighting vehicles were already in position and smothered the flames with foam. All the passengers escaped injury and the fire was immediately extinguished.

Over the last fifty years (ICAO celebrated its fiftieth anniversary in 1994) there have been a number of occasions where the effect of ICAO's intervention in seeing its Standards and Recommended Practices adhered to, has resulted not only in the raising of civil aviation safety standards, but also in the saving of lives. Such occasions rarely come to the notice of the travelling public.

Globally, more than a billion people board an aircraft for a flight each year. Statistically, flying is the safest means of transportation; in terms of statistical probability, it is much safer to travel by air, for example, than to travel by road. To the extent that the majority of the flying public takes aviation safety for granted, this is a reflection of, and a tribute to, the disciplined professionalism and dedication of those who work in a broad spectrum of activities in the aviation industry. If aviation safety is to be maintained, there is only one standard – the highest.

Fig. 25   The arrival of the 'big bird' not only illustrates cultural and technological contrasts; the aeroplane is the main link with the outside world and its arrival can be cause for a party.

Fig. 26   *Imaginative conceptual planning in airport site selection, taking a multitude of engineering, economic and other factors into account, is of far-reaching importance.*

Fig. 27   *Completion of the runway represents a major step in the construction of the airport and its facilities.*

Fig. 28   *A newly constructed air traffic control tower - the nerve-centre for the airport's operations. In the foreground is a highly sophisticated rescue and fire-fighting vehicle.*

Fig. 29   *'Selling' ideas - the constant preoccupation.*

Y.Y.Kim, Resident		*Turhan Mangun, formerly of*
Co-ordinator,	*The author.*	*the Economic and Social*
United Nations		*Commission for Asia and the*
Development		*Pacific, later to become*
Programme		*Resident Co-ordinator,*
		United Nations Development
		Programme.

Fig. 30   *The first powered aeroplane to fly in Canada; Baddeck, Nova Scotia, 1909 (picture by courtesy of the National Museum of Science and Technology, Canada).*

Chapter Sixteen

Mission for Flight Safety

The signatories to the 1944 Convention on International Civil Aviation agreed on arrangements aimed at developing international civil aviation "in a safe and orderly manner... " Within the aviation community, if one were to ask someone how he or she would describe the mission of ICAO, the Convention's offspring, the response would usually be: 'flight safety'. Flight safety means safety in the widest sense; practically every component of the aviation system ultimately contributes to flight safety.

The developing world tends to see ICAO in a rather different light to that of the developed world. The countries of the developed world are the leaders of technology and systems; in general, the developing world follows.

Although the developed countries normally deal with the Regular Programme of ICAO, many of the developing countries are mainly interested in ICAO's Technical Co-operation Bureau. Some of them consider the TCB to personify ICAO, primarily because the professional ICAO personnel to whom many developing countries are most exposed are the staff fielded under development co-operation arrangements, usually with third-party financing.

And when we discuss the developing world, in terms of the number of countries which are categorised as 'developing', what is the ratio between developed and developing countries? Although with the currently fashionable nationalist fervour one cannot be precise in terms of numbers, there are roughly thirty countries which, depending on the criteria used, could claim to be regarded as developed; in addition, there are some hundred and fifty developing countries in our world. This gives a ratio of one to five. Or one could say that rather over 80% of the number of countries in our world are developing countries. In varying degrees, most of these countries look to ICAO for practical assistance and advice, based on ICAO's Standards, Recommended Practices, Agreements, Information Circulars, Manuals and other guidance material.

Within the aviation community, ICAO is particularly important for the developing countries. When projects are planned to support civil aviation development, ICAO is often a catalyst between the national Director General of Civil Aviation, the financing ministry and (as is often needed) the external funding institution. It is ICAO's objectively knowledgeable information and advice which will often affect the critical decision whether to proceed or otherwise.

Working in the field of civil aviation development co-operation with the Third World, as one's career progressed one increasingly 'lived' the work. It was not a question that someone might become a workaholic; a workaholic is often a person who sees work as some sort of refuge. Workaholics are sometimes people with marital problems, or perhaps they may experience complications in their relationships with their children. There is a difference between the workaholic and someone who, because of the demands of his or her job, has to spend long hours dealing with issues, consciously sacrificing the enjoyment of family life.

So why should I, for example, find that increasingly I was 'living' my work? First, I was dealing with the development and implementation of projects in Asia. The time difference between Montreal and Bangkok, for example, is twelve hours. Although a number of telephone calls were received during our office hours, if the caller in Asia wanted to speak with me from his office, then his call would come to my house at night; it was not unusual, therefore, to receive telephone calls at one a.m. or two a.m. Second, the projects with which ICAO was involved were in the nature of hands-on, operational activities, which meant that issues would need early discussion and resolution, if dislocation and delay in the work was to be avoided. With eighty projects under implementation and another thirty in various stages of negotiation, the need for discussion on certain points could arise at any time. Third, as the confidence factor with civil aviation administrations would grow over the years, increasingly there was a tendency for Directors General of Civil Aviation, or their colleagues, to call us for objective, independent advice.

In such a dynamically active working environment, a component which would prove to be of critical importance was the undertaking of properly organised official missions to various countries. How did the need for an official mission arise; how would it be planned and carried out?

Within some organisational entities, missions (or tours) by senior executives are carried out at regular intervals, say once or twice each year. Within the field of technical co-operation, we ran a 'lean' ship; unless there were sound reasons, then there would be no basis at all for undertaking a mission.

However, missions would always be needed. In practice, only so much can be achieved by the written word; in order to 'move' a situation, face-to-face discussions with senior people were essential, especially since, if a project were to proceed, officials from such ministries as transportation and communications, planning, economic affairs, external assistance or foreign affairs would all need to agree on a certain course of action.

We were also conscious of the reality of the nature of progress. The signing of important agreements usually takes place in appropriately fine surroundings, sometimes in the presence of important invited guests. However, before this point can be reached, an enormous amount of work has to be undertaken by officials; based on a basic idea, a project has to be drafted and costed. Over the following months, sometimes years, the draft is considered and shaped to take account of government priorities; in the end, it has to be financed.

Sometimes, after exhaustive discussions on a proposed project, a point of deadlock might be reached. I recall such a situation arising in one of the least developed countries. After two years' negotiation, when various parties found that they were unable to reach a final consensus, the Minister of Civil Aviation invited all those concerned to a cocktail party. During the party, he announced that he had arranged for a river cruise for all the involved officials the following day. Once on the large boat, the Minister announced that we had a good day's work ahead of us. He would authorise the return of the boat only when he had received definite information that the project objectives and activities had been finally agreed; he would also need confirmation that full financing arrangements were in place. In terms of aviation safety, the proposed project was important; and it was clear the Minister strongly supported the project. At last, all aspects of the project were agreed. And the boat returned to port.

In practice, apart from project development possibilities, we found that over the months different types of situations would build up in various countries. For example, a proposed project which had been under negotiation for three or four years, might be unexpectedly held up at the time it should have been finally approved; in such a case, we would want to prepare the ground for discussions aimed at clearing the way for the project's signature.

Again, there was always the possibility that an ICAO project co-ordinator was experiencing some local problems; these could involve the funding organisation or, possibly, a member of the national counterpart personnel. If the project co-ordinator over-stepped the mark, he might find himself placed in an untenable position; once a certain stage had been reached, it was far preferable for the matter to be discussed and resolved by an ICAO visiting official from the regional office or from ICAO headquarters. On other occasions, reports of a detailed project review would be discussed between the government, the funding organisation and ICAO; in such cases, representation from an ICAO regional office or from headquarters would be desirable.

The need for an official mission would arise in a natural way, in the sense that as one reviewed the civil aviation project development and implementation situation at any given stage, well-substantiated reasons would surface which, eventually, would convince us that the undertaking of the mission would be warranted and, we hoped, would be cost-effective; apart from the issue of resolving problems, because we needed to conduct our operations within the limited overhead which we received, the factor of cost and likely resultant effectiveness always had to be taken into account.

Once the proposed official mission had been discussed and agreed internally, we would then plan the mission; this would be done, at worst, to the nearest half-day and at best (depending on flight schedules), to the nearest two hours. Messages would then be dispatched through the United Nations Development Programme (UNDP), which maintained lead offices in the various countries, proposing the dates of a mission and the subjects to be discussed. Typically, the mission would include meetings in four to six countries; although we sometimes felt justified in visiting more countries, we recognised that the fatigue factor would almost certainly lead to diminished performance as the mission progressed.

On one occasion in an Asian country, I had been having discussions covering a proposed expansion of a civil aviation project. Between meetings, the local project co-ordinator asked me whether I would be prepared to address a group of students who were attending a course at a regional civil aviation training centre; the group comprised students from a number of countries in the Asia and Pacific regions. I responded I would be happy to do so; the problem was that a schedule of meetings had been arranged which would continue up to the time of my departure for the next stage of the mission. However, I mentioned that there would be about a half hour available during a lunch period; if the students were prepared to assemble at that time, I would be happy to address them.

During a lecture period of some twenty minutes, I endeavoured to describe the civil aviation development situation generally and, specifically, as it related to Asian and Pacific countries. I left ten minutes for questions.

The first question was voiced along the following lines,

"You seem to have landed yourself a very nice job and I suppose you are paid a bomb. All you seem to do is to globe-trot. And think of all the interesting places you visit! How did you manage to get that job? But what a waste of money!"

I thanked the questioner for the directness of his question. I would be equally direct in my response. First, it was quite true that I visited many interesting places; my problem was that time was never available to see the sights. The only part of the geography of Asia where I felt that, through first-hand experience, I was a real expert, was the geography of meeting rooms in various countries. In a period of eighteen days, I would be involved in forty-seven high-level meetings in five countries. Each of the in-country meetings would be related to trying to reach a certain objective; some of the meetings would be concerned with reaching an agreement which would impact on a certain course of action in other countries. Would the questioner like to try my job for a few days? Did he know what it was like to maintain a peak performance during a gruelling schedule of travel and meetings. Did he know that to command respect, one should not only be thoroughly conversant with a subject, but during the discussions it was expected that the ICAO representative would normally know more about, or shed a new light on, the subject than anyone else in the room. And did he know that projects do not just 'happen'; individuals have to discuss concepts, which in turn are followed by detailed discussions and negotiations. Had he ever tried to convince a finance ministry to support a project for civil aviation knowing that, before one had entered the room, the finance officials had agreed that they would not finance the project; after all, with a limited budget, what about health, food and education? Why not take safe aviation for granted; it is safe, is it not? Somehow, one must help to inform, to 'sell' ideas, taking into account the national politics of the country; to sway, until eventually one would overcome stubborn resistance and eventually the officials would change their minds.

The costs of my questioner's airfare, tuition, board and lodging were met by a civil aviation training project; did he understand that such a project needed to be financed? Did he understand that technical assistance practitioners from ICAO spent their working lives helping to identify civil aviation weaknesses, discussing how they might be overcome, outlining a project proposal, seeking agreement on the key features of the proposed project, assisting in the drafting of the project documentation and using their good offices to see the project financed and approved?

Once the project had been approved it would need to be implemented. Some projects were large and complex. Many problems would arise during the implementation phase, which might extend over a period of several years; and timely monitoring and evaluation work would have to be undertaken. Typically, during a mission to Asia, someone like myself would spend sixty-five to seventy hours sitting in an aircraft; for most of this time, one would either be preparing for the meetings ahead or compiling concise reports on meetings which would now be 'history'. Although I could have continued the question and answer period, my time had run out and I was driven to my next meeting.

About two years later, on behalf of ICAO I attended a regionally-convened meeting. One of the participants was the questioner whom I had met during that lunch break at the regional training centre. He had now risen to the rank of Deputy Director in his civil aviation administration; I congratulated him on his appointment. With a sense of humour and some charm, he recalled his question of two years previously. Since then, he had learned a lot and he wanted me to know that he understood what I was doing; no repetition of my explanation was necessary! We became good colleagues and firm friends.

When we hear of 'Asia and Pacific', what sort of image does this conjure in our minds? Perhaps many would think of the Buddhist temples and culture of Thailand, the skyscrapers of Singapore, the rich variety of the geography and peoples of the vast country of Indonesia, the temples of India, the sand and sea of the Maldive Islands, the archaeological sites or the beauty of the valleys of Northern Pakistan, the Himalayas of Nepal and Bhutan, or the welcoming tranquillity of the Pacific Islands; the images seem endless.

However, in the field of technical co-operation, we concentrated on areas of weakness in the network of civil aviation facilities and services. This meant that, often, we were travelling and working in countries which, for the tourist at least, would be regarded as off the beaten track; it was in these countries that the need for support to the civil aviation infrastructure was clearly evident. The countries had sometimes been the victims of political upheavals or they had not yet been able to raise themselves from a state of poverty.

If one is to make an effective contribution to the field of development co-operation, a pre-requisite is a knowledge of the politics and culture of the countries of a region, linked with an understanding of what is, or what may not be, possible in the given circumstances. As we all know, even with the most thorough preparation possible, factors may well intervene which will prevent the achievement of objectives of development co-operation.

Sometimes, on my return from an exhausting mission, I would meet a friend who would say,

"You've been away again, Colin; did you have a successful mission?"

Apart from recording that, in conjunction with my colleagues, all I could do was my best, I would say,

"Success? We shall only know that in four or five years' time!"

Although much serious business was discussed during missions, the lighter side sometimes intervened to take one's mind off the relentless pace of consultations. For example, on one occasion I flew without a stop-over from Montreal to Manila in the Philippines. As I made my way out of the airport, I was already relishing the idea of a comfortable hotel bed. A driver met me and commented that the aircraft's arrival had been an hour late; I responded that within an overall flight time of nineteen hours which had brought one to the other side of the world, perhaps the delay was acceptable. As we reached the city, the driver made a detour; we were first to visit the project co-ordinator's house. There, a large party was in full swing.

The project co-ordinator explained that the following evening we would be attending an official function; during the late afternoon on the day after, I would be departing for Bangkok. So he had decided that the first evening was the only time available for a party. Eventually, when I was dropped at the hotel at 2 a.m., the driver mentioned that I would be picked up at 7.30 a.m. for the first official meeting.

Two days later, with several meetings behind us, before departing for my onward flight to Bangkok I managed to write a letter to the government confirming the understandings reached. Now I could relax; as the following day was a Saturday, I would go straight to bed in the Bangkok hotel. I could be asleep by 10.30; what a wonderful thought!

When you are really tired, sometimes you remember that moment when true relaxation would begin. And so it was in this case. Consumed by fatigue, I remember my head sinking into the softest pillow in the world! Within seconds, with a feeling of deep relaxation, I sank into a serene slumber.

As I slept peacefully, in the distance I could hear the faint sound of the ringing of a telephone. It persisted. Was I dreaming? Now it should stop; let me sleep properly. Gradually, my consciousness began to rise; the ringing became louder. I suddenly realised that the ringing was next to my bed.

"Hello," I said.

"Hello, Colin."

I recognised the voice of one of my Thai colleagues.

"Good evening," I said, "How did you know I had arrived? Our first meeting is not until Monday."

"We like to keep an eye open for our guests, you know. You sound fine! I am ringing to say that we have arranged a game of golf; we are the first to hit off in the morning. So we'll pick you up at your hotel at 5 a.m. I suggest you arrange a wake-up call at 4.30 a.m. We are looking forward to having you with us. Good night."

We had a great game!

As the ICAO Civil Aviation Purchasing Service developed, demands were increasingly made on our time to respond to a number of requests for assistance; in a nutshell, the objective of CAPS was being achieved. Today, over fifty registrations have been made by various civil aviation government agencies to utilise CAPS.

One request involved an African country which sought ICAO CAPS assistance in obtaining some complex and expensive aeronautical equipment.   As always, the requirement for the equipment was urgent.

In fact, however urgent the need for certain equipment might be, early delivery of major equipment was rarely achieved; the case in point was no exception. If money was to be spent properly on equipment, studies were essential to identify the parameters and potential degree of usage of the equipment, after which the equipment would need to be specified in detail; a statement of requirements might well have extended to one or two hundred pages.   The documentation would then be circulated to qualified bidders, who typically needed about three months (sometimes longer) to prepare their detailed technical and commercial offers. The offers were then evaluated;   and the more complex the equipment, the longer the evaluation would take.   From the commercial aspect, financing arrangements had to be considered, discussed and agreed. It would only be on completion of all of this work that the contract could be issued.

Depending on the equipment to be delivered, another one to two years would elapse before the equipment had been manufactured to the specification and this would be recognised only after the completion of a factory testing procedure; once the equipment arrived at the operational site, it needed to be installed and, after testing, finally accepted for commissioning.

It was also necessary to take into account that the contract work was not confined to the contractor.   Often, specially designed buildings had to be erected by the buyer to house the new equipment; apart from assuring a stable power supply (a requirement which frequently presented a problem in developing countries), interior environmental conditions (temperature and humidity) had to be strictly controlled.

Although all of these factors were explained at length in a letter to the responsible officials in the African country, from their responses it was clear that they were under pressure within their government to obtain the quickest results possible. In order therefore to help move the project forward, it was agreed that I should visit the country and discuss with the civil aviation authorities how best to proceed. After several exchanges of telegraphic messages, the date of my visit was established. On arrival at my destination, I would stay overnight in the capital city and the following day I would be contacted in the hotel; I would then be driven to the airport where a light aircraft would bring me to the up-country town where the initial discussions would be held.

Two weeks later, I arrived in the country and took a taxi to the hotel. Routinely, I completed the check-in card; I was then asked to show it to the cashier a few steps away. This man checked over the card in great detail and seemed to act more in the nature of a suspicious immigration official than an employee of the hotel whose job it was to serve the clientele. After a few points had been clarified, he looked up sharply and stated with an air of finality that I should pay in advance for the period of my stay. I responded that I was carrying traveller's cheques and would normally expect to pay on departure. The man became rather irritated and said,

"Mr. Everard, you have two choices; you can pay now in advance, or you can return to the street. This is a busy city and all the hotels are full."

As I began to sign the first traveller's cheque, we were plunged into darkness; the power supply had failed. Immediately, my traveller's cheque was illuminated by the light of a torch; apparently, breaks in the power supply were common and the cashier was well prepared for the eventuality. Once the necessary payment had been made, I was escorted to my room by a porter. Even though the journey had been tiring and the hotel checking-in procedure trying, it was not easy to sleep properly since the air-conditioning system was not working.

I had expected to be contacted early the following morning by the pilot of the light aircraft. Since no one appeared, I asked at the reception whether there was a message for me. On being told that there was no message, I requested assistance in making a telephone call to my final destination. Since it was a Sunday, I suggested that it would be better to try the number of a personal house first; should there be no response, then one could try the office number. I was asked to wait a few minutes while an attempt was made to make the telephone call.

I sat in the lobby and re-read my briefing papers. As the delay in making the call persisted, I read various newspapers and magazines. After two and a half hours and having made several enquiries, I was beginning to wonder whether another method might be considered which would result in success.

Just at that moment, a young hotel employee approached me from the Bell Captain's area.

"Good morning, Mr. Everard," he said, "I have been watching you for almost three hours. You are one of the most patient men I have ever seen. You want a telephone call, don't you?"

"Yes, I do."

"I am sorry to disappoint you, but if you ask the reception to help you with a telephone call, it will never go through. May I suggest, sir, open the door over there, walk down the corridor and when you come to the second door on the right, knock twice."

When I reached the second door I was confronted by the following sign:

HOTEL TELEPHONE EXCHANGE
POSITIVELY NO ADMITTANCE
NO EXCEPTIONS

I knocked twice. The door was opened by a large, confident-looking woman; she was smiling broadly, which revealed a set of perfectly white, shining teeth. Although I am six feet tall, I found myself looking up at the welcoming, almost motherly, expression on the face of the woman; her beautiful, lively eyes positively shone as she looked at me expectantly. She was of heavy build and her generous, colourful dress made her look broader than was probably the case. Her puffy sleeves reflected the influence of the early missionaries. She said,

"You must be Mr. Everard. I am so pleased to meet you. Please come in." The door was firmly closed behind me.

"Would you like a cup of tea, sir?" The tea had already been made; as she poured it into the cup, she smiled again and said, "I understand you have a very important call to make up-country."

"Exactly."

"I should love to help you, Mr. Everard and I can certainly do so. I hope you won't mind if I mention that it is the custom in our country that if we give a special favour, then we receive a reward."

The woman had placed me in a predicament. I had never paid a reward in my life and, in principle, I would never countenance such an unsavoury, wasteful practice. On the other hand, I needed the telephone call; unless my travel arrangements could soon be resolved, the cost to my Organisation of achieving precisely nothing would far exceed a small bribe; on reflection, perhaps I was considering a tip!

I had sometimes heard bribery being discussed outside ICAO; I had never participated in the discussions and, as soon as the subject was approached, I had walked away. What was I to do now? By ignoring the local custom, was I being a pompous Englishman; should I, like the proverbial ostrich, immerse my head in the sand?

I recalled that the previous evening, at the time that the traveller's cheques had been extracted from me by the cashier, I had taken the opportunity to obtain some local currency. I turned away from the woman, looked into my wallet and pulled out a large note. Although I had not been able to check the notes properly the previous evening due to the lack of light, I could see in the corner of the note a somewhat bent '1'.

Turning round, I handed the note to the large woman and said that I hoped this would be considered appropriate as a gesture of appreciation for making my important call. The woman took the note and held it in front of her. Her pleasant face was transformed into an expression of ecstatic happiness. She began to giggle and the smile seemed to get wider by the second. The woman embraced me; my initial effort to resist the hug was ignored. I was powerless in the grip of this strong woman; there was no contest. As the hug strengthened, my face was pressed to her generous bosoms; within a few seconds I was wondering whether I might suffocate. In an endeavour to escape the hug, I began to jump up and down. At last, I had been released.

Breathlessly, I suggested that while I drank some tea, perhaps the woman could try and make the telephone call. Within two minutes she had made contact with the first, personal number.

''Oh! He is still in bed. Is that so! You mean he has overslept. Wake him up and tell him that Mr. Everard is on the line.''

A minute or two later my sleepy colleague spoke to me. He was sorry there had been some confusion about the dates; he would arrange to send the aircraft. Since it was a Sunday, perhaps I would stay for another night in the hotel and I would be picked up the following morning.

As I came to the end of my call, the door opened and a man entered.

"Can you please tell me what is going on? Several hotel guests have complained to me that they cannot get a response from the switchboard. What is happening?" The large woman looked at the intruder with scorn.

"Nothing is happening, except Mr. Everard and I are engaged in highly important business! Until the business has been done, nothing else will happen."

The large woman then advanced towards the man, placed her hands under his armpits, raised him a few inches above the ground and transported him through the door which he had just entered; as she replaced him on the floor, I was reminded of a shop model being moved from one place to another. The woman closed the door and turned to me.

"I want you to know, Mr. Everard, that as long as you stay in the hotel, your calls will receive the highest priority. Is there anything else that I can do for you now, sir?" I explained that my travel problem had been resolved and I hoped I would not have to seek further assistance.

"Incidentally," I asked, "Who was that man who was complaining?"

"He is only the Manager – but *I* look after the switchboard!"

When I had returned to my room, I examined the contents of my wallet carefully, especially the local currency which I had obtained in the torchlight the previous evening.

I soon realised that the basic currency unit was the '1'. There was also a larger note which represented a unit of '10'; just as the '1' was bent, so the '0' was printed in irregular form; I had not noticed the '0'. My intended gesture of appreciation had been multiplied by ten. Since, through the efforts of this large, affectionate woman I was enabled to pursue my professional endeavours successfully in her country, I did not begrudge the personal donation I had made to her happiness.

Although, looking back, there were numerous incidents which were laced with unpredictable humour, one also recognised that, in their own way, they were often essential ingredients of progress. In this particular case, the catalytic telephone call enabled an important multi-million dollar project to be discussed, planned and implemented. Another positive step had been taken on the road to aviation safety.

There were also incidents which were devoid of humour. Occasionally, they might be dangerous. It was on these occasions that the attentive eye of the Guardian Angel reminded me that he had not become bored and fallen asleep; he never failed me.

Chapter Seventeen

Relax to Recharge

From time to time, all of us need a rest. For those who do not accept this fact, or lack the discipline to detach themselves from their work to generate new strength, it is only a matter of time before nature will intervene; heart attacks, strokes, nervous breakdowns or simply grinding to a halt, are often signs that a worker has neglected his or her mental and physical health. There are few more embarrassing, or sometimes irritating, situations than to see someone pathetically pursuing tasks with a 'burnt out' energy system. The maintenance of good health should be regarded as a personal responsibility, especially for those in positions of executive leadership.

A person dedicated to making a significant contribution to a certain field of endeavour will have to work hard if the contribution is to be realised. Especially if one works in an operational capacity, there will be many stresses and strains; and normal working hours are rarely sufficient to fulfil all of the pressing requirements of one's job. It is in these circumstances that good management, organisation and discipline come into their own. The job must be managed in such a way that, on the one hand, all of the work demands are met and, on the other, time is still available to 'recharge the batteries' through recreation and the occasional holidays.

If one lives in the eastern half of Canada, for example in Montreal, there are a number of ways in which one can enjoy recreation. However, if the enjoyment is to be pursued in the vicinity of Montreal, then the seasonal climate factor will need to be taken into account.

Although brief summers can be hot, in general one could argue that although Canadians are a warm-hearted people, the eastern half of Canada is a cold country. Even leaving aside the Arctic wastes to the north, if you live in Quebec, then you know that the winter period will usually last some six months. The first snow will fall in early or mid-November. You should not expect to play on a golf course until well into the following May; in the hilly areas, the opening of the golf courses will be delayed until the end of May or even early June.

Canadians often assert that their country has virtually no spring; although this is not always the case, quite frequently spring-like weather is indeed brief. At the beginning of June, the temperature will sometimes rise significantly and one is persuaded that, at last, spring has arrived. I have known many occasions when ten days later there is a sudden drop in the temperature; once again, the heating would be brought into operation.

After a three-month summer it is already time for the commencement of autumn, or fall. Many believe the fall to be the most beautiful period of the year. Sunny days and crisp nights are a time for enjoyment. As you drive, cycle or walk through a Canadian woodland in the fall, the colours of the leaves will overpower your mind by sheer beauty; the depth, richness and variations of these colours could never be adequately described. They have to be seen to be believed.

Towards the end of October, as the temperatures sink and rough weather approaches, often from the Great Lakes, one may be saddened by the falling of the leaves. Soon, the first snow will arrive.

Between spring and fall, apart from enjoying a game of golf or tennis, one of the finest recreations which one can pursue in Canada is fishing. For fourteen consecutive years, I would drive with our children for a few hours northwards to spend three or four wonderful days in the Park de la Vérendrye.

When we had left East Africa, I had imagined that we would never again experience anything similar to the wild country, dusty roads, limitless horizons and the roaming wild animals. I was wrong. As one drives northwards from Montreal through the Laurentian Mountains, one leaves behind the farmland; the transition to the landscape of virtually uninhabited bush, rivers and lakes is rapid. If you turn off the main road, you soon find yourself in an environment which seems to have several of the characteristics which one had imagined had been left behind in Africa. For example, you may walk up a dry river-bed strewn with dry roots and trunks of trees. You may, as we did, practically step on to a good-sized viper.

When driving on a bush track, the wheels will throw up a cloud of dust, a few grains of which will also find their way into the car and, perhaps, on to your tongue. On our first fishing trip, after leaving the main road we headed down a track bound for Lake Cabonga. The children were happy and sang as we bumped along. As I looked in the mirror I could see the dust belching out behind us; lowering my eyes, I expected to see a row of happy children's faces. To my surprise, Marci looked a little sad and I could see a tear rolling down her cheek. "You were so happy, Marci; what is it?" The response was poignantly direct,

"It is so beautiful here, Daddy, and we are so happy; and the dust reminds me of Kenya. I loved it there!"

Although some of the characteristics of the countryside were reminiscent of East Africa, there were others which one would always associate with Canada. For example, the vast expanses of water in Canada and the northern part of the United States, in particular, are nothing less than astounding. We are not only talking of huge expanses of water as typified by the Great Lakes. There are many areas, such as the Park de la Vérendrye, where lakes of all sizes abound. I have made reference to Cabonga; this is an expanse of water of a hundred square miles. There are probably another hundred lakes, each ranging in size from one to several square miles in extent.

The type of wildlife which one finds in Canada represents another difference. When you have been visited by a large bear at night, intent on stealing a catch of fish, you will carry the image in your memory for the rest of your life. On hearing the arrival of the bear, one would shine a torch and be surprised by the large, loping form of the visitor caught in a shaft of torchlight; soon, it would disappear in the thick, dark woodland. The excitement, including the challenge of overcoming fear, is something that the children will never forget.

The moose was also an inhabitant of the Park. Returning to camp in our small boat in the early evening, sometimes one of us would have a sighting of the largest deer on earth. Measuring 8 feet at the shoulder, we would watch this impressive animal as it would majestically appear from the forest and wade into the shallows of the lake, attracted by water lilies. As we would quietly approach, the moose would raise its head, crowned by massive antlers; it would pick up our scent, turn and disappear into the forest.

Marci was our mentor during our fishing excursions. With her knowledge and encouragement we were to catch some fine Walleye and Northern Pike. We always camped (something to which I needed no introduction) and over the years we acquired good equipment, which enabled us to be comfortable and self-sufficient during our stay in the wilderness-like surroundings.

For thorough relaxation and recreation, one could not ask for more than the serenity of a few days' fishing, occasionally punctuated by the added interest of hooking a fish. On the water, a change of weather could also generate excitement and a sense of adventure, as our lonely boat would hug the lake shoreline on our slow return through the choppy waves and rain to the warmth of our camp.

The most important element of these recreational excursions was that you were out of reach of the office; out of contact, the frequent ringing of the telephone was put to rest. The recharging of the batteries meant that one returned to the busy world of technical co-operation with renewed vigour.

During the winter months, along with thousands of Canadians, one would ski for recreation. Because of the severe winter conditions which so often included low temperatures, wind and ice, the challenge which was faced was considerable; one felt that if one could ski to a reasonable standard in those conditions, then probably one should be able to ski with competence in virtually any skiing area of the world.

It was during difficult conditions that I had a skiing accident. A few days later, I felt it might be interesting if I were to record the circumstances of the accident and the feelings which were uppermost in my mind at the time. The following passage is the diary that I wrote:

THE SKI PATROL

(or the diary of a bureaucratic skier)

I have always enjoyed physical challenge. For the desk-bound bureaucrat, whether in industry, commerce, a vocation or a government, skiing offers not only relaxation but as much instantaneous physical challenge as anyone could seek. It was with these thoughts in mind that a short while ago, after a particularly hectic three months in the office, I decided to put it all behind me for one glorious day and ski with one of my charming daughters, Marci. Although that particular Friday was not exactly one of the more inspiring in terms of the weather, we were however fortunate in that it was not incredibly cold, nor was a blizzard imminent; and the fact that Marci had acquired a fine pair of new ski boots that week provided us with a good reason to try them out.

We chose a big mountain. As we sat in the chairlift we occasionally caught a glimpse of blue sky as the rather low veils of cloud were blown rapidly across the wintry sun. I always think of a chair on a cable as an island in space. You are out of contact with Mother Earth and, except for your companion sitting next to you, you are cut off, if not remote, from your fellow human beings. For me, the chairlift is a place for thought, a seat from where, as you rise up the mountain, if you purse your lips you can 'drink' in the wonderfully clean, crisp mountain air; and it is a pedestal from which you can indulge in sheer visual pleasure, whether looking down at a sea of soft green fir trees (a scene which often changes to a silvery white wonderland as you reach higher altitudes), or looking up to the azure above. Sometimes, when the green and blue meet on a brief horizon one is reminded of the saying, 'Blue and green should never be seen'. When you have seen them meet on a mountain, you can have no doubt that they should.

The wind was blowing quite hard on top of the mountain and we found that, with it blowing on our backs, we could traverse the white expanse effortlessly; I watched little Marci, like a figurine, moving gracefully in the icy conditions high up on the shoulder of the mountain. Soon we would be below the top and perhaps it would be more sheltered.

"Let's try that run over there," I tried to shout above the wind. Marci nodded and we traversed towards it. As we were about to descend, I noticed the ski patrol helping a young girl on to a stretcher. We have all seen the ski patrol, but few of us have contact with them. Perhaps we have thought from time to time that they are undoubtedly excellent skiers; we know they can help in an emergency, but happily this particular *raison d'être* does not concern the majority of us.

I hesitated. The first part of the descent was a little steep and uneven. It must be tricky, I thought, for the ski patrol to manipulate the stretcher down a section like that. Marci and I watched them for a few moments.

"Instead of going straight down here, we can easily ski by the side of the main run over there, down that narrow trail through the trees; we can cut back at the bottom and we shall be ahead of the ski patrol. Then we won't press them or distract them. Let's go."

Down we went, back and forth, descending rapidly, rather as though we were plunging down a huge, uneven stairway. Now and then the skis were noisy as they bit into and scraped the icy patches. Three-quarters of the way down that stretch, I stopped to watch Marci a short distance above me. She was descending safely and looked elegant in her new boots. So I went on.

Then it happened. What happened? I do not know exactly and the details will remain, as far as I am concerned, one of the unsolved mysteries of the world. In those few seconds, a ski loomed up in front of me and I found myself incredulously wondering why the safety binding had not yet opened. My glasses were smashed. And my ankle was first twisted one way and then ripped the other. A thought flashed,

"Now you've really done it." And I was right.

I lay in the snow, perhaps a little dazed, and noticed the red droplets around me in the virgin whiteness; then, I thought, I should at least sit up. My boots were still firmly held in the bindings; like any other average skier, I had fallen from time to time and those bindings had opened without fail. Now Marci was next to me. In a helpful, gentle way, Marci opened the bindings and released the safety straps. Now we could take stock of our suddenly new situation. Raising my right leg to test the strength in my ankle, I was reminded of lifting a solid, heavy lump of sirloin when bargain hunting in a supermarket a week previously. It was heavy, lifeless and apparently cold. The ankle was useless and it was pointless to pretend otherwise.

While we were discussing our quickest approach to the ski patrol, a band of young people appeared above us. In turn, each stopped next to us on the narrow trail, gave us a quick glance – and sped on. I was obviously an obstacle which needed careful circumvention. Another young skier then studied me for several seconds and seemed to wonder if I had hurt myself. She was evidently not convinced; having satisfied her curiosity, she quickly disappeared from view.

Three thousand feet up on a windy afternoon, and lying helplessly on a thinly covered patch of ice on a little-used trail, is not the most encouraging of situations. Marci would have called the ski patrol, but she was not certain that she would again find our spot; so we decided to stay together for the moment.

And then we received our most welcome visitor, an excellent skier who stopped in an instant and said little; but he had an expression on his face which said, "I've seen this before".

"Broken?" he asked.

"I don't know." As he fleetingly left us I heard the words,

"I'll let them know."

Half an hour went by. We talked a little, agreed it was getting colder and every couple of minutes we glanced above us at the narrow, empty, darkening slope. As always there was hope; but as time passed, it was not easy to avoid a feeling of apprehension and, perhaps, a trace of anxiety. Then a heavy form appeared at the top of the slope.

"Here they are, Marci."

Of course our instant friend had kept his word; he has the right to know that I shall feel eternally grateful. The ski patrol had found us.

Jim and Peter were physical opposites. Jim, who managed the stretcher, was tall, lanky and blue-eyed; Peter was short, compactly built and dark, but they worked in perfect unison. Chatting amiably, they asked me a few questions and, within five minutes, the lower part of my leg was in a splint. After the other leg was secured to the injured one, they carried me gently on to the stretcher, wrapped me in blankets and firmly battened me down. After a brief enquiry about my comfort, Jim held the sledge boom and announced,

"Now we are ready for the voyage."

The sledge stretcher began to move, initially slowly, over the hard packed powder. We were *en route*. Marci would meet us later at the bottom of the mountain.

The trip down was uneventful. At one stage, Jim suggested I should raise my head to see for myself a particularly tricky stretch which had just been negotiated. I was full of admiration. As we reached the lower levels, we seemed to move faster. We seemed to be moving so rapidly that I wondered if my guardians were still there. Could I be travelling ever faster down the mountain, like a canoe caught in a quickening current? Lying on your back, firmly secured on a stretcher and with your head lower than your feet, is not a position in which you should permit the imagination to exploit a shocked personality. Suddenly, we were slowing down and the periodic enquiry after my comfort broke the relative silence. The reassuring figure of Peter appeared at my side; I noticed he was carrying my skis and poles.

Now we were down. The stretcher was manhandled into a hut and, while Jim asked me my name and other details, Peter carefully sponged off my face. The girl whom we had briefly seen in an accident at the top of the mountain was already in the hut and she seemed concerned about the blood on my face. I explained that it was superficial. But the ankle was another matter. Five minutes later, Jim and Peter were gently sliding me into an ambulance.

I thought of the promising beginning to that afternoon, of the lonely spot on the little-used, narrow trail, and of Marci's level-headedness. But above all I thought of the ski patrol. How can you express your gratitude adequately? In circumstances such as these I prefer the simple, 'Thank you for all your competence and kindness' approach. The response was equally simple, "It's nothing, sir; it's our duty."

With two broken bones and torn ligaments safely encased in plaster, using crutches I returned on Monday morning to the world of business and bureaucracy. A friendly soul opined that,

"You never really think it could actually happen to you, do you?"

After many years of skiing, I could only respond that I had never thought about an accident at all. Does a motorist think of a possible accident when he is *en route*? Does a pedestrian think he will be run over when he crosses the road? Does a pilot think of an impending air disaster with himself at the controls? God forbid! So why should the humble skier countenance an accident?

With hindsight, after an accident you may blame yourself; you might conceivably blame others. But it is pointless to torment yourself with academic thoughts of this nature, because whatever the reason for the accident, you have to come to terms with a *fait accompli*. If your accident happens to occur on a ski mountain, be grateful for the ski patrol. Like a Guardian Angel they will be there in your moment of need. From ordinary skiers like myself they will always have respect and gratitude. They will also receive an annual financial contribution. They are more than worth it.

Marci agrees.

* * *

Looking back on twenty years of living in North America, as far as recreation was concerned, one could easily escape the daily work pressures in order to recharge one's batteries. In the process one would not only enjoy a wide range of healthy and delightful recreational activities; one would also collect many happy memories.

Chapter Eighteen

A Search for Reality –
Truth and Progress in the Third World

About a year ago, I attended a course at the University of Vienna which was conducted for teachers of the German language; twelve countries from Europe and North America were represented by the participants. One of the course requirements was that each participant should conduct a period on a certain chosen subject; from a list of some ninety-two possible subjects, I chose to talk about the Third World. After twenty minutes, before inviting comments, I asked the group several basic questions relating to the Third World.

I was taken aback by the degree of ignorance exhibited by my fellow participants with respect to the Third World; after all, they were members of the teaching profession. Most were in their late twenties and some were in their thirties or forties. And it was not only a question of ignorance; with the exception of one of the participants, the level of interest shown in the subject was low.

When the period was completed, the professor stated that he had conducted over two hundred language courses at various levels and this was the first time that a participant had chosen the Third World as a subject for presentation and discussion. When one considers that the vast majority of the world's population lives in the Third World, I for one found this statement to be a somewhat sad commentary.

When considering the Third World, as a starting point it may help us if we endeavour to see developing countries in the perspective of history. For example, the colonial period which is currently in the process of drawing to a close is just one among many. Colonisation of weaker countries by the great powers of the day has occurred in so many instances since the beginning of history. And we know that, frequently, colonisation brought to less developed countries not only a degree of subjugation, but also civilisation, culture and development possibilities.

As we know from our personal experience, life often does not seem to treat us fairly. The fact is that the spectrum of nations, like humanity, will always include those which are rich and often strong, and those which are poor, and frequently weak; some of the rich do not deserve their wealth and some of the poor are not properly rewarded for their labours. However interesting a discussion on what constitutes a fair reward for our work might be, to the average practical person such discussion tends to be academic. Whatever our circumstances we tend to escape into rationalisation; it is usually easier that way.

I hold no brief for colonisation; I was invited to participate in a colonial administration but declined the offer. However, I had contact with colonial administrators and sometimes watched their performance first-hand. It has become fashionable over the years for countries which were involved in colonisation to feel uncomfortable or to harbour feelings of guilt. An objective assessment of the results of colonisation, however, would often reveal a number of positive factors.

Although we frequently hear the convenient chant that colonisation destroyed cultures, in fact the degree of dislocation of cultures has almost certainly been exaggerated. As far as pastoral, nomadic and sparsely distributed populations were concerned the impact of colonisation on their culture was, with certain exceptions, minimal. The main positive effect of colonisation on these segments of the population was that violent conduct between tribes and clans was not only discouraged, but often prevented.

Certainly, to the extent that any system produces excesses, the effects would clearly be negative; and colonisation was no exception. We live in a dynamic, constantly changing world and inevitably the stronger will try to influence, or dominate, the weaker. Colonial-type systems, in one form or another, will continue to exist, whether in some form of political, physical or economic activity; and like all systems, they will have both positive and negative effects. Looking back, however, when one considers the relatively peaceful state of many of the less developed countries during the colonial period, to condemn those involved in the colonial process ignores the truth of the situation.

Looking back over the last forty years, what has been the experience of formerly colonised countries? The eastern African area I have referred to in the first part of this book typified the situation at that time. Forty years ago, the countries of the Somali Peninsula and of East Africa were subjected to some form of colonial-type administration, with the exception of Ethiopia; some countries were directly colonised, others were called a 'Protectorate', while Somalia was an Italian Trusteeship of the United Nations. Ethiopia had been militarily liberated from foreign domination in the forties.

During our lifetime, as bystanders we have watched the picture of decolonisation unfold. Unfortunately, there are a number of countries where, in contrast to the relative peace which prevailed during the colonial period, the picture we see today is one of degeneration into violence, mismanagement, corruption and persistent poverty.

We also see examples of stunning success. During the next century, some of the Newly Industrialised Countries, especially those in East Asia, will represent a strong challenge to countries of the developed world.

One of the most serious problems created during the era of decolonisation was the unpreparedness of some of the colonised countries to assume the responsibilities of independent countries. The colonising powers must, to a large extent, be held responsible for departing from some of the colonised countries prematurely. It is acknowledged that the colonial countries were under tremendous pressure, through the UN system and from some great powers, to bring the colonial system to an end. Nevertheless, the human dangers inherent in this idealistic, often pseudo-intellectual, approach could have been properly recognised. In practical terms, if a programme of say, twenty-five years of infrastructural development had been established, then, whatever the pressures, it made no sense to reduce the period to five years, which is the type of situation which occurred, for example, in the Somali Republic. Apart from other factors which will be touched upon, the lack of effective infrastructural development has been a primary reason for the inability of certain developing countries to govern themselves effectively.

Unfortunately, stemming from the current wave of nationalism, the deleterious effect of lack of effective infrastructure in critically important areas of government administrations will become increasingly evident; this will apply particularly to technical areas. In the field of civil aviation, for example, if a newly-created small country finds itself without experienced expertise in airworthiness or flight operations, how will air safety be properly maintained? If the country does not have the right human resources, then normally the required expertise would have to be purchased from the international market-place. And if the country is short of foreign exchange to finance the expensive service? The potentially tragic results are not difficult to imagine.

Whereas formerly larger national geographic units had at their disposal the human and material resources to create and develop the required infrastructure, in cases where these units have become politically fragmented, the new, often relatively weak governments are suddenly faced with a crisis of lack of qualified and experienced specialists. To the extent that the gap affects safety-related activities, human safety will be compromised.

In a nutshell, the clear fact is that for any government to operate effectively, properly trained and experienced personnel must be available as part of the basic infrastructure. To ignore this fact, regardless of whether the country has the status of developed, developing or somewhere in-between, leads to, at best, degraded essential services and at worst, life-threatening situations.

While the lack of infrastructure development in many Third World countries continues to represent an enormous handicap at the administrative level, at the political level countries have often suffered miserably through instability. Even in countries where good progress had been made in developing an infrastructure, political extremism could nullify the progress achieved; Uganda was a case in point. The suffering of large segments of Third World peoples has surely far exceeded any suffering which may have arisen during the colonial period.

Leaving aside the aspect of direct physical violence which is, unfortunately, so prevalent in our world, let us consider the aspect of drought and resultant starvation. We could be forgiven for believing that drought and famine represent a new, dreadful element of African life. The fact is that one heard little of the threat of starvation during the colonial period. This was mainly because, once it was clear that rains had failed, the colonial administration took precautions to protect the population against the impact of lack of water and famine. I well recall such situations, when all necessary resources were brought to bear to establish centres (such as Abdel Kadr in the Somali Republic) which provided food, drink and succour to those parts of the population which had been afflicted with famine conditions. The colonial administrators were not only well-chosen men with a mission, but they were skilled in large-scale administration, usually having the confidence of the population of the district for which they were responsible. In their place, at enormous cost, today we have the worthy efforts of relief and other organisations, many of whose dedicated workers are quite unused to the conditions and cultures of the populations they aspire to serve.

One of the key elements which is responsible for political instability in so many countries is the supply of arms and ammunition, either to governments or other political factions. Over the last forty years, we have heard of the sacrifice of hundreds of thousands of individuals for one political cause or another; the arms industry is big business and economically important to a number of countries. But, whether viewed from the moral or material aspects, can the death of one innocent human being be justified by the existence of an industry which has, as its primary aim, the export of arms to foreign developing countries?

Notions of nationalism, which often lead to conflict, constitute another significant element in the mosaic of political instability; and wherever this occurs serious damage to the human infrastructure is at risk. Especially where specialised knowledge is involved, the impact can be catastrophic.

On the general subject of nationalism, apart from the ever present ingredient of political greed and exploitation of people's minds, one of the ironic tragedies of nationalistic concepts is that, frequently, an examination of the history of the last few hundred years would reveal the weakness of adopting narrow nationalistic attitudes. Of course, we should be proud of the achievements of groups of people who constitute a population of a defined geographic area which bears the name of a certain country; no one should criticise success, nor begrudge those associated with it. In its positive connotation, nationalism constitutes a healthy attitude which centres on constructive human endeavour.

Then we have another, darker side to nationalistic attitudes which centres on selfishness and fragmentation. To the extent that nationalism 'succeeds' (that is in the eyes of the nationalists), the result is often negative. A weakened entity takes its place in our world, often amongst relatively more powerful neighbours; a new centre for political exploitation is created. Apart from other drawbacks, the birth of the new country immediately results in great strain caused by lack of human infrastructure. It is worth repeating that the existence of an effective infrastructure is a pre-condition for development.

Many of us seem to assume that the current stage of development of the country in which we were born is a continuation of the achievements of our forebears of that particular country. This is frequently a far cry from the fact. Mankind has roamed our planet over a protracted period of time, which in turn has led to wide dispersal of members of population groups. For example, if each of us were to trace our family back through history we might well be surprised to find that few families have in fact remained within the confines of a certain country; on the contrary, it is more likely that we would find that over the years branches of our family would have been dispersed over perhaps several countries. We should not delude ourselves that we and our kinsfolk have forever been confined to a limited geographical area and we should not be surprised to find that our ancestors came from countries which, today, we regard as 'foreign'.

If we were to face up to the fact that we stem from ancestors who through the ages have wandered, sometimes far afield, then less credence would be accorded the current concepts which are enunciated with regard to nationalism; and the emptiness of so many political pronouncements on the subject would be clearly exposed. For example, I refer to myself as an 'English European'. In using such a term, I recognise that branches of my family could be traced back to such countries as Germany, France and the Netherlands. It therefore makes no sense for me to claim that I am English in the narrow, nationalistic sense of the term. I have no doubt that this fact also applies to many of my countrymen.

If populations of the world's countries could, in addition to asserting their sovereign rights as well as retaining (and maintaining) important elements of their cultural heritage, also recognise that their ancestors resided within an overall geographic area which was not limited to their current particular country of nationality, then the generation of narrow nationalistic feelings, which so often are negative by definition and attract radical or fanatical elements, would be discouraged. To the extent that these negative feelings could be eradicated, the world would become a happier place in which to live.

In-country and international co-operation is unquestionably one of the keys to the well-being of our world; conversely, narrow nationalistic feelings almost inevitably cause political instability and conflict.

Those whom I would label 'negative nationalists' will reject the co-operation approach and will assert that the price of political upheaval (usually accompanied by economic malaise) is worth it – whatever might constitute 'it'. My response is to implore an examination of history, to step out of passionately held sentimental feelings and then with a hard-headed, realistic attitude to assess the likely results of so-called nationalistic 'success'; surely most of us have already seen too many of these 'success' stories, accompanied by images of bitterness, misery, strife, the breakdown of the rule of law, economic decline and chaos caused by lack of an effective infrastructure.

And to those who believe in co-operation with their neighbours (both within and outside the country), but who seem so often to have given up on promoting the benefits of co-operation, we should tell them to sound their trumpets loudly and clearly. There is nothing to hide in their conviction and they speak with the benefit of experience. Although it may well be the more challenging and demanding option, in the end it is co-operation which produces the best overall results for populations. Apart from other benefits, the avoidance of fragmentation and strengthening of the integral parts of the nation state, in the context of the related geographic area, results in the retention of existing human infrastructural resources and facilitates their future development.

We live in a world of 'haves' and 'have-nots'. Over the last hundred and fifty years or so, a relatively small group of countries has developed great material wealth based on industrial technology. In these circumstances, the rest of the world, by far the majority, has two basic options: it can try to stand still in terms of culture and material development; or it can try to board the 'bandwagon' as a means of development. As far as the opting out of the race for development might be considered as a possibility, in isolated instances this has been tried but, since true independence as such is found in practically no case in our world, the results have not been encouraging; by far the vast majority of the 'have-nots' have decided to try and jump on to the development 'bandwagon', with its associated inter-dependence. With all its complex distortions, the Third World today mirrors the current status of a large-scale, world-wide attempt by developing countries to aspire to the standards achieved by the handful of developed countries.

If we continue to look at developed and developing countries in the context of history, there can be little doubt that we live in an age of enlightenment. In spite of the contradictions and hypocrisy of international politics, it is indeed remarkable that since the last war the developed world has invested so much in assisting the developing world. Although much bilateral aid is 'tied', multi-lateral aid, in theory at least, is not. To some extent, the vacuum left by the completion of decolonisation has been filled by the activities of bilateral and multilateral assistance, the latter partly through the UN Specialised Agencies. In this way, work on bridging the gap in infrastructure development can continue. But so much more could be done in pursuit of this aim; because the role of the UN Specialised Agencies is important in a number of developing countries, their role deserves to be expanded and more fully utilised. At the same time, certain Agencies need to be reformed in terms of organisation and their capability to participate more effectively in development co-operation.

One often hears reference to the UN system as though it is an organisation which has some foreign status. For example, we hear that in a certain country 'the UN did not manage very well'. We are all part of the UN system. The UN system membership includes practically all countries of the world; and the UN system is only as strong as its members. Unfortunately, the United Nations Organisation is mainly in the news at the political level, which means that its actions will often be perceived as contentious. In these circumstances, the Organisation would almost certainly reap a greater reward if its member states would agree to place stronger emphasis on the activities of its Specialised Agencies in contributing to a narrowing of the gap between the developed and the developing worlds.

And the staff of the UN Specialised Agencies, are they of good quality, or does the staffing system need reformation? Any system benefits by constructive reviews and, provided the results are properly analysed and sensibly received, adjustments for the better should follow; the UN staffing system would be no exception to this rule. Especially in large-scale organisations, firm rules need to be established regarding recruitment criteria. Although the UN system has rules in this respect, they are not always observed. For example, unless a post is designated to require 'political approval', then political influence to see a post filled by a certain individual should not be permitted; if it occurs, the affected application should be disqualified. National administrations have learned this lesson long ago and its observance by the UN system would sometimes mean the recruitment of better staff. Another aspect which needs to be thought through and tackled, is the question whether members of governing bodies should be permitted to apply for, and subsequently be appointed to, posts within the Organisation they serve. In certain circumstances, these individuals will have the 'inside track'; if the procedure leads to lack of fairness in what should be fair competition, then the recruitment procedure becomes distorted to the detriment of the quality of the overall staffing situation.

Apart from a few wrinkles which need to be ironed out, it seems unlikely that a major reformation is justified. In general, the UN system is served by able and dedicated staff. With stronger support at the political level, the quality could be even better. As Javier Perez De Cuellar says in the foreword to the second edition (1994) of the 'Who's Who' of the UN:

> A detail that is often overlooked is that this is an organisation
> meant to serve its constituents – the peoples of the world. Its
> rise and fall is equally tied to those individuals who dedicate
> their working lives to the organisation.

The editors of the 'Who's Who' include the following comment in a preface:

> ...the bulk of those who work with the UN are not concerned
> with war (peacekeeping), but with the day-to-day lives and
> welfare of the more then five billion people whom its
> Agencies... serve.

It is in any case worth noting that, whatever perception the member states may have of the United Nations Organisation, recent history has clearly shown that member states will act unilaterally, in their own perceived interests, when important national issues are at stake. The stronger the member state, the more likely it is to act unilaterally.

Why should a backward country not seem to wish to develop as rapidly as possible? Again, we often have to fall back on the historical context. If we take a country with a relatively low population, which had been fairly isolated until the last fifty years or so and which, probably, may not have been endowed with an abundance of natural resources, the chances are that the country in question was colonised during the last part of the nineteenth century. Its population grew used to a colonial administration (paternal or otherwise) until the late 1940's or 1950's. Suddenly, the country is to be brought to independence. A programme of infrastructure development is drawn up and initiated. However, within a year or two the colonial power announces that, under external pressures, it will (in effect) abrogate its responsibilities and depart.

The international community then shows, to a greater or lesser degree, some interest in the country; to the extent that foreign investment, for example in tourism, might be attracted, this occurs. But as far as the population of the country is concerned, little development in the wider sense of the word is in fact taking place.

The United Nations system establishes itself in the country, as do diplomatic missions; between them, development assistance is channelled to the country. With its former colonial status now superseded by the benefit of significant aid schemes, there is little real incentive within the government, or amongst the population, to develop into a truly independent state. The challenge of self-sufficient independence is blurred by the aid schemes, which help to sustain the country and its population, albeit at a level which is lower than many of its citizens would prefer. The country lapses into a type of somnolence under which it is not only mainly sustained by international development assistance, but it actually expects to receive the assistance on an indefinite basis; from time to time the country demands, and often receives, more from the donors.

We know that there is no clear definition of a developing country. What we do know, is that some countries manage to develop more effectively and quickly than others. Although a number of complex factors are inevitably involved in the development process, it seems that every country maintains a certain development tempo. In the case of some developing countries, once the tempo reaches a certain level, the process of development is accelerated. However, there are many countries, regrettably, which still chiefly rely on aid schemes to sustain their populations and little progress seems to be made in reaching the stage where they will be able to develop increasingly on their own. In other words, the *will* to develop and to become independent using their own national resources, as opposed to relying on external aid schemes, is patently lacking.

I believe that the most single important element in development co-operation is the generation within a Third World country of the *will* to develop. Ironically, in the poorer countries the larger the amount of money which is made available for development co-operation, the less the tendency often exists within that country to develop a will to achieve progress through its own efforts. So long as foreign aid makes the critical difference between, say, economic collapse and the ability to limp along, those in the government often tend to opt for the *status_quo*.

There is no question that the poorest countries deserve relatively enhanced support; at the same time, it is essential that development co-operation is geared to stimulating the *will* in these countries to reach a point of self-sufficiency within the shortest (but realistic!) time-frame.

When we watch our television and see the plight of our fellow human beings in the Third World, we are certainly moved by compassion. At the same time, perhaps we should also feel anxious. History has taught us that where the gap between rich and poor is wide, trouble awaits us around the corner. Can anything be done to accelerate the process of development in the Third World, in order to narrow the gap?

The blunt answer to the question is that not very much can be done to narrow the gap significantly between the rich and poor countries. There are those who believe, in general, that by diverting more money for investment in projects in developing countries, the process of development in these countries will be accelerated. This approach can only be valid in a relatively small number of cases, for example where a developing country has already 'taken-off', as it were; in any case, the process of effective development implies substantial investment in wealth-creating projects.

But if we look at the poorest countries which are most in need of development, the premise that larger investments in development assistance will accelerate the process of development is, almost without exception, false.

Unfortunately, governments of most developed countries which contribute to development co-operation, emphasise the sums of money invested in the Third World in any given period. To some extent, this approach is understandable, since the developed countries concerned wish to maximise the size of their contribution in comparison with contributions made by other countries; image enhancement must play its part. However, by simply emphasising the sum of taxpayers' money of the developed countries which is used to support development in the Third World, whether the contribution involves bilateral grant aid, soft loans or the channelling of funds through multi-lateral institutions, ignores the aspect of value. The most important benchmark in gauging the effectiveness of development assistance is not the amount invested, but the *value* obtained from the investment; it is the value which is the acid test and which needs to be analysed and emphasised.

When we look at the question of value derived through development assistance, implicit in the answer is the absorptive capacity of the country being assisted. At this point, we inevitably return to the issue of infrastructure development. Unless the minimum degree of infrastructure required to absorb a development project is in place, the project cannot wholly succeed.

I have observed many projects which were highly successful during the period when the project was assisted by the injection of foreign specialist expertise. The project may have been thoroughly planned and well-executed. However, if one were to review the impact of the project a few years later, unfortunately, too often those who had been trained in various technical specialisations had, for one reason or another, moved on; inevitably, some degree of vacuum was created, which in turn reduced the effectiveness of the dedicated efforts of those who had been directly involved in the project in the first place.

So, if the gulf between developed and developing countries will remain for the foreseeable future, what might be considered in terms of improving the present system of development co-operation?

If we first take the position of the developed countries, there needs to be a much higher degree of general consciousness of the problems facing the Third World. Understandably, the developed countries are greatly preoccupied with problems within their own countries and which affect hundreds of millions of their citizens. For example, endeavouring to come to terms with the fact that large-scale unemployment in the developed world will persist for years to come is an unpleasant subject which, correctly, preoccupies a large number of leaders in both government and industry. In such circumstances, the latest outbreak of civil war or the occurrence of massacres in the Third World tend to take second place to significant problems which exist at home.

Apart from the need for the direct efforts of all governments to inform their citizens objectively and systematically about problems and developments in the Third World, the international press also has an important part to play. The power of the media is awesome. On the one hand it can, and does, produce excellent, well-informed, journalism; on the other, especially where vested interests are concerned, it can misrepresent and distort facts. Those in control have an opportunity to participate in informing the world-wide public, and in a constructive way, regarding the situation in various Third World countries. They should grasp the opportunity with enthusiasm and contribute to a raising of the general consciousness on this subject.

Then there are those who adopt an attitude of scorn towards the development problems of the Third World. However, a glance back by these individuals through the histories of their own countries during the last few hundred years will remind them that the countries of the developed world also experienced tremendous political and social problems which, all too often, resulted in civil disorder, strife and bloodshed. The fact is that material development requires a high degree of conceptual planning, detailed professional knowledge, the harnessing of industrial technology and financing. Above all, as I have already emphasised, development requires the *will* to develop.

If the developed world would give a stronger moral emphasis and commitment to assisting in the resolution of some of the major problems of the Third World, the existing institutions which are responsible for development co-operation would function more efficiently. This could be achieved by providing higher quality representation at the policy level. After all, if a country supports international development co-operation, why not assure the highest possible intellectual and practical participation?

Unfortunately, those who represent their countries on governing bodies of international organisations and financial institutions are not always of the quality required to assure effective governance. Too often, a selection system (which may include patronage) can result in the appointment of unprofessional or unknowledgeable persons to positions of high responsibility. Not only does this result in lack of effectiveness, but an obstruction can sometimes be created to the business of development co-operation. As always, there exist some country representatives who can be relied upon to do their 'homework', but these tend to be the minority; certainly amongst the UN Agencies and development institutions, one hears dissatisfaction voiced by the professional staff *vis-à-vis* the quality of those who serve on governing bodies.

Members of governing bodies should have a clear understanding of their role. They are members of an overall management body and the execution of their decisions needs to be left to professionals who are involved in their specialised fields on a continuing basis. Members of governing bodies should primarily be concerned with policy. They should not themselves closely participate in the day-to-day work of the officials they oversee; and they should not pretend to have current, highly specialised knowledge which, usually, they do not have. In the world of today, if a specialist is to remain current, he or she will be thoroughly involved in the specialisation on a continuing basis; if a specialist leaves the field for even a few months, the dynamic nature of the specialisation will usually ensure that the former specialist is left behind. A good specialist will be the first to admit, and to accept, this fact. Whatever our training, there is one certainty which applies in today's world: once we have left a specialised field, even for a short period, we are out of date!

Over the years, in discussing Third World development co-operation with national representatives whether of developed or developing countries, I have sometimes been astounded by the lack of basic knowledge relating not only to problems in the Third World, but also with respect to the system of development co-operation as a whole; and sometimes, one could only be saddened by the mindless rhetoric which may be produced to provide a smokescreen for ignorance.

As one aspect of effective representation in international fora, we should focus on management. For any endeavour to have a chance of success, an essential ingredient is effective management. Many of us have read the management literature, headed by such esteemed practitioners as Peter Drucker. For all our reading and study, how effective are we as good managers?

According to Professor Charles Handy of the London Business School, there are three types of skills or cleverness which are required in organisation and management. He asserts that these can be divided into three groups:

"Technical, that is you have to be good at something; human skills, working with people; and conceptual cleverness, the ability to make the unlikely seem obvious."

Professor Handy states that good managers have all three types of cleverness and skills. Technical skills can be taught and learnt, but human skills can only be learned. Conceptual skills can be neither taught nor learnt, but only developed if you are fortunate enough to have them.

Professor Handy might also have touched on the critically important element of the need for sound judgement. We should not confuse high academic accomplishment with the ability to judge situations effectively. There are many people in our world who, although they may not have a strong academic record, nevertheless demonstrate great ability in judging complex situations. There are others who have had the benefit of a thoroughly sound academic education, but they appear to be devoid of the ability to judge situations rationally. Their colleagues endeavour to help them by widening their work experience to develop their ability to judge in different types of situations, but it makes little difference. The ability to judge rationally is simply lacking.

If international governing bodies could be manned by more representatives who have at least a reasonable degree of understanding of the Third World and its problems, linked with sound judgement and the conceptual management skills which Professor Handy refers to, this should certainly lead to improved performance.

In a nutshell, I believe that there needs to be much stronger recognition of the crucial importance of good management within international organisations, such as the United Nations and the Specialised Agencies. Good management means not only analysing problems and reaching rational decisions on necessary solutions; decisions made must be documented in unambiguous, clear-cut terms. Currently, certain high-profile activities of the United Nations' system frequently attract criticism; this in turn leads to a poor image and disenchantment with the system as a whole. We often find that UN officials are criticised for acting inappropriately or at levels of performance which are below those required to see a particular problem solved. On closer analysis, too often one finds that the empowerment of the officials in question has been nullified to a substantial degree, because the policy decision of the governing body concerned has been couched in restrictive or sometimes ambiguous terms; this prevents the responsible officials from doing whatever may be necessary to assure effective solutions. In such cases, it is the management body which is at fault and this fact needs to be properly recognised. In some cases, the management procedures and practices of a management body can be overhauled with the objective of achieving a higher level of management efficiency. In other cases, the problem may centre on the individuals who participate in the work of a management body. In this context, I believe that a rigorous review by all countries of their representation on international governing bodies would lead to an enhancement of the quality of representation, which in turn would facilitate the better delivery of effective development assistance.

Continuing on the subject of improving the quality of development co-operation, we can now transfer the spotlight from the developed world to the Third World. I have already emphasised the critically important element of developing the *will* to become more self-sufficient until the country concerned can 'fly on its own'.

In addition to the generation of the will to develop, with all that is implied by reaching this crucially important stage, in the context of the creation of a solid infrastructure, human resources development linked with the transfer of technology needs to receive special attention. Certainly, within the multi-lateral development co-operation system, there is strong recognition of the importance of this particular basic requirement; even stronger efforts are needed to achieve enhanced results. Unless more people can be trained for a wide range of specialisations, the present situation which often prevails, where staff seem to be constantly on the move between fields of work, will continue to cause dislocation and the loss of continuity.

The issue of continuity deserves further emphasis. Certainly in many developing countries, and especially in the least developed countries, far too little attention is paid to continuity at the executive level. Some countries require senior civil servants to be transferred between ministries within a specified period; apparently, it is considered undesirable that senior personnel should spend too long in one position. However, in practice, one often finds that a man or woman is transferred just when the individual has obtained a grasp of the work responsibilities involved; in other words, crucially important knowledge and experience at the executive level is needlessly lost.

Another cause of dislocation of continuity is political change within a government; this happens frequently. How can government business be effectively conducted when Ministers and senior officials are shuffled every few months? The negative effect on a country's development of a break in continuity can be devastating.

I recall a discussion with a senior official in a Newly Industrialised Country on the subject of the importance of continuity. I had commented that the man in question had, I believed, held his appointment in a certain ministry for several years. He confirmed that he had remained in that particular post for about seven years. He was aware of his government's policy *vis-à-vis* an array of important issues and he understood the ramifications involved in all the important current situations; in this way, at the executive level he was in the best possible position to make a thoroughly worthwhile contribution to the work of his ministry. Then he became thoughtful,

"You know, even with a good education and many years of government experience, it took me four years to really understand and gain a proper grasp of the full range of my duties and responsibilities."

It is through the attitude and realistic honesty of officials such as this man that his country has become a success story in many respects. Conversely, those countries which fail to recognise the crucial importance of continuity at senior levels within their governments will inevitably suffer, through lack of specific knowledge and experience at the executive level, in their development efforts.

Of the many problems which confront countries of the Third World, one of those of the greatest significance involves the export of national expertise. In certain countries, the export of professionally-trained personnel is encouraged as a method of obtaining foreign exchange through the remittances of the personnel involved. In one country, the policy was effective to such an extent that a request was made by the government on the World Health Organisation for a number of medical doctors, to replace the nationally-trained doctors who had departed for foreign countries!

If developing countries continue to export their professional technical and managerial personnel, how do they expect to raise themselves in terms of development? As with so many problems, the definition is not difficult; the challenge is to solve the problem. Today, this fundamental problem remains unresolved; until the size of the problem can be significantly reduced, the 'brain-drain' will persist to the detriment of the developing countries.

As an observation and simply to fill in an important part of the overall picture, in many developing countries the main requirement is the maintenance of law and order, so that the process of development has the opportunity of bearing fruit. The world is currently afflicted by organised crime of one sort or another and the ramifications seem endless. Some large-scale violence is the direct result of the political exploitation of weaker countries, which find themselves used as pawns in a political power game. I have already referred to the lamentable effect of the operation of the arms industry. Unless and until the level of violence can be reduced in many developing countries, it is inevitable that effective economic and social development of these countries will be severely curtailed.

It is natural that the minority of the world's population which lives in the developed world should, on the whole, exhibit a tendency to avoid the challenge of making a really strong, dedicated and worthwhile contribution to bridging the gap between their world and the Third World. This short-sighted attitude, so prevalent amongst the populations of developed countries, needs to be replaced by a conscious attempt to understand the nature of the Third World and to produce ideas which will contribute to bringing the Third World closer to the small group of nations which constitute the developed world.

If the combined intellectual and practical resources of the international community can be more effectively harnessed through the participation of high quality individuals in representational and managerial functions, there will be some hope that the process of development co-operation can be accelerated. This is not to say that achievements so far have been insignificant; on the contrary. But especially with respect to the poorer countries, much remains to be done.

Some hundred and thirty years ago, an American author and poet called Josiah Gilbert Holland wrote the following lines:

> God, give us Men! A time like this demands
> Strong minds, great hearts, true faith and ready hands;
> Men whom the lust of office does not kill;
> Men whom the spoils of office cannot buy;
> Men who possess opinions and a will;
> Men who have honour; men who will not lie;
> Men who can stand before a demagogue
> And damn his treacherous flatteries without winking!
> Tall men, sun-crowned, who live above the fog
> In public duty and in private thinking.

Can we not be inspired by the sentiments expressed in those lines? Although they were written in the last century, they could well have been written for our world of today.

In the context of time, the thoughts which I have expressed in the chapters of this book were gathered during the last forty years; the situations I have described remain crystal clear in my remembrance. For a young person, forty years seems a long time; but when you later look back, those years seem to have passed in a flash. And if for a moment you dwell on the fact that you can look back for almost half a century, then perhaps you could be forgiven for feeling that time takes on a new meaning: time seems timeless.

Looking ahead, whether we live in a developed or developing country, why should each of us not consider becoming involved in some practical aspect of 'the other world', in pursuit of co-operation and the development of international understanding? And let us not forget that, in facing the many difficult challenges which will surely arise, in times of need we should not feel alone. The Guardian Angel will always be there.